WESTMAR COLLEGE

AUTOBIOGRAPHIES of TEN RELIGIOUS LEADERS

ALTERNATIVES IN CHRISTIAN EXPERIENCE

AUTOBIOGRAPHIES of TEN RELIGIOUS LEADERS

ALTERNATIVES IN CHRISTIAN EXPERIENCE

RADOSLAV A. TSANOFF

*Professor Emeritus of Philosophy and
Professor of Humanities,
Rice University*

TRINITY UNIVERSITY PRESS  SAN ANTONIO

To my young fellow-students of Autobiography
at Rice University

AUTOBIOGRAPHIES
of TEN RELIGIOUS
LEADERS

ALTERNATIVES IN
CHRISTIAN EXPERIENCE

St. Augustine — St. Teresa of Ávila

George Fox — John Bunyan — John Wesley

Cardinal Newman

Ernest Renan — Count Tolstoy — Albert Schweitzer

Pope John XXIII

CONTENTS

THE STUDY OF AUTOBIOGRAPHIES

The purpose of this book is to examine principal varieties of Christian experience as they have been expressed in the intimate autobiographies of great religious leaders. It seems advisable by way of introduction to consider the character of the autobiographical literature of which this work represents one selection. The scope of this sort of life-stories is largely limited to our Western world, and it is mainly a modern self-revelation. There are scarcely any Oriental works in this field and very few of ancient origin, East or West. As the meaning of the word indicates, autobiographies are accounts of the authors's own lives. The study of them gives us a deeper understanding of personality; they are works of most searching self-exploration. On the other hand, they are also living reflections of the various aspects of human experience—social, intellectual, artistic, religious. They are furthermore open windows of the broad human vistas in various periods of history. Note how this is illustrated in our first and in our last chapter. In the *Confessions* of St. Augustine we are reading the most intimate self-probing and self-revelation, but we can also feel on every page that we are at the crossroads of history, with the great imperial Roman system collapsing, and a new, Christian civilization emerging out of the decay and dissolution of classical antiquity. And where can one be confronted more sharply with the spiritual aspect of the contention of ideologies, the conflict of purposes and ideals, and the grave need of fair and productive dialogue in our time than by reading the *Journal of a Soul* of the saintly Pope John XXIII who convened the Second Vatican Council? Our study of the great autobiographies gives us these intimately personal but also social-historical revelations.

This study may be described as a biographical approach to the humanities. That is to say, instead of undertaking a systematic examination of principles and problems, we are concerned here primarily with persons. Our inquiries are throughout a series of conversations—conversations with persons of high spiritual rank. There are literally hundreds of autobiographies by men and women of some stature, many of them quite sincere in their intimate accounts and revelations; but what do they have to reveal? Sincerity is not enough: compare, for instance, the great love lyrics of poetry with the usual packets of love letters. So we have to make our selection. The mention of great lovers brings to mind directly the name of Dante. Dante said that he wrote his *Divine Comedy* "to procure him full experience," and among the fullest and choicest experiences available to us are those of sharing in the confessions of the great autobiographers. Selection, choice is essential to any humanistic study. It is of prime importance in good sound history, which Burckhardt defined as "the record by one age of what it finds worthy of study in another." Now, to be sure, not all that is worthy of study has been recorded autobiographically: that is the reason why some great religious leaders have not been noted in this study. We are examining here intimate religious autobiographies, a choice of those that have been deemed most worth studying.

The importance of studies of autobiographies has been recognized by literary men and critics, philosophers and historians. John Dryden wrote: "Biography excels history." Victor Cousin was quite positive: "Give me the series of great men, and I will give you the history of the race." Goethe proposed and perhaps

planned making a collection of the great self-confessions in literature. He thought it worth his while, in his studies of the Renaissance, to translate the *Autobiography* of Benvenuto Cellini. In
their broad biographical approach Carlyle and Emerson showed
deep concern with the heroes and representative men in history.
Wilhelm Dilthey, outstanding student of the philosophy of civilization, expressed his estimate in enthusiastic terms: "Autobiography is the highest and the most instructive form in which the
understanding of life comes to us." Discount the truth of this
statement by half, and still it leaves us with a most interesting
prospect of worthwhile study.

The student of what William James called "the varieties of
religious experience" is bound to deal with the problem of
understanding the intense expressions of it reported by the
mystics. In this study a cardinal source book is the autobiography
of St. Teresa of Ávila. The historian of Protestant movements
must give serious consideration to the rise and spread of nonconformist denominations within the Protestant fold: Quakers,
Baptists, Methodists. Here again three autobiographical works
prove to be of the first importance: George Fox's *Journal,* John
Bunyan's *Grace Abounding to the Chief of Sinners,* and the
Journals of John Wesley. On the opposite side of these dissidents
from the Church of England, the so-called Anglo-Catholic current
in the Episcopal faith calls for careful note, and here the capital
work is the *Apologia pro Vita Sua* of Cardinal Newman. The
modernist trend of liberal scholars and critics in the various
Christian churches is an important aspect, especially of religious
thought and action of the past century and a half. Three of
our autobiographies record its various expressions in a Roman
Catholic (Renan), Russian Orthodox (Tolstoy), and Lutheran
(Schweitzer) setting.

We should recognize fairly some of the difficulties and problems of our study. They are initially problems of the autobiog-

rapher himself. The self, his real self, which he probes and reveals, is not one but various. This complication is familiar to any biographer, whose interpretation is bound to emphasize some aspects of his subject while ignoring or neglecting other aspects. An autobiography is itself a biography, of the author's own life, with all the advantages but also some peculiar difficulties of a direct personal account. The most immediately intimate character of the subject matter may itself interfere with a fair account of it. Consider, for instance, the two-volume biography of Lord Tennyson by his son. Hallam Tennyson knew a thousand details of his father's life and character as he knew his alphabet; he did not require any scholarly research. His problem was a different one. He was writing the biography of his own father, yet he was resolved not to write simply as his father's son but as a fair critical student of the poet's life and works. This kind of problem is accentuated in the autobiographer's work, which is bound to have a living intimacy but may be deficient in objectivity. Edward Gibbon, after completing his monumental history of *The Decline and Fall of the Roman Empire,* undertook to write of his own life, "the truth, the naked, unblushing truth" about himself. But as we read this work, which is a little masterpiece, we meet not a single one but several Gibbons. And maybe this was the real truth about Gibbon, that he was various. Is not this the kernel truth about oneself, that one does not have a single kernel? We may recall the scene near the close of Ibsen's drama *Peer Gynt,* where Peer is peeling an onion and finds only layer after layer, but no kernel. To him this is a shocking quandary: "Where was I, the one man, the true man!" In Montaigne's *Essays* we find the same realization, but not shocking; rather most interesting, this variety of selves, and all of them Michel de Montaigne. His "most universal quality is diversity." If he wrote variously of himself, it was because in him were all turns and manners and contrarieties; and he proceeded to expatiate. Goethe for his part summed it up in two lines:

> Nothing living is but one:
> Always it is various.

An autobiographer may aim to give us the whole truth about himself, the main central truth, but his work may illustrate the conviction of John Donne: "No man is an Iland, intire of itselfe." The grasp of this basic truth about ourselves is one of the humanizing gains in the reading of autobiographies. We may learn that we should not try to reduce our view of a person to a simple formula. Real personality is versatile and even sinuous. It slips and wriggles out of our stiff efforts to grip and incase it. So Robert Browning tells us in his lyric about a husband's vain attempts to constrict his wife to a single definition:

> Range the whole house from the wing to the centre,
> Still the same chance: she goes out as I enter.

This seemingly ever-various self-disclosure is not due to insincerity or pretense; indeed, precisely the opposite is true. The candor may be genuine; actually there is self-discovery as well as self-disclosure in the portrayal. Rembrandt is said to have drawn or painted some sixty portraits of himself. If we could study and understand these threescore portraits, we could read them as chapters in the "painted autobiography" of the many Rembrandts.

There is another problem which should not be overlooked. We say that we may not doubt the autobiographer's candor, or at any rate his sincere intention. But is not his self-portrayal also affected by his own attitude? He is, so to say, reenacting the drama of his life: can he avoid being to a certain extent an actor? We should not forget the original meaning of personality, in the etymology of the Latin word *persona*. It signified the mask which an actor on the stage wore in playing a certain role. Some autobiographies are certainly apologies motivated by the purpose of self-defense, as is Cardinal Newman's *Apologia pro Vita Sua,* in which he would justify the course of his life and thought and conviction which led him from the Church of England to Rome. Other autobiographies are stamped with the penitential note. St. Augustine reflects on his former sinfulness; St. Teresa is also terrified by the anxiety that she is not altogether assured of her complete deliverance from the perils of backsliding. In some autobiographies the apologetic note may be almost absent. This is the deep impression we get from the frank and forthright self-penetration of Count Tolstoy's *Confession.*

The marvel of great autobiographies is that, in revealing the various recesses of the inmost self, they deepen and expand our humane understanding. And more; beneath the depth of character which we are probing we may see, or at any rate vaguely sense, still unsounded abysses. We get a baffling but also a challenging and a truly humanitarian recognition of boundless personality. Precisely in the field of religion this recognition is most important.

CHAPTER I

ST. AUGUSTINE

Historians of ideas distinguish two main periods in the development of Christian-medieval thought; Patristic and Scholastic. These two terms may need some explanation.

The spread of Christian teaching and the organization of the Christian Church moved rapidly from its first centers in Jerusalem and Galilee to the large world of Mediterranean civilization, a Gentile world speaking mainly Greek or Latin and trained in the culture and thought of classical antiquity. This expansion was initially the work of the great missionary apostle St. Paul, who has been called the second founder of Christianity. Converted to the Christian faith during his journey from Jerusalem to Damascus, he spread the new gospel in Asia Minor and Thrace and Greece and Rome. His letters to the churches which he established became the first writings of the New Testament. St. Paul was a Roman citizen from Tarsus in Cilicia, where he had studied in a Stoic school before proceeding to Jerusalem for his training in pharisaic doctrine under Gamaliel. The Christian teachers who followed in St. Paul's footsteps, in appealing to the large Gentile world of classical tradition, had to make themselves understood in classical terms. The increasing numbers of them had been Platonists or Aristotelians or Stoics before their conversion to Christianity. They found it necessary, for their own conviction and for their effective preaching, to formulate their own Christian beliefs. When they de-

1

clared, in the first words of their Fourth Gospel, that "in the beginning was the Logos, and the Logos was in God, and the Logos was God," they were using a term of long and varied connotation in Greek philosophy. What was their own Christian understanding of the Christ-Logos—and likewise with the other basic Christian beliefs concerning the relations of the world to God, of the soul to the body, of man's sinfulness and salvation and destiny? This—the formulation, or better, the gradual formation of the true and right Christian teaching, orthodoxy—this became the first task, and problem, of the so-called Fathers of the Church (in Latin, *Patres,* whence the term Patristic).

After the fall of the Roman Empire under the blows of the barbarian tribes from the North in the fifth century, a period of cultural stagnation and indeed collapse ensued, some five centuries of "Dark Ages." Then began a revival of learning, a culture of ecclesiastic-theological domination of thought. This second period of medieval civilization has been called Scholastic, a culture of the schoolmen and doctors of the Church. Its guiding principle has been expressed in the words: faith seeking an intellectual statement, *fides quaerens intellectum.* Scholasticism started with the established and authoritatively unquestionable doctrines of the Church and sought, by rigorous analysis and logical elaboration, to develop them into a comprehensive system of beliefs and principles. The greatest of these Scholastic systems was the *Summa Theologica* of St. Thomas Aquinas in the thirteenth century.

The life and work of St. Augustine (354-430) mark the culmination of the first of these two periods. He was incomparably the greatest of the Patristic thinkers. In his formulation of Christian doctrines he became a pillar of orthodoxy. Harnack, the historian of dogma, declared: "Between St. Paul the Apostle and Luther the Reformer, the Christian Church has possessed no one who could measure himself with Augustine; and in comprehensive influence no other is to be compared with him."[1] Augustine's autobiographic account of how he was brought to Christ is therefore not only an outstanding personal document of self-portrayal but also all-essential to the study of the formation and exposition of Christian beliefs.

Christianity is a religion of salvation, the salvation of men from sin by divine Grace; and Augustine's *Confessions* are primarily the most intimate accounts of a sinner's life; depravity, repentance, conversion. As he tells us on his first page, he would bear testimony to his sins and to his misery in straying from God: "You have made us for yourself, and our heart is restless until it rests in you."[2]

The opening parts of the *Confessions* portray Augustine's childhood, boyhood, and youth. He was born in the North African city of Thagaste, the son of a devout Christian mother, Monica, and a pagan father, Patricius. Monica brought up her son in the Christian way; her devout prayer was that he should cling to Christ. But she postponed having him baptized, for she shared the belief of many Christians, especially in North Africa, that while baptism wipes out the stains of earlier wrongdoings, it makes subsequent sinning doubly grievous. During a very severe illness which threatened his life the lad cried out in his fever for baptism, and his distraught mother was on the point of calling the priest. But he suddenly recovered, and so the blessed rite was postponed until after he had sown his wild oats. He seemed to have sown quite a crop of them, to judge from his account; some of them scarcely damning, but significantly revealing in his contrite mention of them. In all seriousness he confesses his childish sins, mere pranks and petty thievings, but then does proceed to relate more flagrant offenses.

Patricius, noting his boy's brilliant mind, was resolved to spare no means to give him the best education in classical eloquence, for he knew that the profession of the so-called *rhetor*,

expert in literature and oratory, yielded both honor and affluence. From the small-town school of Thagaste the youth proceeded to Madaura and then to Carthage. The African metropolis
of vaunted culture opened to him the vista of classical mastery
but also, as he writes, "a caldron of shameful loves seethed and
sounded" about him on every side.[3] He was gaining excellence
in his studies but also drifting into various dissipations. Later
in his thought he was to grapple with the abysmal problem of
evil, but first of all he recounts his own evil practices. Pride and
lust swayed his work and his leisure: the thirst for glory and the
drag of sensual indulgence; eloquence and profligacy claimed
him in turn. A devout bishop in his forties when he wrote, he
is recalling with dismay the sins of his wild youth. He is not writing
for himself; he knows that others will read his book, the large
public; but how can he cover up anything? For he is writing
in the sight of God, God right there beside him, from whom
nothing can be hidden. His whole book is as it were a succession
of prayers of confession. He stands before the Lord, stands in
his memories, tainted and defiled. There he was in his youth
training for the career of a *rhetor,* a master of classical eloquence,
yet all along wasting himself in debauch. His father was spend-
ing his utmost to support him in school, and he himself was
keeping a mistress and with effrontery calling their son Adeodatus, God-given. He was winning prizes for leading his class
in oratory, but also keeping the worst company of dissolute
youths who vied with each other in their vile excesses. Thus
writing in his sober manhood, he would not silence, he would
rouse and drive home the black memories:

> I wish to bring back to my mind my past foulness
> and the carnal corruptions of my soul. . . . In the
> bitterness of my remembrance, I tread again my most
> evil ways. . . . For in my youth I burned to get my fill
> of hellish things. I dared to run wild in different dark-

some ways of love. My comeliness wasted away. I stank
in your eyes, but I desired to be pleasing to myself and
I desired to be pleasing in the eyes of men. . . . Why
do I tell these things? It is that I myself and whosoever
reads them may realize from what great depths we must
cry unto you.[4]

In his murky tempests of sin he was not without beacons of
upward light. When he was seventeen he heard that his father
had died having abjured paganism and embraced the Christian faith. With the support which his mother was managing to
provide he was continuing in Carthage his studies of the
Roman masters, when he experienced the first turning point in
his view of life. He read the *Hortensius* of Cicero, in which the
greatest of Roman orators advocated the study of philosophy, the
striving after wisdom and the higher life. The *Hortensius* is no
longer extant; we can judge only from some short passages which
Augustine cites how it must have burned its truths into his wayward soul. "To will what is unseemly," Cicero wrote, "is in
itself the height of wretchedness; nor is it such misery to fail
in obtaining what you want, as to wish to obtain what you ought
not."[5] It was a searing rebuke as if directly to him, Augustine.
"Love of wisdom has the name philosophy in Greek, and that
book set me on fire for it."[6] It urged him to seek further and
higher, but yet not decisively. This was the beginning of almost
fifteen years of struggle between his better and his lower nature,
the urge for truth and righteousness and the drag of indulgence
and corruption.

Untowardly at that stage of his spiritual career, he made the
wrong turn. Had he, directly after reading the *Hortensius,* proceeded earnestly upward from Cicero to Plato and Plotinus and
to the Bible, his radical change of mind and heart might have
been reached earlier. He did in fact decide to sample the Holy
Scriptures, but in his proud rhetorical manner he found their

humble style lacking in his favorite Ciceronian dignity. Their inner meaning was beyond him, but he felt himself above them; "disdained to be a little child and, puffed up with pride," as he writes, "I considered myself to be a great fellow."[7] Quite astray now in his misdirection, he became attached to the teachings of the Manicheans, which presented to him a plausible explanation of evil, a sort of sedative to a problem which was to him a keenly personal quandary as well as a basic spiritual perplexity. He groped in Manichean ways for some nine years.

Manicheanism resisted Christianity as a rival religion; in its westward spread north and south of the Mediterranean it was also a heretical incursion into the Christian churches. Its main doctrine was dualism: the contest of God, absolutely pure and perfect light, and Matter, the dark corruption and counterforce of evil in all existence. It had issued out of Persia, a fusion of the Zoroastrian doctrine of the cosmic dualism of good and evil, Ahura Mazda and Ahriman, with the Greek dualism of God and material existence: a pretentious cosmological muddle. For all its disdain of matter, Manicheanism had a materialistic outlook. Good and evil, perfection and corruption, were identified literally with light and darkness. These two, light and darkness, were viewed as ever contending in the cosmic process. From dismal terrestrial abysses light radiates toward the sun and the moon, is held back by the roots of plants but bursts forth in blossom and fruit—and thus much further, with elaborate rituals intended to overcome the darkness and material corruption.

In its heretical promotion within the Christian churches Manicheanism followed the Gnostic sectarian dismissal of the Old Testament idea of God as creator of the material world; it vaunted its own purely luminous ideal of Deity. What especially gripped Augustine was the Manichean account of evil. Man's sinfulness was explained as inherent in his bodily nature. Augustine was enticed by the doctrine; it lulled his grievous sense of personal blame for his foul wickedness. "It was not ourselves who sin, but . . . some sort of different nature within us commits the sin. It gave joy to my pride to be above all guilt, and when I did an evil deed, not to confess that I myself had done it."[8] The initial lure of the Manichean teaching gradually lost its power over his mind, but only gradually and not altogether. His critical judgment could not entertain seriously the esoteric mysteries of Manichean ritualism, for he was not unfamiliar with pagan superstitions. In the doctrine itself he saw pitfalls. The lesser priests of the cult could not quiet his doubts about the ceremonial marvels nor about the doctrinal confusions. They promised him better grasp of their truths, should he confer with their leading sages. But his discourse with one of the wisest of them, Faustus, proved of little avail.

There still was the lulling Manichean explanation of the evil strain in our nature. Year after year it kept him in his attachment to the cult. But all the time the disdain of his better self for his foul profligacy was embittering his life. He describes this self-splitting and the torture of it in unmistakable words: "I carried about my pierced and bloodied soul, rebellious at being carried by me, but I could find no place where I might put it down. Not in pleasant groves, not in games and singing, not in sweet-scented spots, not in rich banquets, not in the pleasures of the bedchamber, not even in books and in poetry did it find rest."[9]

The words bespeak not only his disgust with his dissipation but also his failure to find peace and true satisfaction in any worldly pursuit—his spiritual restlessness. Outwardly he was a pronounced success; he had won a prize for poetry and gained such provincial eminence in Carthage that he proceeded later to Rome where he soon attained intellectual distinction. His philosophical studies and his reflections led to his dismissal of the Manichean account of nature and human nature, though he still did not sever his connection with the cult, and its leaders were proud to claim so famous a master of eloquence.

Though in many ways Manicheanism was losing its hold on him, Augustine could not yet fulfill his mother's hope of advancing to Christianity. After the death of her husband, Monica kept close to her son, never despairing of his eventual conversion. She had a vision in which she was assured from on high that her son would be saved. But his own spirit seemed to be losing its intellectual anchor. His gradually renounced Manichean delusion left him in general quandary. He turned to Platonism; not, however, to Plato of the *Dialogues* but to the Platonists of a later period who had become affected by skepticism. How could he commit his life to any teaching when there was no assured basis of validity to which the least item of belief could appeal? All alleged truth or error seemed to waver in clouds of incertitude. His rhetoric and oratory were convincing to loose-textured minds, but not to his own. His inner life was a trackless wilderness.

Manicheanism could not hold him, but on the other side his mother's church doctrine also was beset with barriers to belief. The Church demanded unquestioning commitment to its doctrine; but how could he assent to its Old Testament stories of a God with hands and feet who in the cool of the evening walks in the garden which he had planted like a farmer? And if he disowned some of these notions, what could assure the binding truth of others? His own judgment?—but it had already betrayed him during his years of Manichean delusion! Augustine demanded clear august truth and found his mind and soul groping in a dust cloud of doubts.

While he was thus entangled in his mesh of uncertainties, an important turn in his outward career was to lead him to utter spiritual reversal. The city of Milan—second in importance in Italy only to Rome, long the seat of the imperial vicar, and in Augustine's day the residence of the Roman emperors of the West—applied to Rome for a municipal professor of eloquence. Symmachus, who had been proconsul in Carthage and was a stout opponent of Christianity, was urged by the Manicheans to select Augustine. He attended a public discourse by Augustine, strongly supported his candidacy for the post, and in fact, as Augustine wrote, sent him to Milan. The intention of the Roman sponsors, pagans and Manicheans, had been that Augustine with his eloquence would rival and prevail over the influence of the great Ambrose, Bishop of Milan. Divine Providence or the blessed irony of events pointed otherwise. Augustine visited Ambrose, fourteen years his senior who, as we read in the *Confessions*, received him in fatherly fashion and as an exemplary bishop welcomed his pilgrimage. It was to become a pilgrimage to Christ; but Ambrose's first impression on the younger orator was that of professional mastery. He listened to the bishop's sermons, at first mainly admiring their rhetorical excellence. He writes: "I was not anxious to learn what he said, but merely how he said it."[10]

Ambrose was not the usual Christian preacher, but a classical master in his own right. The son of a Roman prefect and with the most thorough literary education, he had held high official posts in the Empire—a consular prefect in North Italy with his seat in Milan. Although not a Christian in his personal outlook, he so swept the populace by a public address that by loud acclaim he was chosen to fill the vacant episcopal see of his district and was forthwith baptized and consecrated bishop. That was ten years prior to Augustine's arrival, and in that decade Bishop Ambrose had shown both utmost devotion to his office and outstanding leadership, ecclesiastic and theological. The former rich prefect had followed the words of the Gospel by distributing his goods to the poor; the former master of worldly literature and philosophy had adopted a daily schedule of the most thorough study of Biblical and Patristic writings, and had brought to his interpretation of Church doctrine a spirit of critical reconstruction.

The influence of Ambrose on Augustine was not through personal contact and direct exchange of ideas, for which the bishop's packed schedule afforded little leisure. Ambrose's door was hospitably open to visitors, but they found him immersed in his official duties or in his engrossing studies, in which Augustine as well as others felt that he could not be disturbed. Far different was the impression made by his sermons. Augustine had begun by admiring the bishop's rhetoric, but more and more he got from Ambrose's homilies a new insight into the deeper meaning of the Biblical writings and of the essence of Christian truth. Bishop Ambrose, proceeding on St. Paul's words, "the letter killeth, but the spirit giveth life,"[11] was subjecting to a reasonable reinterpretation many Scriptural accounts which had been stumbling blocks to Augustine's acceptance. "This was especially the case after I had heard various passages in the Old Testament explained most frequently by way of allegory, by which same passages I was killed when I had taken them literally."[12] In his sermons Ambrose was showing Augustine how a Christian mind could become a man's mind and put away childish things.

Listening to Ambrose, Augustine was confronted with the basic truth that spiritual things must be spiritually understood, that God is Spirit—the very opposite of the Manichean deity of literal light. His grasp of the Christian verities required a genuinely spiritual outlook. "If I were only able to conceive a spiritual substance!"[13] So he writes on his way to his conversion—on his way, but not yet on his arrival. Before entering into the spirit of Christian truth he studied classical spirituality in Plato and Plotinus. When his mother came to be with him in Milan, he could tell her that he was no longer a Manichean, although not yet a Catholic Christian. Realizing what Ambrose had done to forward her hopes for her son's conversion, she zealously hastened to church and would hang upon the bishop's words. She watched over Augustine as if to nurse him through sickness to health, with a premonition of "a more acute danger intervening, through that paroxysm, as it were, which doctors call the crisis."[14]

While her being under his roof was renewing Augustine's sense of the meaning of utter Christian devotion, Monica herself was being led through loyal obedience to Bishop Ambrose's orders, if not through understanding of his reasons, to a more spiritual form of Christian worship. "One time when she had brought to the saints' memorial shrines pottage and bread and wine, as was her custom in Africa, she was forbidden to do this by the doorkeeper. As soon as she learned that the prohibition came from the bishop, she accepted it in so devout and obedient manner that I myself wondered at how easily she became an accuser of her custom than an objector to his command."[15] On a deeper level or on a higher plane Augustine himself would be expounding later his doctrine of the Church's sacred authority under divine Providence.

In a passage expressing his admiration for Ambrose, Augustine reveals also his own spiritual state at the time. "Ambrose himself I believed to be a happy man, as the world judges such things, because so many powerful persons showed him honor. His celibacy alone appeared to me a hard thing. But what hopes he held, what struggles against temptations arising from his exalted station, what comforts amid adversities, how sweet the joys of that secret mouth within his heart, . . . such things I could not guess at, nor had I any experience of them."[16]

Monica, hoping and daily praying for her son's conversion to the Church, was not yet thinking of his following Bishop Ambrose in a churchly career. Augustine had declared openly that he could never lead a celibate life.[17] But in his high position as municipal *rhetor* he should regularize his homelife in a socially appropriate way. Marrying his mistress was, in Monica's judgment, quite out of the question. The poor simple mother of Augustine's son was worldly enough to realize that she was not fit to be the *rhetor's* wife, and Christian enough to submit loyally to her humble lot. It was not the brightest episode in Augustine's career. He kept his son, whom he cherished, but sent the boy's mother back to Africa, alone, even with the definite promise that she would not be joined to any other man. Monica for her part would find a suitable bride for Augustine, and in her plans she was successful. But the young lady "lacked almost two years of the age of consent."[18] Augustine sought solace for his grief over his lost mistress and for the unavoidable delay of his marriage, by procuring another mistress. These details in his autobiography add some documentation to his dark comments on man's depravity.

His barriers to godliness were not all sensual. The seventh book of the *Confessions* opens with these sentences: "My evil and abominable youth was now dead, and I was passing into early manhood. But the more advanced I was in age, so much the more was I defiled by vain things."[19] His mind was struggling, and making headway, with basic problems: of spiritual substance, free will and the problem of evil in relation to God's omnipotence, time and eternity! And of much of this and more his reflections revealed their sources in his studies of Plato. Yet all of it was to him still intellectual speculation; it lacked the deeper note of true devotion. Thus in his later recollections he opens his heart to God:

> I was made certain that you exist, that you are infinite, although not diffused through spaces either finite or infinite, that you are truly he who is always the same, with no varied parts and changing movements, and that all other things are from you, as is known by one single most solid proof, the fact that they exist. Of these truths I was most certain, but I was too weak to find my joy in

you. I prated as if I was well instructed, but I did not
know enough to seek your way in Christ our Savior.[20]

What he did not find in the Platonists—the face of piety, the
tears of confession, the contrite and humbled heart—he recognized it all in his reading of the Scriptures. With the most intense
zeal he seized especially the Epistles of St. Paul; "in a wondrous
way all these things . . . penetrated my very vitals."[21] But still he
could not really surrender himself to Christ, not utterly. "I marveled that now I loved you. . . . Yet I was not steadfast in the
enjoyment of my God. I was borne up to you by your beauty,
but soon I was borne down from you by my own weight, and with
groaning I was plunged into the midst of those lower things."[22]
His soul swung from almost holy exaltation to wayward and cold
backsliding. "The storm tosses seafarers about, and threatens
them with shipwreck; they all grow pale at their coming death.
Then the sky and the sea become calm, and they exult exceedingly
as they had feared exceedingly."[23] His soul was split and riven.
"This debate within my heart was solely of myself against myself."[24] "What was there that I did not say against myself? With
what scourges of self-condemnation did I not lash my soul? . . .
Yet it drew back; it refused to go on, and it offered no excuse
for itself. All arguments were used up, and all had been refuted.
There remained only speechless dread, and my soul was fearful,
as if of death itself, of being kept back from that flow of habit by
which it was wasting away unto death."[25] So the wretched wavering left him desolate. "When on all sides you showed me that
your words were true, and I was overcome by your truth, I had
no answer whatsoever to make, but only those slow and drowsy
words, 'Right away—right away. Yes, right away. Let me be for
a little while.' But 'Right away—right away' was never right now,
and 'Let me be a little while' stretched out for a long time."[26]

This state of wracking indecision was intolerable; it was bound to reach a crisis of resolution. Augustine has portrayed this climax in what is one of the greatest pages in the entire psychology of religion. "When deep reflection had dredged out of the secret recesses of my soul all my misery and heaped it up in full view of my heart, there arose a mighty storm, bringing with it a mighty downpour of tears."[27] He turned aside from his friend Alypius, and in his solitude with God he flung himself under a fig tree, gasping forth mournful words:

> "How long, how long? Tomorrow and tomorrow? Why not now? Why not in this very hour an end to my uncleanness?" Such words I spoke and with most bitter contrition I wept within my heart. And lo, I heard from a nearby house a voice like that of a boy or a girl, I know not which, chanting and repeating over and over, "Take up and read. Take up and read.". . . I checked the flow of my tears and got up, for I interpreted this solely as a command given to me by my God to open the book and read the first chapter I should come upon. . . . So I hurried back to the spot where Alypius was sitting, for I had put there the volume of the apostle when I got up and left him. I snatched it up, opened it, and read in silence the chapter on which my eyes first fell: "Not in rioting and drunkenness, not in chambering and impurities, not in strife and envying; but put you on the Lord Jesus Christ, and make not provision for the flesh in its concupiscences." No further wished I to read, nor was there need to do so. Instantly, in truth, at the end of that sentence, as if before a peaceful light streaming into my heart, all the dark shadows of doubt fled away.[28]

He opened his soul to Alypius, who had been going through his own crisis. Alypius turned to the page which Augustine showed him; the following sentence read: "Now him that is weak in the faith take unto you." These words he applied to himself and joined Augustine without any painful hesitation. The two proceeded forthwith to Monica and told her the story, to her great rejoicing. For Augustine now a new life was beginning: henceforth he would seek neither wife nor ambition in this world but would stand firmly on the rule of faith. Beyond the pursuit of any worldly wisdom, he would probe his inmost soul in the presence of his Lord: "Who am I, and what am I? Is there any evil that is not found in my acts, or if not in my acts, in my words, or if not in my words, in my will? But, you, O Lord, are good and merciful, and your right hand has regard for the depth of my death, and from the very bottom of my heart it has emptied out an abyss of corruption. This was the sum of it: not to will what I willed and to will what you willed."[29]

Augustine's total inner transformation was followed by a thoroughgoing change in his daily career. He could no longer pursue his schedule as a master of eloquence in Milan. The "vintage vacation" was approaching; he would then resign his municipal post. As it was, his lungs were giving him trouble; deep breathing was difficult; public speaking was painful. He had a good excuse for ceasing his worldly program without any further explanations. A countryside retreat at Cassiasicum was made available to him, and to it he withdrew with Monica, Adeodatus, and his close friends and some students, for some four months prior to his intended baptism. Private meditation on his own spiritual future alternated with intimate discussion in which literature and philosophy were directed towards their religious concerns. It was Augustine's Platonic-Christian symposium.

Augustine's baptism took place at Eastertide. The prayers of his mother had been answered; her life had reached its goal. Keenly aware of this, Augustine at this point of his *Confessions* devotes several chapters to a filial eulogy of Monica. Did he feel that his symposia at Cassiasicum were not quite free of their pagan-classical air? He needed utter concentration on unmistakably Christian themes. He would leave Milan and Rome and retire to his rural

Thagaste. But while waiting at Ostia, the port of Rome, for a ship to take them across the Mediterranean, Monica fell desperately ill. Realizing that her death was imminent, Augustine was in a quandary how he was to take her back to her African home, for he knew that she had always planned to be buried alongside her husband's grave. But now she expressed utter indifference: "Put this body away anywhere." And so it took place in the autumn, at Ostia. The bereaved Augustine returned to Thagaste, where before long he found himself alone indeed, for he lost his son Adeodatus, on whom he had set his earthly hopes. Settling down on a piece of property which still remained of his father's estate, he gathered about him some devout souls into a small community of hermit-monastic withdrawal from all worldly pursuits.

The plainly autobiographical part of the *Confessions* ends with Book VIII. The remainder of the work is devoted to discussions of problems which engrossed his Christian reflection: of memory, time and eternity, form and matter and creation. Deeply concerned to clarify and establish firmly the doctrines of the Church, he had no personal plans for a churchly career. But Providence, he felt, had other plans for him. On a visit to Hippo his presence was recognized at a church service. His reputation must have been widespread in the province, for the congregation with one voice acclaimed him as their choice for priest and successor to their aging Bishop Valerius. The monk-hermit of Thagaste bowed to the popular demand in which, as he was assured, he should note the finger of God. He begged for some time to prepare his soul for his forthcoming duties. The delay could not be extended long; he was ordained priest, and within four years, in 395, he was consecrated bishop, first as assistant to Valerius and then as his successor in Hippo. In this office he served for thirty-five years, dividing his time between his manifold episcopal duties and an immensely productive career of writing systematic works in Christian philosophy and theology which, as he felt profoundly, were one in their fundamentals. The *Confessions,* notably the latter part, may be regarded as the beginning of this work of formulating Christian orthodoxy, to which he was devoting his mature reflection.

It has been stated that to understand the successive versions of the Church creeds, from Nicaea to Toledo, we should keep in mind the doctrines deemed heretical which they were intended to refute. In Augustine's works also, the exposition of orthodoxy required the exposure of misleading errors. Of necessity he was involved in manifold controversies. His own personal career had been one of groping from darkness towards the light, from the foul swamps of sin to the heights and solid rock of Christian devotion. To make this unmistakably clear to himself and to others, he wrote his *Confessions,* and it is the basic conviction which he wrote explicitly at the beginning of his *Colloquies:* "God and the soul: that is all I want to know. Nothing else? Nothing whatever, *Nihil omnino."* The soul without God—the soul with God: this is the issue which concerned him above everything else.

Augustine was never tired of repeating that his salvation was nowise in any degree his achievement or due to his merit. It was Christ alone who raised him, an undeserving and depraved sinner, to the blessed state of grace. But how was he, and how were all Christians to understand this divine gift of redemption, redemption to righteousness for some, but eternal damnation for multitudes of recalcitrant sinners? This problem involved the interpretation of the nature of God's creative activity, of God's relation to the world, and of the basic character of evil, its actuality in a world created by omnipotent and perfect Deity. The religious meditations of St. Augustine involved him in the entire gamut of philosophical inquiries. Some of his proposed solutions expressed profound insight which has influenced theologians and philosophers through the ages. Other Augustinian ideas have embroiled the churches, Roman Catholic and later also Protestant, in perplexity and controversies. St. Augustine, the pillar of orthodoxy, has also had an unsettling influence on Christian piety.

It was to be expected that Augustine, saved by the Christian truth from the fallacies of Manicheanism, should have undertaken to expose and refute those fallacies, to save others from going astray. This resolution he carried out in several ways. The basic Manichean error was a double one: a wrong conception of the nature of God and of the world structure, used to sustain a wrong explanation of the origin and the nature of evil. First of all, then, he attacked the Manichean cosmic dualism of God and Matter. Matter is not coeternal with God. The truth is in the Christian doctrine of the one and only creative agency in the universe, God, by whom all things were brought into being. This creative activity of God was not exercised merely for a certain period, as if it were a single important chapter in the biography of Deity. To believe in God as the creator means to believe that all existence is throughout all time subject to God's creative power. And the creative agency of God is not like the work of a craftsman who fashions materials that are already at hand. God is the absolute creator of all that there is; the world is *per Deum de nihilo*.

We can see that the problems of evil will be confronting us, the actuality of evil in a world created by almighty and perfect God. But Augustine turns his more immediate attention to God's infinite and eternal nature which transcends the limitations of time. Eternity does not signify boundlessly extended longevity. It means timeless reality. We may not ask: what was God doing before He created the world? We should probe the misconception which leads men to raise such a question, a misconception regarding the nature of time. Time is a category of finite existence. Temporal distinctions, of past, present, and future, can apply only to finite things and processes. We may say that in creating the world God made possible time itself. In the timeless eternity of God there can be neither before nor after. The world is in time, and time is of the world, but God is truly and timelessly eternal.

Keep this and related ways of thought, and see how they apply to other problems, namely to that which engrossed St. Augustine: the explanation of good and evil. Here he attacks the second basic Manichean error: the view of evil as due to the eternally anti-divine reality of dark materiality. But if God is the one and only creative cosmic power, bringing forth all that there is, how can we regard God's perfect creation as sullied by any evil of corrupt existence? Augustine's treatment of this thorny problem has embroiled pious minds in theological tangles. His theodicy is dual, but it does not point two ways because of his wavering orthodoxy. He finds the Christian truth, as he sees it, confronted by two counter-heresies, between and against which he must hold firm.

Resisting first the Manichean error, Augustine maintains that the actuality of evil is not due to any essential depravity in nature itself. All that God created, in its essential character, is good: both matter and spirit, body and soul. Evil is and can only be in the perversion and degradation of our will in its inappropriate and misdirected preferential choice. So St. Augustine wrote golden words of truth in his masterwork, *The City of God:* "When the will abandons the higher and turns to what is lower, it becomes evil—not because that is evil to which it turns, but because the turning itself is perverse—*perversa est ipsa conversio.*"[30] In the *Confessions* the same conviction is expressed in more emphatic terms: "I asked: 'What is iniquity?' and I found that it is not a substance. It is perversity of will, twisted away from the supreme substance, yourself, O God, and towards lower things, and casting away its own bowels, and swelling beyond itself."[31]

On almost every page St. Augustine's writings are punctuated with Scriptural verses cited in support of his interpretations of doctrines. In this important case the explicit Bible verse would not be forthcoming, but St. Augustine's view was nowise alien to

Scripture. It could be read in the old account of creation in the Book of Genesis: "God saw everything that he had made, and behold, it was very good."[32] Likewise St. Paul had contemplated the various glories appropriate to different levels of God's creation: "there is one glory of the sun, and another glory of the moon, and another glory of the stars. . . ."[33] And we can read Augustine's truth in the parable of the prodigal son who one day "came to himself," so that he abandoned his swinish life—quite fit for the swine, but not for him—and turned his steps homeward, to his Father.[34]

The great passage in *The City of God* was an eminent example of that happy interfusion of Scriptural and Classical wisdom manifested in Patristic thought at its best. Here we may note the direct influence of Neoplatonism on St. Augustine. While nowise following Plotinus's doctrine of God's emanation in the structure of the cosmos, St. Augustine shared with him the conviction that if there was to be a world at all, there were bound to be different types of being manifesting in different grades or degrees the consummate perfection of God. Thus there was bound to be "a least" of perfection in nature, matter, a zone of corruption indeed, but having its place in the divine process: "Every string [of the lyre] is set in the precisely right position for the due production of the tones within its capacity."[35] Man's soul lives its life which points two ways; along the radius of its being the soul can reach towards the divine center of perfection, or stray away towards the abyss. Thus St. Augustine was led by Plotinus in his Christian reflection on the problem of evil. The Neoplatonists for their part had high praise for the opening words of the Fourth Gospel: "The light shineth in the darkness; and the darkness apprehended or overcame it not." The two clauses in this verse interplay, and also contend, in the endeavor to achieve a theodicy.

Once having read St. Augustine's truth clearly, we may hear it shared by sages and poets through the ages: evil consists in the misdirection and degradation of the will in its preferring the lower to the higher values. So St. Thomas Aquinas defined sin as being fundamentally in our turning away from the godly course, the *aversio* of the will. That some values are higher and therefore worthy to be chosen and preferred to the lower, that is the alphabet of the wise and good life. The rejection of this insight is the devil's folly in men's lives. Thus Mephistopheles in Goethe's *Faust:*

> Step down;
> I might have said: Step up. 'Twere all the same.

Thus also Shakespeare's witches in *Macbeth:*

> Fair is foul, and foul is fair.

Thus, preeminently, Hamlet in his discussion with his adulterous mother:

> This was your husband. Look you now what follows—
> Here is your husband. . . . Have you eyes? . . . What
>   judgment
> Would step from this, to this?

A sage definition of philosophy applies to theology also. In continual solutions, it is an unending problem. St. Augustine and those along with him have defined the nature of evil as the perverse turning or misdirection of the will. But the persisting problem still confronted the saint: Whence this perverse misdirection of the will in us all, sin-tainted children of Adam? In his rejection of sin as a cosmic eternal principle in nature itself, in his distinction of good and evil as due to right or wrong choices of the will, Augustine was expounding on principle a doctrine that might lead to an optimistic view of the moral capacities of man's free will. But his contemplation of our spiritual career was solemn, never sanguine. He had to confront squarely what he deemed an opposite kind of heresy, the doctrine of the British monk Pelagius.

For some ten years in Rome that sturdy moralist had been preaching that man's will has a positive capacity for pursuing and attaining righteousness. God makes no holy demands on us which are altogether beyond our moral power. Christ's saving grace acts on our will as a holy example and sustaining, completing aid. This teaching was spreading through many churches; its influence was notable in Africa. St. Augustine was aghast at its blind misapprehension of man's woeful depravity and at its flagrant depreciation of the solemnity of Christ's redeeming grace.

A thorough examination of St. Augustine's doctrine of divine Grace is beyond the reach of the present discussion. We can mention only some of its main principles. Up to a certain point Augustine would have agreed with Pelagius, but only to condemn the more sternly the further Pelagian thought as fatal heresy. According to St. Augustine our first parents did have the capacity to choose the good by their own free will; for if Adam had lacked this power his choice would have lacked moral value. But Adam misused his freedom and chose the wrong course. God in His omniscience foreknew Adam's choice, which, however, he did not predetermine; and in all justice he preordained the solemn retribution, in which all of us children of Adam have always been involved. Grace and salvation the divine Judge owes to no one, yet he mercifully accords it to us. To us all, or only to some?—the sentence is hard to complete.

Here is the point where Pelagians contested sharply with Augustine, some of them even more sharply than Pelagius himself. They held that we all share Adam's capacity of free choice between good and evil: a flagrantly unchristian arrogance, according to Augustine. The Pelagians insisted that God's punishment of the recalcitrant sinners can be regarded as just only if we recognize their sinfulness as due to their own free choice rather than as their inherited doom as children of Adam.

But both Pelagians and Augustine were confronted with a basic problem in theodicy which can scarcely be regarded as overcome. Recognizing Adam's responsibility for his particular choice, they saw that his choice did disclose his moral character. The further question in theodicy is still baffling: Was it impossible for God to create an Adam who could freely choose the good, rather than to create an Adam who, in the solemn exercise of his moral freedom, actually preferred the evil course? How would the strict Augustinian deal with this dilemma? And how does the justice of gracious but also punitive divine Providence operate in the lives of us countless children of Adam who lack his moral capacity? We can readily see why Augustinians, Pelagians, and Semipelagians have been engaged in agelong controversies. Is it possible to keep in the same logical head the doctrine of the universal taint of original sin, with its stern implications, and the conviction of man's genuine moral capacity and career? Even those who do not reject outright the strict Augustinian position may find themselves reacting positively to a Pelagian affirmation of man's moral ability to choose, as in Emerson's well-known "Voluntaries":

> So nigh is grandeur to our dust,
> So near is God to man,
> When Duty whispers low, *Thou must,*
> The youth replies, *I can.*

Critical students of Augustine have held that he did not abandon altogether the doctrines to which he had adhered in his youth. This judgment may not be taken in a derogatory sense. Has it been said that every truth, Janus-like, has also its aspect of error? This statement may apply also to error: it also may have its aspect of truth, be it important or minimal. Harnack, the historian of Christian dogma, maintained that we can trace in St. Augustine's thought some still persisting traces of his Manichean and of his skeptical attachments. As a Christian *thinker* the great orthodox theologian retained a certain skeptical reluctance. He did not trust to sovereign reason for his pious assurance but to his devout faith sustained by the authority of Holy Church. Faith precedes understanding.[36]

With regard to Manicheanism, likewise, while Augustine renounced its fatal errors, the basic conviction of contrast and conflict did continue to color the Bishop of Hippo's Christian outlook on life: both in broadly human-historical range and in the most intimately personal experience. This strain in St. Augustine's thought repeatedly comes to mind in reading *The City of God*. He could have borrowed his title from Marcus Aurelius who also wrote "Dear City of God." But to the Stoic Roman Emperor those words signified the *Cosmopolis,* the rational system of nature, and in his meditations we can share his contemplation of the Eternal City, the Roman *Imperium*. In Augustine's Christian outlook, the Roman Empire was man's stupendous monument of corrupt worldliness, tainted at the core and already being swept to ruin.

The Christian saint sees the history of mankind as embroiled in the contention of two "cities," two ways of life. "Two cities have been formed by two loves: the earthly by the love of self, even to the contempt of God; the heavenly by the love of God, even to the contempt of self."[37] Augustine traced this tainted strain through the course of history: in the vaunted but foul Oriental empires and in the most vain majesty of imperial Rome. Its pride and pomp would not predominate over the godly City of saintly devotion. Great is truth, and it will prevail. Later ecclesiastic minds might view this contrast and contest as the issue between State and Church, the higher sanction of spiritual authority over any temporal power. To Augustine it was the expansion of his personal tension between worldliness and piety, viewed in a world-historical perspective.

Ten Centuries Later: St. Augustine and Petrarch

The influence of St. Augustine's life and thought is manifest through history. His poignant and luminous words grip the memory; they can be read in later writings, sometimes literally, or else uttered in a fresh paraphrase. One example may suffice here. We all remember Dante's supreme line, in the third canto of the *Paradiso:* "In his will is our peace—*In la sua volontade è nostra pace.*" Augustine had written in his *Confessions:* "For us, peace is in a good will."[38] Likewise the Bishop of Hippo's stern argument with the Pelagians may be pursued in modern version, in the issue between Luther and Erasmus regarding the bound and the free will, in Calvin's doubly rigid Augustinianism, and once again in the long Jansenist controversy which led Pascal to write his *Provincial Letters.*

One particular instance of Augustine's enduring influence calls for closer attention by students of autobiographies. At the beginning of our chapter Augustine was signalized as the greatest and the conclusive Patristic mind. But several historical scholars have found reasons for calling him "the first modern man." This title would surprise most of us, for general preference has reserved it for Petrarch (Francesco Petrarca, 1304-1374). Petrarch died just one hundred years after St. Thomas Aquinas, but long ages seem to separate the life outlooks of the two men. Petrarch was quite beyond the medieval-Scholastic range of interests. He was emulating ancient-classical models; he aspired to rival Virgil in poetry and Cicero in prose. He was the acknowledged poet laureate of his day and master of "the more humane letters" which were to claim public devotion during the Renaissance which he was inaugurating. For all this early modern resurgence of classical ideals, however, Petrarch's heart was still gripped by medieval-Christian compunction. He carried in his pocket Augustine's *Confessions,* and in reading them, as he wrote, he followed the story not of another man's pilgrimage but his own.

One of Petrarch's works, entitled *My Secret,* is a sort of autobiographic essay, presented as a vision in which St. Augustine appears before him, to admonish him sternly against his further surrender to his two strong passions: the supreme love of his life which he had given not to God but to a mortal woman, and she another man's wife; and second, his lifelong pursuit of worldly fame instead of humble devotion to God. We have as it were another chapter of Augustine's confessional self-condemnation, this time addressed to Petrarch. The imaginary dialogue expresses the still persistent Christian-medieval conscience which must have haunted Petrarch in his worldly glory, even though it could not check his chosen course.

The *Secretum Meum,* written in Latin, is a work of very dramatic writing. The saint's conviction is that man's felicity or infelicity depends upon the choice of his will. Petrarch questions this as a description of the effective direction of life. He has admired St. Augustine; does he not read constantly the saint's *Confessions?* He feels and shares the saint's travails, yet his own life has been quite different. Augustine replies: Yes, you have sought salvation, but not resolutely. What has possessed you has been a worldly love and devotion. You have even used the term divine to describe the beauty of your lady-love. But Petrarch protests: Surely there is a difference between noble and ignoble love. "Love may be described either as the vilest passion or the noblest action of the soul."[39] Of his love for the Lady Laura he remembers only what is most noble. "Neither in the object of love nor in the manner of loving am I guilty. . . . It was she who turned my youthful soul away from all that was base, . . . and forced me to look upward." But, Augustine insists,". . . she has detached your mind from the love of heavenly things and has inclined your heart to love the creature instead of the Creator: and that path alone leads, sooner than any other, to death." Along this line of thought the holy Father of the Church would drive Petrarch to remorse and repentance. We are reminded of Dante's *Inferno* in which the poet of medieval Christianity portrayed a region in Hell for the sinners of incontinence who had wasted spirit and body in excessive love for earthly things: in gluttony, in avarice, in lust. Only we are now told that not only adulterous passion, like that of Paolo and Francesca, is to be condemned, but also noble and pure devotion, when it turns our hearts away from God and Christ.

In the other parts of the reported colloquy the saint continues his charge against Petrarch by condemning his zeal for worldly fame. "Ambition has too much hold on you. You seek too eagerly the praise of men, and to leave behind you an undying name." This Petrarch admits but cannot give it up. But, Augustine insists, "this pursuit of a false immortality of fame may shut for you the way that leads to the true immortality of life." Petrarch confesses: "That is one of my fears also, but I await your discovering to me the means to save my life." He even recounts his lifelong thirst for glory. Augustine tells him that even now he is worried lest he die before having finished the epic *Africa,* on which he relies for immortal fame. But this glory, this reputation which he seeks, it is but "a breath, a changing wind; and what will disgust you more, it is the breath of a crowd." He should put virtue above glory. But Petrarch maintains that his life is a human life, short of eternity. He doesn't seek to embrace heaven and earth. Such glory as belongs to man is enough for him. "But then how wretched you are!" the saint exclaims. "If you have no desire for things immortal, if no regard for what is eternal, then indeed you are of the earth earthy; then all is over for you; no hope at all is left." Petrarch replies: "Heaven defend me from such folly: . . . never have I ceased to love the things eternal." If so, Augustine urges, then he should follow after human fame as knowing that himself and it will perish.

St. Augustine pursues this idea, to convince Petrarch that he should give up his zeal for his great epic and for his lesser literary *opericole* and meditate rather on death, on his eternal destiny, on God and God's plan for him. Petrarch is moved to contrition, but not to resolution strong enough to alter his life. "I will be true to myself, so far as in me lies. I will pull myself together, collect my scattered wits, and make a great endeavor to possess my soul in patience. But even while we speak, a crowd of important affairs, though only of this world, is awaiting my attention." So we perceive Petrarch's self-portrayal, the two sides of his personality pointing in opposite directions. And we note St. Augustine likewise, recalling his own cleft spirit, as he recorded it in the eighth book of his *Confessions:* " 'Right away. Yes, right away. Let me be for a little while.' But 'Right away—right away' was never right now, and 'Let me be for a little while' stretched out for a long time." But in Petrarch's case the cleft spirit did not proceed to a decisive crisis and a radical conversion.

CHAPTER II

ST. TERESA OF ÁVILA

St. Teresa (1515-1582) has been called the greatest Spanish woman, and her *Life* has been described as probably the most widely read book in Spain after the *Don Quixote* of Cervantes. The enduring popularity of this autobiography indicates a certain basic human appeal as well as the spirit of a particular age. While we should remember that in Teresa's day one fourth of the Spaniards were reckoned as clerical and that the mentality of the great saint was not unique in sixteenth-century Spain, the larger European setting of her age was that of the Renaissance. Her childhood followed the lifetime of Leonardo da Vinci; she was a contemporary of Michelangelo and Montaigne and Giordano Bruno; her old age saw the youth of Galileo; she died only fourteen years before the birth of Descartes; yet it would be unthinkable to group her with that modern company. She is rather with St. John of the Cross and Jacob Boehme, her younger contemporaries, but also with medieval predecessors: St. Bernard of Clairvaux, St. Francis of Assisi, and St. Bonaventura. To understand her life and character and her intimate experiences we should recognize her kinship with this company of saints; then we should also see her in her larger setting of religious contemplation in many ages and various faiths. The spirit which marks them all is that of mystical rapture and ecstasy, and we should have to consider its meaning and importance in the study of religion.

29

But mystical absorption does not exhaust St. Teresa's experience. She was also marked by tireless and widely productive activity, preeminent in the history of Spanish monasticism. She undertook a drastic reform of the Carmelite order, to realize strict unworldly cloistered devotion. Her "discalced" or barefoot nuns and friars were to live in complete withdrawal from any secular pursuits of power or pleasure or profit. Her *Book of the Foundations* is a detailed record of indefatigable struggle to achieve this holy purpose, despite discouragement and outright opposition by prelates and laity who did not share her convictions. Starting with her first foundation of barefoot nuns, in her native town of Ávila, within twenty years she established sixteen more convents throughout Spain. Fourteen monastic houses for barefoot friars were founded through her efforts or influence.

The story of her organizing zeal and energy becomes doubly impressive when we consider that she was a continually and often very gravely sick woman. The eight-page chronological outline of her career, with which Professor Peers prefaces the first volume of his translation of her *Complete Works,* is as depressing in its record of her many illnesses as it is inspiring in the sheer magnitude of her listed achievements. When she was twenty-four she suffered an attack of catalepsy so severe that she was given up for dead, and even her grave was dug. Left an invalid for three years, she long endured the effects of paralysis, which recurred for about a dozen years. This was the worst of many ailments which included a fractured left arm, numerous attacks of high fever, digestive ills, a quartan ague, neuralgia, quinsy— a generally disordered bodily constitution. Her accounts of perilous cross-country travels over swampy roads or over rough and precipitous terrain—and she feverish and upset digestively and badly shaken by the heeling wagon—make exciting reading, enjoyable only because one is aware of the eventual safe outcome. The episode related in greatest detail, of her journey to establish her convent in Burgos, is particularly impressive.

The thirty-one chapters of her *Book of the Foundations* recount her more important successes in establishing her convents and monasteries of barefoot Carmelites: in Medina del Campo, in Valladolid, in Toledo, Pastrana, Salamanca, Alma de Tolmes, Segovia, Beas, Seville, Palencia, Burgos. Her hardships were not due only to bad roads, or filthy and vermin-infested inns crowded with unruly, drunken, and swearing travelers, or futile inquiries about houses for her nuns, or plain unholy poverty and frustration in getting sponsors for her projects. When starting her convent in Toledo, "on that first day we had not so much as a scrap of brushwood to broil a sardine on."[1] She had also to reckon with hostility to her plans of Carmelite reform. The "calced" Carmelites of less strenuous and more "practical" piety, nuns and friars alike, were a powerful organization which resisted Teresa's policies as unreasonably strict and unwarrantably critical of themselves. Powerful prelates and officers of the Inquisition distrusted her reliability in theology and ecclesiastic conformity; some of them regarded her as morbid and unsound, especially suspecting the reports of her supernatural visitations.

For three years her active work in Carmelite reform was delayed by her appointment, which she had obediently to accept, as prioress of the "calced" Carmelite Convent of the Incarnation in Ávila, which she had left about ten years earlier to start her convent of barefoot nuns in that city. She needed both piety and statesmanship in meeting the initial resistance of the nuns whom she had to direct: "My ladies, have no misgivings as to how I shall govern you; for, though I have thus far lived among and governed nuns who are discalced, I know well, through the Lord's goodness, the way to govern those who are not."[2] When the convent of St. Joseph of Carmel, Segovia, was being established, apparently with the permission both of the Bishop and of the city, "the Vicar-General . . . came out at once in a great rage, and refused to allow Mass to be said there any longer. He also tried to imprison the priest who had said it. . . ."[3]

The ignorant crowds did not welcome at first the arrival in their midst of the barefoot nuns; the Mother Foundress sought safety for the devout sisters in initial secret settlement and seclusion. In the course of time, however, Teresa's convincing saintliness and the genuine and devout piety of her nuns turned early resistance into positive and even enthusiastic support. Instead of having to slip unawares into their rented rundown houses, they were welcomed on their arrival, as for instance in the village of Beas, where they were cheered by the entire population in a festival procession.

Some powerful church leadership resisted her reformatory efforts to the last years of her life. In her endeavors to overcome the ecclesiastical antipathy to her barefoot Carmelites she dared to appeal to King Philip II himself, and it was owing to the royal support of her cause that she was able to prevail eventually in gaining decisive favor in Rome. For all that, some high prelates continued to put obstacles in her way, as she relates it in the longest and concluding chapter of her *Book of the Foundations*. She had shown deference to the views and orders of her confessors and bishops, but she also minced no words in expressing her estimate of the most revered but not reliable Archbishop of Burgos who forgot his initial promises and refused to license her projected foundation. Later he sent her with seeming reassurance to the Vicar-General, "but the devil must have paid a visit"[4] to him also. As it turned out in the end, however, the prelates were dilatory because they wanted her to convince them that she had secured the means needed for the support of the convent; this point she acknowledged in all candor. But still she made a plea for her faith in holy poverty. A convent supposedly endowed may be disappointed in its patrons, and in any case it would be unlikely to get any popular contributions; but barefoot nuns that were known to be without means could always rely for their support on godly people.

The Foundress Mother must have shown remarkably good judgment in selecting her nuns from the large number of those who came to her. (Five of the six daughters of her patroness in Burgos, Catalina de Tolosa, joined her convent as barefoot nuns.) Her account of her various foundations is one of steady praise of her nuns. They showed loving obedience to her strict rule, which is formulated in her *Constitutions*. The conventual regime was most exacting. Fasting was to be observed, except on Sundays, from September to Easter, and "no meat must ever be eaten, except in cases of necessity provided by the Rule."[5] For all her saintly austerity, however, the Foundress Mother did have her weakness for some specified dainties. Her *Letters* contain grateful acknowledgment of toothsome gifts, "sweets, sardines, partridges"[6] Of course she rued her lapses—were they a part of her remorseful "wicked sinfulness"? Like St. Francis she meant to be and to stay poor, but people did insist on sending her presents. Quite contritely she confessed: "It must be my nature— I could be suborned with a sardine."[7]

The barefoot requirement was relaxed when they had to cross muddy ground, for the Foundress Mother had high regard for cleanliness; but "sandals must be hempen-soled." The nuns's habit was of "frieze or coarse black woolen cloth," of the plainest design; the beds were only straw pallets, mattresses were not allowed to the nuns except in case of sickness; carpets were limited to the church.[8] No decoration, no color, no mirrors, no finery whatever. The entire convent was to bespeak the consecration of the nuns and their prioress to the holy life, renouncing all worldly attachment to anyone and anything. Within the convent a friendly spirit of communion was to prevail, but no personal intimacies: "no sister must embrace another, or touch face or hands, and there must be no special friendships among them but each must have a general love for all the rest, as Christ often commanded his Apostles."[9]

The daily program of the convent was outlined in strict precision, both as to hours of common worship and private meditation and ready sharing in the many tasks and chores of the house. Each nun was to pursue her chosen godly path with joyful concentration on piety, without worldly amusements or desires or regrets. While thus describing the ideal conditions for her nuns St. Teresa was aware of their occasional straying, and her *Constitutions* included a sort of penal code for the correction of faults which were classified in detail as slight, of medium gravity, graver, and gravest. The stipulated penances were of duly graduated severity; one instance may suffice:

> If any nun be convicted before the prioress of having borne false witness against any other, or of having habitually slandered her, let her do her penance as follows. At the hour of dinner, without her mantle but wearing a scapular on the back and front of which have been sewn two tongue-shaped strips of red and white cloth, one of each on either side, let her sit on the floor, in the centre of the refectory, and take bread and water as a symbol of punishment for her great sin of the tongue, and let her be taken thence to the prison.[10]

Even this brief survey of St. Teresa's career as Foundress Mother of Reformed Carmelite convents and monasteries should suffice to indicate her genius for organization which has few parallels in the annals of monasticism. We are reminded of St. Bernard who in the twelfth century championed a monastic reform, whose founding of the Cistercian Abbey of Clairvaux was followed within thirty years by almost one hundred allied cloisters throughout Europe, who urged the Second Crusade and was the acknowledged holy statesman of the Church. But Bernard's deepest concern was not centered on his outward career; rather, on his inward loving devotion to the Lord. Medieval tradition called him "the Man of Love," and his supreme hope was to experience the "heavenly conversation" of utter absorption in the Divine. St. Teresa likewise, through all her tireless labors and achievements, found the real summit of her being in her most intimate mystical experiences, in that upper chamber of her soul, or as she called it in her great book, *Interior Castle,* where she was one with the Lord, Teresa of Jesus. The Church that has been duly wary of occult visionaries has likewise accorded exalted tribute to its tested and true mystics. We may well surmise that it was as much Teresa's Carmelite Reform as her mystical preeminence which led to her canonization as a saint within forty years of her death.

It has been written that the blessings of a satisfied conscience are least experienced where they are most deserved. Surely one good reason for doubting the saintliness of a person is if he regards himself as a saint. The converse inference may also have merit. The reader of Teresa of Ávila's works cannot fail to be impressed by her contending estimates of herself; her ardor for cleaving to the Lord and her devastating sense of unworthiness as a wicked sinner. This, her spiritual duality, characterized her in her early life, and she never surmounted it. So she wrote: "It really frightens me to remember how little I could do by myself and how I was so tied and bound that I could not resolve to give myself wholly to God. When I started to read the *Confessions,* I seemed to see myself in them. . . ."[11] But how could she ever experience St. Augustine's assurance after his conversion, of his utter peace in the Lord? As she read not only St. Augustine's *Confessions* but also the lives of other saints, she reflected: "There was only one thing that troubled me, . . . namely, that, after the Lord had once called them, they did not fall again, whereas I had fallen so often that I was distressed by it."[12] Teresa's *Life* records her spiritual ascent, but also her swaying between the higher reaches of the godly life and the nether levels of worldliness.

She was born in Ávila in 1515, the daughter of Don Alonso Sanchez de Cepeda and his wife, Doña Beatriz Dávila de Ahumada. She wrote of them both in the highest terms: "It was a help to me that I never saw my parents inclined to anything but virtue."[13] Although, as she confessed, she alone among her nine brothers and two sisters failed to resemble her parents in virtue, she felt herself to be her father's favorite, hoped to deserve his approval, and was intent on consulting him in everything. She failed to do so in everything, however; for she and her elder brother Rodrigo had been reading the lives of saints and martyrs and had glorious plans of running off to the land of the Moors and begging their bread for the love of God, "so that they may behead us there."[14] That missionary plan was followed by the decision of the two young devotees to become hermits, and they would build hermitages in their orchard by piling up heaps of small stones. She played at building convents with her girl friends, all pretending that they were nuns.

She lost her mother when she was thirteen, and in filial devotion she called herself Teresa de Ahumada. The mother had been fond of books of chivalry, and to these Teresa turned from her lives of saints. She began to cultivate romantic ideas, decked herself out, using perfumes and all the vanities she could get. Unluckily at that time she came under the influence of a cousin, a young woman of unclean mind and tongue. The taint of this companionship would have been deeper had she not been taken as a boarder to an Augustinian convent in Ávila, where she remained for a year and a half. Her personal charm quickly made her a favorite with the nuns, and their good example turned her own thoughts and desires to higher things. She began to consider plans of becoming a nun, wavered for and against the idea but reached a decision by entering the Carmelite Convent of the Incarnation in Ávila as a novice. At the end of a year's stay there, at the age of twenty-two, she was a professed nun.

It was at that time of her life that a succession of grave illnesses, which we have mentioned earlier, laid her so low that, a cataleptic for more than eight months, she was regarded as dead, and only her father's persistent refusal kept her from being interred. When she regained consciousness, as she wrote much later:

> Only the Lord can know what intolerable sufferings I experienced. My tongue was bitten to pieces; nothing had passed my lips; and because of this and of my great weakness my throat was choking me so that I could not even take water. All my bones seemed to be out of joint and there was a terrible confusion in my head. As a result of the torments I had suffered during those days, I was all doubled up, like a ball, and no more able to move arm, foot, hand or head than if I had been dead, unless others moved them for me. I could move, I think, only one finger of my right hand.[15]

Months and years of slow and not consistent recovery followed; for almost fifteen years she suffered periodic effects of her paralysis. While she was gradually regaining her energies, she suffered another blow, in the death of her father. Thus shaken, body and soul, she yet continued in her cloistered devotion, and what was more important, she began to feel dissatisfied with what she regarded as the laxity of the Carmelite convent. It had affected her, and she had recoiled in remorse. The nuns did not observe the rule of enclosure, a mere formality; along with the straying in and out of the world went other amusements and pastimes and sundry indulgence. It was then that "Christ revealed himself to me in an attitude of great sternness, and showed me what there was in this that displeased Him. I saw Him with the eyes of the soul more clearly than I could ever have seen Him with those of the body."[16] Could we regard this experience as the inception of her "interior castle" of mystical states, as well as of her eventual plans for the Carmelite Reform with her barefoot nuns?

We have come now to the most important part of St. Teresa's self-portrayal which marks her special preeminence in studies of religious experience. Preeminent she is in her most detailed reports of the soul's gradual ascent to the supreme state of rapture or ecstasy. Her accounts are bound to leave most of us deeply perplexed. Our quandary, but also our religious outlook, if not cleared up, might be expanded significantly if we first consider some broadly analogous accounts by other saints in the Christian tradition and in other faiths.

The term mystical has had a eulogistic but also a derogatory connotation, and one may test one's own spiritual temper when reading St. Teresa's reports. Mysticism has been used to signify the summit of religious contemplation, but it has also described morbid religious aberrations and also hysterical delusions. In German these opposite intensions are expressed by two different forms of the word, *Mystik* and *Mysticismus*. Our own speech also has a corresponding pair: mystical and mystifying; the latter term is loaded with a further derogatory implication.

If we try to define mysticism, we find a variety of proposed formulas. "It has been used to designate the striking manifestation of supernatural activity, whether it be occult possession of savages by demonic powers or divine intervention in human life and in the course of nature. It has described religious experiences of intense emotional fervour, elusive intimacy, and blinding clarity of direct intuition. The mystical soul has been regarded as not putting its trust in formulated doctrine or in ecclesiastic or ceremonial regime but using or dismissing tradition to suit its own quest, relying not on convincing arguments but on its own love and thirst for the Divine."[17]

Even the briefest survey of the evolution of religion may provide significant instances of these various aspects of mystical experience. Anthropological studies of religious ceremonies in primitive societies report not only striking manifestations of alleged divine or demonic possession of shamans and medicine men but also the specific use of narcotics and intoxicants to induce religious trances and frenzy. On a higher cultural level the Greek Bacchanalia disclosed the strong appeal of deep-lying impulses of occult and often morbid emotions; some of them urging the soul on its spiritual ascent, others orgiastic and debasingly pathological. The word enthusiasm, we should recall, signified divine possession; but our words assassin *(hashishin)* and thug are derived from Syrian and Indian practices of violent and criminal religious intoxication.

In our study of the mystical fire we should not overlook the smoke but must not confuse it with the flame. From the shaman and the bacchante and the *hashishin* we should look upward to the great mystical seers, even if we may be inclined to regard the latter as visionaries. We can meet them in various faiths, East and West. In their exalted company St. Teresa's visions can be recognized in more significant perspective. In the Orient India has been the classic land of mystical contemplation, from the ancient seers of the Vedic Upanishads to the lyrical self-absorption in Deity which marks the *Gitanjali* and the other poems of Rabindranath Tagore, the first poet of Asia to receive the Nobel Prize. So we read in the *Bhagavadgita,* the most read religious classic of India: "The devotee who worships me abiding in all beings, holding that all is one, lives in me, however he may be living."[18]

West of India, in Mohammedan lands, a whole school of Persian Sufi poets expressed the strong hold of mystical devotion. One special characteristic shared by them with Christian mystics, such as St. Bernard, St. John of the Cross, and St. Teresa herself, was their use of erotic utterances to express intense religious absorption. Thus, Jalalud'-din Rumi: "One knocked at the Beloved's door; and a voice answered from within: 'Who is there?' and he answered: 'It is I.' Then the voice said: 'This house will not hold me and thee.' Then went the lover into the desert, and fasted and prayed in solitude. And after a year he returned and knocked again at the door. And again the voice asked, 'Who is there?' and he said, 'It is Thyself!' and the door was opened to him."[19]

Christian mysticism has its earliest fountainheads in the Gospels and St. Paul's Epistles. Have we not in our youth learned by heart the words in the fourteenth chapter of the Fourth Gospel: "At that day ye shall know that I am in my Father, and ye in me, and I in you." St. Paul wrote to his church in Corinth of his mystical rapture, when he was "caught up to the third heaven, . . . into paradise."[20] We may read similar words in St. Teresa's pages.

The note of ecstatic consummation is strong in the medieval saints, not only in the pronounced mystics but also in the more characteristically rational devotees. Thus in the thirteenth century the strongly intellectual doctrinal tradition of the Dominican doctors contended with the mystical appeal of the followers of St. Francis of Assisi, the chief of them being St. Bonaventura, who expressed their ideal with eloquent intensity: "Interrogate grace and not doctrine, desire and not knowledge, the groaning of prayer rather than study, the spouse rather than the teacher, God and not man, mist rather than clarity, not light but fire all aflame and bearing to God by devotion and glowing affection."[21] Dante has been called "Aquinas in verse," but in the *Paradiso* the poet's guide in the ascent of the Ten Heavens is not St. Thomas but his adored Lady Beatrice and the mystical St. Bernard of Clairvaux. Dante's spiritual climax is a spiritual vision of the Divine as a river of fire in which the souls of the blessed saints are as flaming sparks; and his concluding line praises God as "the Love that moves the sun and the other stars." St. Thomas himself was not unresponsive to the mystical appeal. As the doctor of the *Summa Theologica* lay dying in the monastery of Fossanuova, he asked the friars to read to him St. Bernard's mystical sermons.

With this very general background of discussion of mystical experience we shall consider St. Teresa's accounts of it in her self-portrayal. We have several versions, notably in her *Life,* in the *Spiritual Relations* addressed to her confessor, in the *Way of Perfection,* and in the *Interior Castle (The Mansions).* These works, as well as the saint's *Letters,* have had wide popular appeal, and not only in Spain. They have been ranked in very high terms for their literary mastery; but St. Teresa had the humblest estimate of her abilities as a writer: "For the love of God, let me work at my spinning-wheel and go to choir and perform the duties of the religious life, like the other sisters. I am not meant to write. I have neither the health nor the intelligence for it."[22] Nor does she pretend to any doctrinal adequacy of exposition. She does not claim to explain, for she does not understand "mystical theology, as I believe it is called."[23]

We should first simply relate what she reports. We are reminded of the story of the blind man by the pool of Siloam whose sight was restored by Jesus. He could not argue it out with the Pharisees, who were learnedly critical of his Lord: "One thing I know, that, whereas I was blind, now I see."[24] Doctrinal "pharisaism" may be of the right or of the left; so far as we can, without prejudgment theological or worldly, we may do well to read St. Teresa's accounts as her personal reports. Such a plain reception of what she has to say may enable us to venture more fairly to some critical appraisal of her "spiritual relations."

The ascent to rapture was to St. Teresa God's consummate blessing to the devout soul, but, as she made it clear, the godly life is not limited to the contemplative exaltation. She recalled the Gospel story of the Lord's visit to the home of Martha and Mary. Martha, "cumbered about much serving," chafed that her sister was not helping her but was simply sitting at the Lord's feet to hear His word. The Lord said: "Martha, Martha, thou art anxious and troubled about many things: but one thing is needful; for Mary hath chosen the good part, which shall not be taken away from her."[25] St. Teresa, the Foundress Mother, urged her sisters to remember that Martha also in her way was serving the Lord.

> Remember that there must be someone to cook the meals and count yourself happy to be able to serve like Martha. . . . If contemplation and mental and vocal prayer and tending the sick and serving in the house at even the lowliest tasks are of service to the Guest who comes to stay with us and take His recreation with us, what should it matter to us if we do one of these things rather than another? I do not mean that it is for us to say what we shall do, but that we must do our best in everything, for the choice is not ours but the Lord's.[26]

In her own life the mystical saint was also the Foundress Mother: like Mary she sat at the Lord's feet, but like Martha also, she was busy, "anxious and troubled about many things," in the endless toils of establishing and directing the numerous convents of her Carmelite Reform. The two directions of her life-career she pursued, the way of Martha and the way of Mary. Yet in her supreme hope she was and remained with Mary.

In St. Teresa's view the mystical ascent is a gradation in prayer or orison: the rise of the soul from itself towards God. To reach unto God and be with God and in God, one must be delivered of one's own self. "The order . . . to observe in prayer is this. First, make the sign of the cross; accuse yourself of all the faults committed since your last confession; strip yourself of all things, as if you were to die that hour. . . ."[27] The stripping of self, it would seem, involves loss of consciousness but is not to be identified with it. Long before St. Teresa had reached states of ecstasy, in her early youth, she had suffered from serious fainting fits. She remembered her protracted catalepsy. We should not confuse bodily failure with the contemplative exaltation.

Through long years of her spiritual quest St. Teresa had gradually recognized the characteristic stages or the main paths which had led her to the supreme experience of Christ's intimate possession and the taste of His blessed love. She had read somewhere of a comparison which helped her to understand the processes of holy self-transcendence, and she would develop it in some detail.

> The beginner must think of himself as of one setting out to make a garden in which the Lord is to take his delight, yet in soil most unfruitful and full of weeds. . . . The garden can be watered in four ways: by taking the water from a well, which costs us great labour; or by a water-wheel and buckets, when the water is drawn by a windlass; . . . or by a stream or brook, which waters the ground much better; . . . or by heavy rain, when the Lord waters it with no labour of ours, a way incomparably better than any of those which have been described.[28]

From her chosen example she turns to the application of it, to describe the four stages of the mystical experience. Her account of them varies somewhat in her *Life,* in the *Spiritual Relations,* and in the *Interior Castle (The Mansions),* but the main outlines are fairly clear in them all. The four stages of the mystical ascent, like the four ways of watering a garden, are four kinds or stages of prayer. For prayer or orison is the soul's ascent to God, or rather it is Christ's way of drawing the soul to Himself; His divine Grace manifesting itself in our own effort and devotion to aspire to Him and to be with Him.

The first stage of the mystical ascent is mental orison, the Prayer of Meditation. Like drawing up the water out of a well, this is a toilsome proceeding. It requires ascetic rigor, austere self-discipline in the holy life, rejection of all worldly vanities, firm resolution to attain indifference to the thousand nothings and to concentrate on the one and supreme All. Had not St. Augustine written: "God and the soul: that is what I desire to know. Nothing more? Nothing whatever."[29] In chosen solitude and mental prayer we should plunge all our meditation on some holy theme, such as Christ's Passion. We should be at the Lord's side in the Garden of Gethsemane, praying with Him: "Not as I will, but as Thou wilt." There is no transcendence of our own thought and consciousness here, not yet, but rather intense concentration on our holy pursuit. This is arduous endeavor, and more than once it may fail of attainment. Perhaps the initial preparation for it was not sufficient; we may have to turn back to our daily discipline in the unworldly life, in godly service and daily tasks of charity, ever hoping that the Lord will graciously incline our soul again to the mental Prayer of Meditation, which may lead us beyond itself to the deeper insight and the higher ascent. For the soul is not to view the Interior Castle from the outside and remain in its outer court; it should enter the castle, dwell in it, in its many rooms and in the chiefest mansion at its center. This holy pilgrimage is a detachment from self that is yet a thorough self-penetration. "For we ourselves are the castle": the soul must reach through its periphery and "enter within itself."[30]

The second stage of the mystical ascent is the Orison or Prayer of Quiet. The mind that has emptied itself of all worldliness and secular knowledge now manifests, in its concentration on the Divine, greater powers and mastery than it has ever before shown in its usual activities. One instance of this holy self-ascendency is cited both by St. Teresa and by St. John of the Cross, and in almost identical words. Thus, St. Teresa: "In this state of Quiet, I, who understand hardly anything which I recite in Latin, particularly in the Psalter, have not only been able to understand the text as though it were in Spanish, but have even found to my delight that I can penetrate the meaning of the Spanish."[31]

It is not by our own effort or merit but by the Lord's grace alone that we can experience this communion with Him. "However hard we try we cannot reach it for ourselves. . . . The soul, in a way which has nothing to do with the outward senses, realizes that it is now very close to God, and, that, if it were but a little closer, it would be one with him through union."[32] This communion with God transforms one's soul so thoroughly that its entire activity is irradiated. Those to whom God has granted this favor may then turn to any daily task with a deep joy that is beyond understanding. "Thus Martha and Mary work together."[33] During the Orison of Quiet, in the intensity of its actual state, "the soul dares not to move or stir, for it thinks that if it does so this blessing may slip from its grasp: sometimes it would like to be unable even to breathe."[34] The blessing is itself a promise of yet greater gifts to the soul; "the flowers have now reached a point at which they are almost ready to bloom."[35]

By divine Grace the soul's communion with God, in the Prayer of Quiet, may in certain cases ascend to the third height, the Prayer of Union. The soul is now wholly yielded to God in worshipful absorption. It is "nothing less than an all but complete death to everything in the world and a fruition of God."[36] In this its union with God the soul has quite transcended its usual reactions of sense or feeling or desire, and feels only of its oneness with its Beloved. "The understanding . . . counts for nothing here; the soul would like to shout aloud, for it is in such a state that it cannot contain itself—a state of delectable disquiet."[37] Speaking most likely of herself in the third person, St. Teresa recalls how in that state she would have joyfully endured any suffering for her Lord's sake. "She would have been glad if she could have been cut to pieces, body and soul. . . ."[38] In this loving bliss of union the soul is self-transcended: like a large and ugly silkworm which, having buried itself in its self-spun cocoon, comes right out of it a beautiful white butterfly. Quite transformed and self-transcended as it is now, we may say, the butterfly is still aware of itself as a butterfly. So the soul is conscious of its oneness with God. "This kind of prayer . . . is quite definitely a union of the entire soul with God except that His Majesty appears to be willing to give the faculties leave to understand, and have fruition of the great thing that He is now doing."[39]

Finally, as peak above peak in the mystical ascent, beyond the climax of Union is the summit of the fourth stage, the Prayer of Rapture or Ecstasy. In this complete absorption of the soul in God, consciousness of oneself is utterly surpassed. Recalling St. Teresa's comparison of the four ways of watering a garden, this is the divine rainfall in which the soul is flooded and swept away. In its very nature this experience overtaxes any effort to give an adequate account of it from within, for while it lasts self-observation and consciousness itself are suspended. In St. Teresa's many states of rapture, often during Eucharist, the sisters communicating with her could note the outward marks of her exaltation, and so she gives us their reports. "The hands become as cold as ice and sometimes remain stretched as though made of wood. The body remains standing or kneeling according to the position in which it was when the rapture came on."[40] How is it that the consciousness, suspended during rapture, and all its faculties—sight, hearing, touch—quite submerged, how is it that, when it returns to itself, it somehow becomes aware of transcended bliss which it has experienced? Of all these marvels the saint does not profess to have an explanation, only the reports of it.

The aftereffects of rapture on some mystics have been described as very upsetting and requiring long recovery. But St. Teresa's accounts seem reassuring; she has felt no serious harm from rapture, with some exceptions. "My body was so exhausted that even today I can write this only with great difficulty, and my hands are very painful and feel as if they were out of joint."[41] In her case the utter absorption in God has more usually been followed by a pervasive tender piety and by a renewed firm commitment to any holy duties. Once again Mary and Martha alternate in her spiritual temper.

When Mohammed had his first life-transforming experience on Mount Hira outside Mecca, when in his illumination he saw the Angel Gabriel holding Allah's Koran and asking him to read it and translate it—and he an illiterate man—he ran back home in a state of utter quandary and asked his wife to tell him whether perhaps he had not been maddened by a demon. St. Teresa likewise was repeatedly beset with this dire perplexity. So many wise priestly minds regarded her as bewitched: how could she be sure that her ecstasies were not in fact only delusions with which the devil was molesting her? These worries were the wormwood aftertaste of her divine feasts. But she had had so many plain clashes with the devil that she had come to distinguish the malign experiences from the blessed.

Some of her accounts of Satanic encounters are of a shattering character. She had a vision of being tossed down to hell to see the special pouch set aside for her. It harrowed her to think that after all her sublime blessings on earth she was to be damned. But her resolute piety protested, and in renewed zeal she reconsecrated herself to Christ. The devils, however, would not relinquish their wiles. She might banish them by waving the cross at them, but like flies they came back; only the spray of holy water made them keep their distance. They appeared most untowardly. Once when a priest was serving the communion plate she saw two devils of most terrible aspect gripping his throat; clearly he must have been guilty of mortal sin. "What must it be, my Lord, to see that beauty of Thine between two such hideous forms?"[42] Only by the renewed experience of Christ's loving possession could she be reassured and enabled to endure and resist the horrors of the demonic infestations.

She was worried that these experiences, ecstatic or diabolical, took place when she was with others who might not be able to understand. But surely, if the Lord vouchsafed to reveal His presence to her, or permitted the devils to molest her, He knew best the times and the seasons. For all that she cherished her divine solitude, "as a sparrow all alone on the housetop," as the Psalmist sang of old.[43] But she also desired the companionship of those contemplative souls who understood, like St. John of the Cross. Yet even in their converse there always remained something, and it the kernel of it all, incommunicable.

As time went on, St. Teresa's intimacy with Christ the Lord assumed very striking forms. She felt his presence at her side, invisible but unmistakable; then somehow more clearly visible than anyone to mortal eyes, with a beauty beyond any powers of description. "It is not a radiance that dazzles, but a soft whiteness and an infused radiance which, without wearying the eyes, causes them the greatest delight. . . . So different from any earthly light is the brightness and light now revealed to the eyes that, by comparison with it, the brightness of the sun seems quite dim. . . ."[44] Amazing experiences, amazing to herself, convinced her of Christ's especial loving concern in her behalf. "Once when I was holding in my hand the cross of a rosary, He put out His own hand and took it from me, and when He gave it back to me, it had become four large stones, much more precious than diamonds—incomparably more so. . . . On the cross with exquisite workmanship, were portrayed the five wounds. . . . To nobody, however, did it look like this, except to myself."[45] This holy bejeweling of hers is repeated with variations.

Her mystical visitations alternated with the most arduous practical endeavors, which proceeded against heavy odds but were finally successful. When she prevailed in establishing her convent of St. Joseph, she had a vision of Notre Dame with St. Joseph beside her, commending her for her holy work, and as a sign of the favor she had gained with the Lord the Virgin Mary threw around Teresa's neck "a very beautiful gold collar, to which was fastened a most valuable cross. The gold and stones were . . . unlike anything that one can imagine."[46] Once when in ecstasy she saw a dove over her head, its wings "made of little shells which emitted a great brilliance."[47] The multitude of divine blessings overwhelmed her. She was enabled to cure others by prayer, to release souls from Purgatory. She was reluctant to confess it all to her priest: "Not, I think, because of humility, but for fear lest he might laugh at me and say: 'What a St. Paul she is, with her heavenly visions! Quite a St. Jerome!' "[48] The deepest mysteries of the Incarnation and the Holy Trinity were clarified to her in direct vision, even though she could not claim the ability to explain them in reasoned language.[49] She saw the very throne of God, with the angelic choir, and glory blends with humbleness in her reports of her raptures: "Oh, my Majesty and Greatness! What art Thou doing, my Lord Almighty? Consider to whom Thou art granting such sovereign mercies."[50] Her language takes often an erotic tone of spirituality; she feels herself the bride of Christ; she, the meanest worm of sinfulness, to whom the Lord's loving grace has been granted wholly undeserved.

This account—paraphrase and direct select citation of passages—is the barest report of a most intimate and intense religious experience. The reader of St. Teresa's *Life* and her other writings is bound to stop and ask himself: What is one to make of these wholly extraordinary and scarcely credible "spiritual relations"? How are we to interpret and evaluate the mystical experience? This kind of question raises the whole problem of the psychology of religion and of our ultimate philosophical outlook. We cannot pretend here to explore fully that boundless field; we can only venture to approach the problem in its relation to other inquiries into the exceptional manifestations of the mind of genius. Wordsworth's lines keep ringing in our memory:

> Oh mystery of Man, from what a depth
> Proceed thy honours?[51]

We should be on our guard lest we be misled by the seem-ing kinship of alleged mystical states of consciousness with some pathological cases of hysteria and mental disorder or trances of narcotic inducement. How are we to separate altogether the saint's visions from the hallucinations of psychiatric patients so as to realize that the mystic's raptures are not to be regarded as fits or seizures? All about us today are people young and old who believe that they can tap unsounded depths or scale sublime heights of experience by taking certain drugs. William James was a hospitable mind who was temperamentally inclined to try the great perhaps. He had been told that the inhaling of a certain diluted chemical could "stimulate the mystical con-sciousness in an extraordinary degree . . . depth beyond depth of truth" yielding "a genuine metaphysical revelation." But the alleged truth faded out, and, when one came out of the trance, whatever words might be remembered turned out to be "the veriest nonsense."[52] Might one proceed to a reasonable sur-mise that the so-called mystical saint also is a type of addict in need of a guardian or a doctor? We are here led to consider again the evidence mentioned earlier of the lurid or morbid aspects of some religious rituals from earliest times. But though we are surely warned, we are not quite confuted in our spiritual quest. As Plato said, "Many are the wand-bearers, but few are the mystics";[53] —both a dismissal and a reaffirmation.

When two series of experiences have some common features, a reasonable inference can scarcely be drawn merely from cer-tain similarities. From the plain evidence that some mystical saints have been known to suffer from nervous and mental disorders and that some hysterical or otherwise unbalanced patients have had hallucinations analogous to some mystical visions, could we rightly conclude that mysticism is a variety of hysteria? We should rather probe further, to consider the entire experience in the two sets of cases: not only some of the conditions or some aspects of the processes but also the eventual results.

One should be careful here not to confuse effects with causes: What in any specific case is the determining condition, and what is the ensuing result? We may have to consider whether the nervous and mental ills of the mystic are the explanatory causes of his visions, or whether the true order is quite the reverse: that it is the overwhelming spiritual upsurge of the religious genius which staggers body and soul and leaves them both limp and helpless. In the case of the hysterical and mentally unbalanced patient, the true order of determining conditions and results may be the very opposite. Here the basically pathological state, while it induces certain hallucinations, is yet spiritually deficient and unable to yield eventual results of any great significance and worth. We should heed Gospel wisdom: "By their fruits ye shall know them. Do men gather grapes from thorns, or figs of thistles?"[54]

Studies of artistic and literary genius may help us to understand better this aspect of the problem of mysticism. We read in *Midsummer Night's Dream*:

> The lunatic, the lover, and the poet
> Are of imagination all compact.[55]

So be it, but still Shakespeare's compact does differ from the lunatic's. Friedrich Schiller is reported to have found the smell of rotting apples a stimulant to poetic inspiration. One day Goethe came to his room unexpectedly and could scarcely catch his breath. Would it follow that you and I need only a bag of rotten apples to start our "Hymn to Joy," which some other person addicted to vile smells could turn into another Ninth Symphony? Did Dostoyevsky write *The Brothers Karamazov* because he was an epileptic, or, despite his epilepsy, because he was a genius?

Coleridge did write his "Kubla Khan" in a drugged state, but where are, not only the "Kubla Khans" but also the "Christabels" and "The Ancient Mariners" that have come out of psychiatric clinics?

Another sort of problem, which cannot be set aside, is raised by the religious seers. It has been pointed out that what the mystical saint finds in his rapture or trance depends on what he brings to his exalted experience. For mysticism is not only Roman Catholic but also Protestant, not only Christian but also Mohammedan and Brahmanic. The Persian Sufi poet had his visions of Allah, but not of Krishna; the ancient seers of the Upanishads had mystical contemplations of the Infinite Brahman but not of Yahveh; and none of them in their raptures felt the immediate presence of Christ the Lord. In our next chapter we shall be dealing with the inner light of the Quakers; but unlike St. Teresa, George Fox had no visions of the Savior's Blessed Mother. Now if we are to take religious experience seriously, we cannot take it uncritically. We cannot regard the mystics of one particular religious tradition as true seers of the Divine and dismiss the visions of the others as delusions. What is the view of the Divine and the Supernatural that would enable us to comprehend fairly the many and so various mystical strains in the far-flung history of religions?

The mystical experience is various not only in the perspectives of different religions. It has various aspects in the raptures of each mystical saint. St. Teresa had her ecstatic vision of Christ the Lord, but she also relates sundry external marvels of which she was the blessed witness. Her divine visions may be interpreted as sublime consummations of her Christian-Catholic piety; but can we also in good plain sanity believe that Christ the Lord really redecorated the cross of her diary with those four large stones much more precious than diamonds and of incomparable brilliance? St. Teresa herself avowed that her cross looked thus bejewelled to nobody else, only to herself. Our most resolute intention to do full justice to the inner spiritual recesses, range and reach, of the mystical saint can scarcely warrant any return to a view of the Divine as a physical power, which would be misguided idolatry. The true miracles are in the inner life, not out there in nature. "God is Spirit," and "spiritual things must be spiritually understood."

Are we not being led in this sort of inquiry to recognize plainly that nature has neither bottom nor top, that reality does not manifest to us either its absolutely ultimate rudiments nor its utmost upper limits? Contemporary physical science would seem to be disclosing to us the former truth; we could be led to acknowledge the latter by our studies of intelligence and spiritual activity in many fields. The ways of genius are beyond our complete inventory, and the range of spirit is beyond any finite computation. Along the various radii of their sublime endowment, thinker, poet, artist, and saint are reaching towards the divine center and summit of reality, and their utmost reach is after all a further vista. The highest peaks of their aspiration, if they ever ascend them, would reveal to them still more exalted prospects. Some of these ascents and self-outreaching powers of spirit are beyond our ordinary comprehension. Goethe was no mean genius himself, but he avowed that the creative marvels of Mozart were past his reckoning. How can we really fathom, not only the inflexible resolution but also the ability of Beethoven, increasingly and then utterly deaf, yet creating the greatest musical masterpieces? The lines from Robert Browning's "Abt Vogler" come to mind:

But here is the finger of God, a flash of the will that can,
Existent behind all laws, that made them and lo, they are!
And I know not if, save in this, such gift be allowed to man,
That out of three sounds he frame, not a fourth sound, but a star.
Consider it well: each tone in our scale in itself is nought;

It is everywhere in the world—loud, soft, and all is said:
Give it to me to use! I mix it with two in my thought:
And, there! Ye have heard and seen; consider and bow the head!

Bow the head, yes—but also consider! Recognition of the sub-limities of genius, which surpass our ordinary formulas of ex-planation, should not lead us, in bowing our head, to forget our wits—to supine surrender to superstitions. We reflected earlier in this chapter that we should not overlook the smoke in the mys-tical fire but should not confuse it with the flame. True—but yet, we should not overlook the smoke. Genius and saint may have their defects as plain mortals or as heirs of a certain tra-dition, with its superstitions or oddities. Did St. Teresa send to her good priest Father Gracian a bezoar (a concretion from the digestive tract of some animal) to wear around his neck as an antidote against poison? Well, so she may have done. But then wasn't Mozart, the master of the most incredibly deli-cate musical lacework at the piano, wasn't he so clumsy with his hands that his wife had to cut his meat for him lest he slash his fingers? In our spiritual appraisals, just as in any good audit, we should note the assets but also the liabilities. And this should be stated also in the converse order.

CHAPTER III

GEORGE FOX

A basic difference between the modern age and medieval thought and life is the contrast between the general uniformity of the Scholastic culture and the variety of new directions and developments which have marked the modern spirit. This variety characterized the Renaissance, which was the age of Benvenuto Cellini, Machiavelli and Leonardo da Vinci; of Montaigne, but also of Copernicus. The seventeenth century, which has been called "the century of genius," was a period of systematic reconstruction of ideas in science and philosophy, in social-political ideas and institutions. The mere mention of the names of Kepler, Galileo and Newton, Francis Bacon and Descartes, Spinoza and Leibniz, Hugo Grotius and Thomas Hobbes, should suffice to signalize this epoch-making achievement of the modern mind.

We should err, however, if we should conclude that the three first modern centuries simply replaced medieval religious faith by modern scientific and philosophical reason. The radical change was more than a turn from theological-ecclesiastic dominance to secular-worldly concentration. The modern age was also a period of alternatives in religion. Contemporary with the Renaissance was the Protestant Reformation. The secularism of the reformers was motivated not by worldliness but rather by a more thoroughgoing spirituality. They preached an all-penetrating Christian spirit that was to infuse the whole of human life and spiritualize it all. We cannot fail to note the contrast of Wycliffe and Huss

55

and Luther and Calvin to Pope Alexander VI and Pope Leo X. During the sixteenth century there was an upsurge of religious intensity which followed a mystical direction. In our previous chapter we studied the Roman Catholic expression of it in the career of St. Teresa of Ávila, but her contemporary, Jacob Boehme, signalized a similar trend in Protestant culture.

The two autobiographies which we shall examine in this and the following chapter are not only most intimate self-portrayals but also reflections of the life and culture of the seventeenth century. We should thus keep in mind that it was an age of religious issues and controversies as well as of social-political conflicts and of systematic intellectual reconstruction. It was the century of the rising royal power in France and centralized monarchical dominance, but, before it, a struggle between Roman Catholics and Huguenots: before Louis XIV and the ministers-cardinals Richelieu and Mazarin were Charles IX and Catherine de' Medici and the massacre of St. Bartholomew's Night. The civil war in the Netherlands between social liberals and reactionaries began as a theological controversy. In Germany the Thirty Years' War, between Protestants and Roman Catholics, reduced the country to a devastated wilderness.

Our present study concerns the British chapter of this period of manifold unsettlement and struggle. Familiar to us all is the story of the conflict between King and Parliament which led to the execution of Charles I, the rise to power of Oliver Cromwell and his followers, the eventual restoration of the Stuart kings Charles II and James II, and the "Glorious Revolution" of 1688, which established William of Orange and more representative and more responsible government in Great Britain. Our present inquiry will not ignore these political changes but will be concerned directly with another struggle of manifold religious alternatives which claimed British conviction and devotion. The initial issue was between Protestants and Catholics, but within the Protestant fold various tensions developed. King Henry VIII and Queen Elizabeth had established and confirmed the dominance of the Church of England. The teachings of John Calvin, through the powerful agency of John Knox, had led to the corresponding settlement of Presbyterianism as the representative Church of Scotland. But in England and Scotland alike, and chiefly in the former, varieties of so-called dissenting or nonconformist religious movements were expressing the demands of multiple thousands for a more intimate and more directly personal Christian experience, resistant to ecclesiastic forms and ritual, less dependent on theological doctrine, and seeking spiritual grace in devout feeling and heartfelt commitment to the Lord. As might be surmised the spiritual emancipation ran the hazard of uncontrolled and often morbid or violent excesses, but in its saner forms it was the promise of significant religious advance.

Students of this period of religious history have distinguished four of these dissenting or nonconformist movements which started in England but spread beyond its borders.[1] (1) The Baptists, represented notably by John Bunyan (1628-1688), whose *Grace Abounding to the Chief of Sinners* is an autobiographic document of the first importance, which we shall examine in our next chapter, resisted ecclesiastical prerogatives. They insisted on the complete freedom of each church community from episcopal or state control. They encouraged preaching by laymen, men and women alike, without settled pay or benefits, without elaborate formal consecration. More particularly they rejected the practice of infant christening. Baptism, they maintained, should be an act signifying the religious conviction and confession of a person of discretion, and it should be actually a baptism, a total immersion, not merely a sprinkling.

(2) A second movement was that of a variety of so-called "Seekers." They were independents who had lost confidence in

the traditional forms of Christian beliefs and practices, Roman Catholic or Anglican or Lutheran or Presbyterian. They were in quest of some direct and burning conviction of Christ's presence in each one of them. They expected some new and light-spreading revelation of the divine power to enter them personally and transform them in unwavering commitment to Christ.

(3) A movement of more upsetting character was that of the "Ranters." They were religious extremists of a sensational sort and in many cases of a violent and morbid outburst. Their services often impressed the sober observer as spiritual orgies. They defied any and all authority: Why could they not write Scriptures as well as Paul? Paul and Christ before him had done their work in their time, but God was directly present in every one of them and could lead them to new light and new truth. Many of the Ranters took an antinomian position, declaring that the saving grace of Christ had emancipated them not only from ecclesiastic and doctrinal conformity but also from the restrictions of the moral law. Like the medieval *Perfecti,* they believed that they had attained a state of sinlessness which could not be tainted by whatever they might do. This pious release of license and "horrid villanies" was bound to discredit and eventually to uproot the rank growth.

Among the group of sectaries the "Fifth Monarchy Men" went the length of extremism. According to their reading of world history, after the four ancient monarchies—Assyrian, Persian, Greek, Roman—a Fifth Monarchy was to be established, and speedily too, in their own day and in their midst. Christ was returning forthwith, and they themselves, the saints, were to reign with him. They might well speed this blessed coming by some stiff uprising.

(4) It is in this setting of ramified religious currents that we should consider the personality and the spiritual career of George Fox (1624-1691), the leader of the Society of Friends, or as

they came to be called popularly, the Quakers. Both during his lifetime and in later judgment, George Fox received extremely contrasting evaluations. Oliver Cromwell and Charles II held him in high regard, but their judges and other officials treated him with cruel hostility and contempt. The great historian Macaulay disparaged him in ironical detail and also in a terse snub as "an intellect . . . too disordered for liberty and not sufficiently disordered for Bedlam."[2] But Edward Everett Hale listed him as one of the eleven outstanding "prophets" in Christian history.[3] Quaker historians have noted Fox's influence on Wordsworth and Coleridge; Carlyle shows his close study of Fox's *Journal*. In our developing American culture, the Quaker impact is notable, above all, in William Penn's career in the establishment of Pennsylvania and also in the poetry and life-mission of Whittier.

Before turning to our closer study of Fox's *Journal* we may note his outstanding characteristic. The first descriptive term which comes to mind is mysticism. But we have been considering the mysticism of St. Teresa, and even on the briefest approach to George Fox we should be bound to see that his mysticism is quite different, different also from that of other great mystics, Christian, Mohammedan, or Brahmanic. As we shall be noting repeatedly, George Fox did experience ecstasy and blessed contemplation, but he was not "a contemplative." The mystical rapture in George Fox's experience was not the final consummation but the great impelling dynamic, impelling him to godly service. He did not find his spiritual summit in "waiting for the Lord"; he "went forth with the Lord," to fulfill the Lord's will. In George Fox as in St. Teresa and in St. Bernard before them, we recognize both practical Christian achievement and mystical rapture; but the prophet of Quakerism differed from the two Catholic saints in his prevailing emphasis on his service in the Lord's vineyard rather than on his visions of the

Divine. His central conviction, which all the Society of Friends were to share, was that the "Inner Light" of God's self-revelation to us is an expression of God's purpose for us. Our true religion must be our daily realization, in godly thought and speech and action, of this living divine presence in us. On almost successive pages in his *Journal* we may note expressions of this characteristic of Fox's active, outgoing mysticism: "I was wrapped up, as in a rapture, in the Lord's power. . . . The creation was opened to me, . . . and wonderful depth were opened unto me, beyond what can by words be declared; . . . And as the Lord opened these things unto me I felt that His power went forth over all, by which all might be reformed if they would receive and bow unto it."[4]

With this broad initial view of George Fox's devout spiritual ascent, we may turn to his detailed self-portrayal and his arduous career as recorded in his *Journal*. He was born at Drayton-in-the-Clay, in Leicestershire, "in the month called July," 1624, the son of a weaver: "an honest man; and there was a seed of God in him. The neighbors called him Righteous Christer. My mother was an upright woman . . . and of the stock of the martyrs."[5] Unlike other saintly confessions of early sinfulness, like St. Augustine's, George Fox's writing recalls the manifestations of God's grace in him from his early years: "I knew pureness and righteousness; for while a child I was taught how to walk to be kept pure. . . . I never wronged man or woman. . . . People had generally a love to me for my innocency and honesty."[6]

He was a young man of indubitable piety, but he was not a churchgoing Christian. The minister in Drayton, one Nathaniel Stephens, was a long-winded preacher who kept going until the hourglass in front of him ran out and then turned it over and kept expounding his doctrine of original sin and man's wickedness and divine predestination to grace or to damnation. Young

George disliked both the length and the doctrine of those sermons, and, instead of attending church service, he would go out into the field with his Bible. At the age of nineteen he left his home and moved from place to place, meeting church people of various persuasions; but none were convincing to him, nor could they understand his depressed condition. They gave him various counsels: to take up smoking, or to try active service in the army, or to take physic and be bled, or to get married. Hearing that his parents were grieving over his absence from home, he returned, but only to distress them by his persisting refusal to go with them to church and listen to the sermon. "Priest Stephens," for his part, came to visit the young man; their discussions did not draw George Fox to the church, and they turned the rector's attitude from initial favor to estrangement and hostility. This confirmed Fox's alienation from clergymen and "professors." He had sought out a number of them, but heard from no one the saving truth which he needed.

In this unsettled state, as he wrote, "I fasted much, walked abroad in solitary places many days, and often took my Bible, and sat in hollow trees and lonesome places till night came on; and frequently in the night walked mournfully about by myself; for I was a man of sorrows in the time of the first workings of the Lord in me. . . . When I had lost all hopes, . . . then, oh, then I heard a voice which said, 'There is one, even Christ Jesus, that can speak to thy condition'; and when I heard it, my heart leaped for joy."[7]

In this emphasis on Christ's religion as immediate and daily personal experience Fox found his central conviction which he felt bound to share with others. "Christ who had enlightened me, gave me His light to believe in; He gave me hope, which He Himself revealed in me, and He gave me His Spirit and grace, which I found sufficient in the deeps and in weakness."[8] This "Inner Light" was all-important; without it, beliefs and doctrines were of no avail, nor any externalities and formal ritual. To Fox church edifices were only "steeple houses." The real church was the devout community itself. This was the true meaning of the verse in the Gospel: "The Kingdom of God is within you."[9] So the mystical direct experience of God's presence was recognized not as an exceptional but as the normal expression of the Christian spirit. "The Lord God opened to me by his invisible power that every man was enlightened by the divine Light of Christ, and I saw it shine through all."[10]

Because he recognized in others as well as in himself the direct presence of God, George Fox upheld the spiritual dignity of every man and rejected any aristocratic exclusiveness or prerogatives, secular or ecclesiastic. The godly man, like God, must be no respecter of persons. This was thoroughgoing Christian democracy, and it expressed itself in the religious organization, in the daily life, and in what seemed to outsiders as sundry oddities of the Society of Friends. Fox did not only reject, like Luther, the rigid barrier between clergy and laity; his religious services dispensed altogether with priest or clergy of any sort. Anyone could speak forth the Lord's truth: anyone, man or woman. This spirit of universal human respect was expressed in the Quakers's firm opposition to slavery. George Fox pled for the humane treatment and the eventual emancipation of the slaves in the Caribbean colonies. William Penn and others followed him by proposing definite measures looking towards abolition; Pennsylvania passed a law in 1711 forbidding the importation of slaves, but it was nullified in London. Fox preached a gospel of peace and avoidance of all strife and violence. Early in his youth he had been shocked when he was advised to enlist in the army. He and his Friends taught pacifism and opposition to war.

Of several other practices which George Fox adopted and firmly maintained, some were dismissed by the general public as oddities, but others were resisted sternly and cost Fox and his followers great suffering. The name by which his Society of Friends came to be popularly known was derived probably from a stern rebuke which Fox gave a magistrate before whom he was on trial: "Tremble and quake at the name of the Lord." "You quake, do you?" the magistrate replied in derision—"Quakers, eh?"[11] Fox objected to the pagan naming of the days of the week, and in speech and writing renamed them First-day, Second-day, and so forth. In the forms of personal address, he remarked, traditional English practice injected definite distinction of rank, in the use of "you" and "Thou," reserving "Thou" for royalty and God, but, strangely enough also for addressing small-type grossly inferiors. Fox, opposing all rank and caste, insisted on addressing everyone, be he king or plain nobody, as "thou" and "thee." "You," he said, must always be plural, never singular.

Other peculiarities of Fox and his followers proved to be of far graver concern. The aristocratic society of his day was marked by much bowing and scraping and doffing of hats. Fox regarded all these flourishes as contrary to plain human dignity and self-respect. He would not bow down to any man on earth, and he kept his hat on, no matter before whom he might be standing. Bareing his head was to be reserved only for the worship of God, even as bowing and kneeling down, to God alone, not to any man. Fox's *Journal* records the repeated berating and punishment for his refusal to comply with conventional practice in this respect.

Much more severe were the sufferings which George Fox endured for his refusal to swear at court or take the oath of allegiance. We should recall that from his early youth he had been marked by strict honesty and truthfulness: "The Lord taught me to be faithful in all things, . . . and to keep to Yea and Nay in all things. . . . I used in my dealings the word Verily, and it was a common saying among those who knew me, 'If George says verily, there is no altering him.' "[12] That was his plain commitment to the truth, and he read and cited dutifully the words in the Sermon on the Mount: "Swear not at all; . . . but let your speech be, Yea, yea; Nay, nay; and whatsoever is more than these is of the evil one."[13] His refusal to take the oath of allegiance was used by those who opposed his preaching in support of their charge that he and his followers were spreading sedition in the land. Fox protested against the falsity of this accusation: neither he nor his Friends had ever been violent or done any seditious act. "My allegiance doth not lie in swearing, but in truth and faithfulness, for I honour all men, much more the king."[14] He affirmed his allegiance to the Government in the most positive terms; but as a loyal follower of Christ's Gospel, he said, he could not swear or take an oath: "Ye have given me a book here to kiss and to swear on, and this book which ye have given me to kiss says, 'Kiss the Son'; and the Son says in this book, 'Swear not at all'; and so says also the Apostle James. Now, I say as the book says, and yet ye imprison me; why do ye not imprison the book for saying so?"[15] His protestations were of no avail; even when all other accusations against him had been refuted, his refusal to take an oath was deemed by his judges sufficient ground for sending or remanding him to prison.

The *Journal* is a frightful record of the unspeakable filth and terror of prison conditions in his day. His account of Doomsdale Prison is too foul to read aloud; but a reader's eyes are more tolerant than his tongue, and one short passage may perhaps be cited here as a harrowing statement of what Fox had to endure for his convictions. And be it remembered that he spent many years in various prisons:

> The place was so noisome that it was observed few that went in did ever come out in health. There was no house of office in it; and the excrements of the prisoners that from time to time had been put there had not been carried out (as we were told) for many years. So that it was all like mire, and in some places to tops of the shoes in water and urine; and he would not let us cleanse it,

nor suffer us to have beds or straw to lie on. At night some friendly people of the town brought us a candle and a little straw; and we burned a little of our straw to take away the stink. The thieves lay over our heads, and the headjailer in a room by them, over our heads also. It seems the smoke went up into the room where the jailer lay; which put him into such a rage that he took the pots of excrement from the thieves and poured them through a hole upon our heads in Doomsdale, . . .[16]

This quotation stops at a comma; there is considerably more of it, but this is more than enough. Fox's sufferings in many jails would have crushed any man of less sturdy physical stamina; in the end they sapped even his strong constitution.

He found in men both wicked betrayal of God's grace and also godly loyalty, and he found them in men of low social station and in high authority, in jailers and constables, and all the way up to Oliver Cromwell and King Charles II. Fox repeatedly gives evidence of the persuasive power that God gave to his words, which often led to men's radical change of heart. At Launceston Castle Prison, where the jailer had derided him as "a hatchet-faced dog," a certain Colonel Rouse came with a large company of attendants to see Fox. After listening to his long harangue, as Fox wrote:

I was moved to speak the word of life to him in God's dreadful power; which came so over him that he could not open his mouth; his face swelled and was red like a turkey; his lips moved and he mumbled something; but the people thought he would have fallen down. I stepped to him and he said he was never so in his life before: for the Lord's power stopped the evil power in him; so that he was almost choked. The man was ever after very loving to Friends, and not so full of airy words to us. The Lord's power came over him, and the rest that were with him.[17]

An interesting part of Fox's *Journal* recounts his relations with Cromwell and Charles II. To both of them he gave plain Christian admonition, and his spoken and written words were not without effect. He had never been a political partisan but had always been a spiritual reformer. Both rulers knew that, though he had suffered under their regime, he had never taken part in any uprising. After his first meeting with Cromwell, the Lord Protector, deeply moved, caught him by the hand and, with tears in his eyes, said: "Come again to my house; for if thou and I were but an hour of a day together, we should be nearer one to the other," and added that he wished Fox no more ill than he did to his own soul.[18] To Charles II, Fox addressed two letters of forthright charge, reporting the persecution of his flock and declaring the need of thorough reform: "Hear and consider, and do good in thy time, whilst thou hast power; be merciful and forgive; that is the way to overcome and obtain the Kingdom of Christ."[19]

Charles II on one occasion did issue an order for Fox's release from prison; but neither he nor Oliver Cromwell before him seemed to have been able to carry out their intended or professed plans for relaxation of religious intolerance. The resistance of the established churches in England and Scotland to the dissidents, and especially to Fox's kind of nonconformity, was strong, and it was exerted by the clergy and more ruthlessly by their laity. The Scottish ministers objected severely to the Quaker conviction of the Inner Light of divine presence in everyone. The first of a number of curses which they drew up, to be read publicly in their churches, was as follows: "Cursed is he that saith, Every man hath a light within him, sufficient to lead him to salvation: and let the people say, Amen."[20] The Conventicle Act, passed by Parliament in 1664, prohibited any nonconformist religious meeting of more than five persons. Thousands of Quakers were imprisoned under that Act, and it was a quarter of a century before the promise of a fair day of religious freedom came, with the Toleration Act after the "Glorious Revolution" of 1688, which put William of Orange on the English throne.

Although, as we have noted, Fox was not a regular churchgoer, he would enter "steeple-houses" when he was moved to speak his Lord's message after the "priest," as he called the rector, had finished his sermon. Sometimes his words met with fair response, but far more often they aroused protests and even led to his ejection from the church. His experiences in nonconformist chapels were less unsatisfactory, but he did realize that he had to do his preaching outside of the churches and chapels. To these meetings, held often in private houses or outdoors, people did come in increasing numbers, not only independent "seekers" but members of other churches. It had not been his early purpose to start another religious denomination, but as the seventeenth century, and his own lifetime with it, neared its close, the Friends were among the most numerous of the nonconformist bodies. Fox's apostolate gained not only followers but also dedicated apostles who spread abroad the gospel of the Inner Light. As early as 1660 their missionary efforts had spread to Holland and Germany, and more outreaching Friends had gone to Venice and Rome and even to Turkey and Palestine.

Their most extensive and eventually most fruitful missionary field was across the Atlantic. On American shores the Quakers met harsh opposition, mainly in Massachusetts, but also found generous welcome, first in Rhode Island and then more widely in Pennsylvania, the colony directed by William Penn, an aristocrat whom George Fox had won to vigorous support of his gospel. The story of the sufferings in New England is a dismal one when we consider that the Puritan clergy and laity who persecuted the Friends were descendants of the Pilgrim Fathers who had crossed the Atlantic to escape from religious repression. The victims appealed to King Charles who hearkened to their plea. Eventually they found reasonable freedom of worship and fanned out from their home base in Pennsylvania.

In their English towns the Quakers had suffered much by being ostracized economically as well as socially. The populace was urged not to trade with them. But the tables were turned in the course of time. In Britain and later also in America the known honesty of the Friends brought customers to their shops, and they prospered. Material success facilitated educational advance. In his youth George Fox had declared that "to be bred at Oxford or Cambridge was not enough to make a man fit to be a minister of Christ."[21] But this did not signify a basic dismissal of education. Having once grasped the true gospel and the true Christian way of life, he and his followers did establish schools of high quality. At the college level, Haverford, Bryn Mawr, and Swarthmore bear witness to the Friends's pursuit of educational excellence.

We have mentioned the very active participation of women in the spread of Quaker preaching. In this work no one proved to be more capable or more devoted than Margaret Fell. Her collaboration with George Fox set a high mark in his apostolic career and also in his more intimate personal life. She was the wife of Judge Fell, Vice-Chancellor of the Duchy of Lancaster and Judge of Assizes for Chester and North Wales. During his absence on circuit his young wife was visited by George Fox who engaged in a dispute with the local rector, William Lampitt. That discussion made a lasting impression on Margaret Fell. She opened her Swarthmoor home to Fox for his meetings. When the Judge returned he also was deeply influenced by Fox's preachment of the true Christian life, and while he never joined the Society of Friends he favored their cause, and his home was at their disposal. On a Sunday morning, while he attended the Anglican service, his wife had a Quaker meeting at Swarthmoor Hall. Judge Fell died in 1658; his young widow devoted all her energies in collaborating with George Fox; not only her means and her time but also arduous work and hardships went into their common service. She used her influence and braved high officials to secure the release of Fox and his followers from prison; erelong she had to share in their sufferings. By court verdicts her own estate as well as that of Fox were forfeited under a writ of praemunire, and she had to endure the unspeakable filth and horrors of prison conditions.

The close collaboration of these two Friends was bound to proceed to more intimate union. George Fox had not included marriage in his planned career. In his youth he had declared plainly that he needed, not a wife, but more wisdom. But after long years of working fellowship he and Margaret Fell were married. Marriage did not mean to George Fox settling down. He continued his work, which took him far afield; only his letters to Margaret show how deeply he respected and cherished her.

Fox's dark days of persecution and court trials and foul imprisonment had been brightened by the devoted fellowship of his fellow workers, Friends indeed. But one shocking exception must be mentioned, for it disclosed another stern aspect of his character. That was the affair of James Nayler's morbid aberration. Nayler had been a close associate of George Fox's, probably the closest next to Margaret. He was a most effective and eloquent preacher; in the judgment of many, more eloquent and winning than Fox himself. Some women enthusiasts overwhelmed him with their admiration; he began to dream of himself in more than apostolic terms. Had he become a religious maniac with visions of himself, as one of his women devotees called him, "The Prophet of the Most High God"? His phantasms proceeded to extravagant extremes as his zealots passed all bounds in their homage of him as "the only begotten Son of God, . . . no more James Nayler but Jesus." He entered Bristol riding on a horse as in another Palm Sunday procession. It was altogether a pathetic story of the mad underside of religious enthusiasm.[22]

Needless to say, there was a morning after this pious debauch.

Nayler was charged with blasphemy; the court condemned him to have his tongue pierced with a red-hot iron and his brow branded with a *B* for blasphemer. He was to be sent back to Bristol, to be publicly thrashed and to ride a horse bareback backward, and then sent back to jail in London under hard confinement. Added to these shocks was Nayler's own coming ruefully to himself. He proclaimed publicly his remorse and repentance; above all he sought reconciliation with George Fox. But Fox's attitude was severe, harsh. He was not ready to forgive what he considered mad blasphemy in one of his principal associates. Nayler had repeatedly to renounce and denounce "all those false worships with which any have idolized my person in the night of my temptation." He knelt ruefully before he finally received his leader's forgiveness.[23]

The Nayler aberration showed certain motives in the intensity of religious enthusiasm which crossed the border of the pathological and which could lead astray and quite upset even persons of less unstable balance. It has been pointed out that the normal and the abnormal "were so combined in Fox that the ultimate result was prevailingly good, both for himself and for his environment."[24] But even Fox, despite his clear declaration of the Inner Light and of God's presence in us all as a purely spiritual experience, was not altogether free from the hazard of straying into morbid explosions or notions of miraculous expressions of divine agencies acting through him. Once, having come out of Derby Prison and walking cross-country, he saw ahead of him the three spires of the "steeple-house" of Lichfield. Though it was winter he was "commanded by the Lord" to pull off his shoes, which he left with some shepherds. He turned towards the city and walked barefoot "up and down the streets, crying with a loud voice, 'Woe to the bloody city of Lichfield!' . . . There seemed to be a channel of blood running down the streets, and the market-place appeared like a pool of blood." On coming to himself he returned to the shepherds and recovered his shoes. Later, puzzled about his behavior, he remembered that during the persecutions by the Roman emperor Diocletian a thousand Christians had been martyred in Lichfield.[25]

There are other aspects of Fox's preaching and related religious activities that are bound to disturb the reader of his *Journal*. Fox reports miraculous cures, not only of raving hysterical men and women, but also of cripples and others suffering from severe physical ills. Many times he wrote how he cast out devils from men's minds and bodies. Fox reported the dread that people had of his piercing eye: "Do not pierce me so with thy eyes; keep thy eyes off me."[26] He was convinced that God's judgment descended upon his enemies, and sometimes without delay. His account of one such instance is characteristic of his style and is a sample also of his manuscript:

> And one time there was a wicked man (which they) gott (to come to ye meetinge & he set) a beares skinn upon his back & hee woulde goe play pranckes in ye Quakers generall meetinge (which hee did: & stoode opposite aginst ye freinde yt was speakeinge with his tongue lollinge out of his mouth & soe made sport to his wicked followers & great disturbans in ye meetinge): & there was a bull beateinge in ye way as hee (returned from ye meetinge) & he stayde to see ye bull beate: & hee comeing to neere ye bull ye bull struck his horne under his throate (& strucke his tongue out of his mouth which hung lollinge out of his mouth as he had used in derision before) & strucke his horne uppe Into his braine & soe swonge him about upon his horne.
> And soe hee yt thought to have donne mischeife amongst God's people was mischeifed himselfe.[27]

Fox kept a record of these visitations of the Lord's doom upon his evil foes. "Most of the justices that were upon the bench at the sessions when I was sent to prison, died a while after"—

a good round dozen of them, or their constables, or the wives of some.[28] Fox was not wholly emancipated from the superstitions of his age. Like Luther and James I, he believed in witchcraft. What is remarkable is the high degree of his resistance to popular or established religious customs and common-law practices.

The core and essence of George Fox's mysticism and more broadly of his religious experience was the outward expression of his inner spirit. He did not blissfully abide in his godly visions; he lived them out: he translated them into actions. Christ's charge to men in the Sermon on the Mount was to Fox also a promise: "Be ye therefore perfect." And the ideal of this divine presence in men's godly living was not an ideal for some distant future; it was a daily prospect and duty. Thus he dismissed sectarian expectations of Christ's second coming. Christ is, or can be, in us all, right now.

We should keep this conviction in mind; else we might misunderstand sundry passages in the *Journal* which have a seeming tone of egotism. Early in his life he felt spiritual elevation: "I was come up in spirit through the flaming sword, into the paradise of God. . . . I knew nothing but pureness, and innocency, and righteousness; being renewed into the image of God by Christ Jesus, to the state of Adam, which he was in before the fall."[29] His self-assurance was an assurance to self, not assurance of self; his blissful sense of daily godliness was his praise of Christ's grace in him. It sustained him throughout his life of the most harrowing torments, and it crowned his life's career in blessed peace; "Now I am clear, I am fully clear."[30]

The following evaluation of George Fox is by the outstanding American Quaker, Rufus M. Jones: "He meant to put vital religion within the reach of everybody. He wanted to make everybody a

priest. He hoped to make religion as free and as universal as sun-
light and air. He tried to reproduce in the world of his day the
kind of Church which the New Testament tells about in its wonderful pages. . . . It would be a Church through which the will of
God was constantly being freshly revealed, a living, growing, expanding, transforming Church."[31]

CHAPTER IV

JOHN BUNYAN

Bunyan's autobiography should be read side by side with the *Journal* of George Fox. They are the two outstanding expressions of the spirit and movement of religious nonconformity in England during the seventeenth century. While both of them were marked by opposition to the formalism of the Church of England, they were also critical of each other. They vied and in several ways disagreed in their appeal to the common people, but the tension was not merely competitive. As we noted in our previous chapter, the religious dynamic of George Fox and his Society of Friends was inspired by a firm conviction of their possession of an "Inner Light," assuring them of God's intimate blessed presence in their lives, without the devastating consciousness of continual sinful temptation and taint. From his early boyhood George Fox recalled his blissful certainty of being in Christ's bosom, pure and innocent. Persecution and imprisonment could not matter to him who was always with God.

Bunyan's religious experience was that of a stormy spiritual career, and he objected sternly to what he regarded as pious complacency in the Quakers, their assurance of an actual and secure holiness. His first published work was against the Quaker serene mystical saintliness. The Christian life, as Bunyan viewed it, was a "Holy War," a desperate and unremitting struggle with the powers of evil. Only through divine Grace could man hope for any victory over sin, and only by ceaseless vigilance

75

might he ward off the renewed assaults of Satan. In his own self-portrayal and in his allegories of the inner life Bunyan was always resisting the notion of any assured holiness. The true saint had always to be a sentinel at his post. He expressed this solemn conviction at the conclusion of his *Pilgrim's Progress:* "I saw that there was a way to Hell, even from the Gate of Heaven, as well as from the City of Destruction." This ever-trustful but also self-warning note was imperative in Bunyan's view of the Christian life.

The title of Bunyan's autobiography sets the keynote of it: *Grace Abounding to the Chief of Sinners.* We are reminded directly of St. Augustine's *Confessions* and of the life stories of other saints continually recalling their long enslavement by the powers of evil. Note St. Teresa's grievous sense of insecurity and unworthiness in her continual lapses of pious devotion. Right here we may anticipate a comment on the differences among the contrite confessors of sinfulness. Augustine does give us reports of his specific vices and profligacy. But, as we shall presently note further, Bunyan's confession as "the chief of sinners" does not record any extensive grave wickedness. His spirit is marked by a ruinous conviction of unspecified sinfulness; it is poisoned by the dread feeling that he is a lost soul. The self-probing account of this contrite piety is thus a spiritual document of major significance to the student of the varieties of religious experience.

As we turn to consider Bunyan's self-portrayed life, we may begin with an outward description of the man which has been provided by a nameless biographer. "As for his Person, he was Tall of Stature, strong boned, though not corpulent, somewhat of a Ruddy Face with sparkling eyes, wearing his hair on his upper lip, after the old British fashion; his hair reddish, but in his latter days time had sprinkled it with Gray, his nose well set, but not declining nor bending, and his mouth moderately large, his forehead somewhat high, and his habit always plain and modest.'"

Unlike the Anglican clergy, and also prominent laymen, who

were well educated and made a point of their learning, Bunyan was one of the unlettered country preachers: "I never went to school to Aristotle and Plato."[2] His writings are not embroidered with classical quotations or allusions; the very occasional Latin phrase is acknowledged as borrowed. We find little evidence of his knowledge of literature or of history beyond his reading of Foxe's *Book of Martyrs*. The only work of which he had mastery was the one on which he decisively relied, the Bible, which he must have known by heart. Rather than make any futile pretense to learning, he tended to overemphasize his low beginnings. As before God he was "the chief of sinners," so in his worldly account of himself he was the lowliest of the lowly. So much the greater be the glory of God who in his mercy reached way down even to him!

We should keep in mind Bunyan's attitude in reading his life story. His biographers observe his tendency to exaggerate his low family station: "For my descent then, it was, as is well known by many, of a low and inconsiderable generation; my father's house being of that rank that is meanest, and most despised in the Land."[3] His father was a tinker, not a trade of any dignity in English social life; but he was not a gypsy peddler of his craft; he was settled in his own house in Elstown in the vicinity of Bedford; his homestead had been in his family for generations. His own and his wife's wills were recorded in the district. As to his outward condition, Bunyan wrote that when he married he did not have in his home "so much household stuff as a Dish or Spoon,"[4] but for his start of a library his bride brought two religious books from her father's shelf. He followed his father's trade, rising from plain tinker to brazier, and when he was out of prison he must have done well at his craft. Later, to be sure, he had success with his writings. The picture of his home at Elstown is not that of a manor, but neither is it that of a hut.

Far more important for our study are Bunyan's reported misdeeds and oppressive sinfulness. He is as emphatic in his general self-condemnation as he is meager in specific confessions. In a book published in the last year of his life, entitled *The Jerusalem Sinner, or Good News for the Vilest,* he described himself as "one of these lowly ones, one of the great sin-breeders. I infected all the youth of the town where I was born, with all manner of youthful vanities." Thirty years earlier he had written: "I was ignorant, self-conceited, surly, obstinate and rebellious. Many a time the preacher told hell would be my portion, the Devil would wreck his malice on me; God would pour on me his sore displeasure. But he had as good preached to the stock, to the post, to the stones I trod on."[5]

What specifically were his varieties of wickedness? He seems to have followed Augustine's boyish pranks of raiding orchards. Coming to more grievous matters, he confessed that he was "filled with unrighteousness; the which did also so strongly work, and put forth itself both in my heart and life, and that from a child, that I had but few Equals . . . both for cursing, swearing, lying and blaspheming the holy name of God."[6]

The more he upbraided himself for his sinfulness, the more he glorified God for lifting him up from his baseness as a brand plucked from the burning. This sort of devout reflection is not at all strange in religious writings; it is in the old Augustinian tradition. But Bunyan was forthright in the English sense of actualities: he did not lay unwarranted and impious claims to any merit of his own in God's judgment of him; neither did he allow any undeserved accusation of his character and conduct to pass unchallenged. Humbly pleading guilty to the general charge of sinfulness, he yet defended himself on grave specific counts. In sackcloth and ashes he confessed his falsehoods, his foul profligacy, and his violation of God's laws and his corrupting influence on his loose companions. But when his critics and foes repeated the general rumors of the deep hold which his preaching had upon

emotional women, quite beyond the devotional response, and accused him of licentiousness, Bunyan defended his unblemished
moral purity in the most emphatic and unqualified terms: "My
foes have mist their mark in this their shooting at me. . . . If all the
Fornicators and Adulterers in England were hang'd by the neck till
they be dead, *John Bunyan,* the object of their Envie, would still
be alive and well. I know not whether there be such a thing as a
woman breathing under the Copes of the whole Heaven but by
their apparel, their Children, or by common Fame, except my
Wife."[7] Whether this abjuration covered his entire life from his
earliest youth, is left doubtful by another passage: "With more
greediness, according to the strength of Nature, I still let loose
the reins of my lusts, and delighted in all transgressions against
the Law of God: so that until I came to the state of marriage,
I was the very ringleader of all the Youth that kept me company, into all manner of vice and ungodliness."[8] But he was
unmistakable in his absolute denial of the least uncleanness after
his early years: "And in this I admire the Wisdom of God, that
he made me shie of women from my first Convertion until now.
Those know, and can also bear me witness, with whom I have
been most intimately concerned, that it is a rare thing to see me
carry it pleasant towards a Woman; the common salutation of a
woman I abhor, 'tis odious to me in whosoever I see it. Their
Company alone, I cannot away with. I seldom so much as touch
a Womans Hand, for I think these things are not so becoming me."[9]

As to his confessed lying and swearing of his early years, do
we have evidence that they were more than the common childish
sidestepping and adolescent loudmouthed bluster? It would be a
gross understatement to say that after his conversion he outgrew
lying. The plain record of his career is that he endured long
years of imprisonment rather than make a false promise that he
would not preach in public contrary to repressive legislation. He

was the epitome of undeviating truthfulness. With regard to swearing, even as a boy he was ashamed and conscience-smitten regarding his foul mouth. "One day, as I was standing at a Neighbours Shop-window, and there cursing and swearing, and playing the Mad-man, after my wonted manner, there sate within the woman of the house, and heard me, who, though she was a very loose and ungodly Wretch, yet protested that I swore and cursed at that most fearful rate, that she was made to tremble to hear me. . . . At this reproof I was silenced, and put to secret shame; and that, as I thought, before the God of Heaven. . . ."[10] He himself once censured a man of a still fouler tongue; as he grew up he abandoned profanity.

There is no mention in Bunyan's autobiography of violence or thieving (aside from the boyish raiding of orchards); murder was not to be spoken of. His violation of the Sabbath, by playing games after church, was contrary to the strict pulpit charge but scarcely beyond the usual ways of "Merrie England"; likewise with his fondness for dancing, to which only the more severe Puritans would have objected. To more worldly, though still generally respectable minds, some of his reported sins, so black in his own self-judgment, would appear not only venial but rather pathetically disturbing in his contrition about them. He wrote that he found ungodly pleasure in slipping into churches to ring the bells; yet he was beset with the fear that the bell might fall upon his head.

Bunyan's spiritual torment was that of a gnawing sense of basic alienation from God. His tragic condition was not so much one of remorse regarding some specific wickedness as a general rueful contrition. Characteristic in his variety of religious experiences is not his particular kind of sin and repentance and redemption, but rather his devastating conviction of utter ungodliness and his deliverance from it. Bunyan felt that the Devil was continually besetting him and that he could never feel the peace of divine assurance. He was "very much afflicted and disquieted" by doubts about his election to grace. Was he not predestined to eternal damnation? "Most unblest of men," he sank into a more treacherous quagmire of devilish incertitude. "How can you tell but that the Turks had as good Scripture to prove their *Mahomet* the Saviour as we have that our Jesus is?"[11] These tireless assaults of the Devil left him stunned in despair. Again and again he would be moved, by reading the Bible or by some sermon he had heard, to a passing assurance that he loved Christ, but the blessed trust would not last. If he really had the love of Christ, nothing whatever could lure him away from it; yet there he was in continual wavering and dalliance, tossed hither and yon by ruinous temptations: "Sell Christ for this, or sell Christ for that; sell him, sell him."[12] The devastating collapse of all hope staggered him: not his fear of failure to master this or that temptation or wickedness, but the more ruinous despair of his utter and irremediable sinfulness. Had he not already committed the unpardonable sin against the Holy Spirit, indefinable and beyond redemption? The reader of Bunyan's pages is moved to pity for this victim of seemingly fatal despair of unfathomable hopeless guilt. "Thus by the strange and unusual assault of the tempter, was my soul, like a broken Vessel, driven, as with the Winds, and tossed sometime head-long into despair. . . . Oh, the unthought of imaginations, frights, fears, and terrors that are affected by a thorow application of guilt, yielding to desperation! This is the man that hath his dwelling among the Tombs with the dead; that is alwayes crying out, and cutting himself with stones."[13]

Through all these wanderings in quest of the Lord's peace Bunyan had been led away from the established Anglican church services, to attend the meetings of nonconformist Baptist preachers. Early in his autobiography he relates how by the grace of Christ he had happened to listen to the conversation of four poor women "sitting at a door in the Sun, and talking about the things of God," telling each other "how God had visited their souls with the love of the Lord Jesus, and with what promises they had been refreshed, comforted, and supported against the temptations of the Devil. . . . They also discoursed of their own wretchedness of heart, of their unbelief, and did contemn, slight, and abhor their own righteousness, as filth, and insufficient to do them any good."[4] He followed these poor women to their meetings; it was a start of his journey towards the light of redemption. But some others of the religious dissenters went to perilous extremes. One group, the so-called Ranters, talked to him in altogether shocking terms. They claimed that they had not only received complete forgiveness but had also attained perfection and holiness, so that no matter what they did, it was not accounted a taint and a sin. That sort of "antinomian" pious vanity before the Lord smote him with terror. Far more ruinous than his own sense of contrite despair was their deluded complacency before the Eternal Judge.

Medieval saints's lives recite how the devil's assaults upon their piety took the most horrible forms: how Satan would magically assume the forms of the bread and the wine of the Lord's Supper, to pollute the divine service itself. Bunyan wrote that in the midst of attending communion he would be smitten with the wicked thought that some deadly thing would happen to the worshipful congregation, and he would struggle to banish the dread idea even as he was partaking of the communion.

The reader of Bunyan's pages begins to wonder whether there could be any end to all this pathetic self-rending contrition. Some good turns in his personal relations helped in dispelling the darkness in which he was groping. By God's grace, as he wrote, he was led to marry a young woman of godly upbringing. One of her greatest joys in life was to read with him the Bible and the two devotional books which she had brought, a pious dowry. In his homelife with her, church attendance also became more regular, and in his relations with the Baptist believers the influence of their minister in Bedford, John Gifford, proved decisive. Like Bunyan, Gifford had served in the army, where he had just missed being shot: the issue of life or death was a harrowing reality to him. Like Bunyan he had wallowed in sin, but by divine mercy he had turned upward and had proved a faithful leader of his Baptist flock. He saw in Bunyan both the true contrition and zeal for repentance and also the power of word and deed to lead others to the saving truth.

Thus both at home and in the meetinghouse and in private talks with Gifford, Bunyan was indeed moving, though not quite steadily, towards the hour of conversion. As it was, he had to be plunged into deepest gloom before the light of salvation streamed into his soul.

> There fell upon me a great cloud of darkness, which did so hide from me the things of God and Christ, that I was as if I had never seen or known them in my life; I was also so over-run in my Soul, with a senceless heartless frame of spirit, that I could not feel my soul to move or stir towards grace and life in Christ; I was as if my loyns were broken, or as if my hands and feet had been tied and bound with chains. At this time also I felt some weakness to seiz my outward man, which made still the other affliction the more heavy and uncomfortable. After I had been in this condition three or four days, as I was sitting by the fire, I suddenly felt the word to sound in my heart, *I must go to Jesus;* at this my former darkness and atheism fled away, and the blessed things of heaven were set within my view. . . . Then with joy I told my Wife, O now I know, I know! but that night was good to me, I never had but few better; I longed for the company of some of God's people, that I might have imparted unto them what God had shown me. . . .[15]

He was thenceforth not only a convert but one who felt

called upon to preach. He was baptized by Gifford in the Ouse river and became an active member of the Baptist group in Bedford. Before long he was chosen as Deacon, ministered to Baptist meetings, and eventually gained such prominence by the power of his preaching that Anglicans would speak of him as Bishop Bunyan. In his sermons he expounded no learned dogmas; he relied on no traditional authority beyond the Bible; he spoke out of his own experience. The emphatic direction of his preaching was autobiographic in tone; he shared himself with his congregation. "I preached what I felt, what I smartingly did feel, even that under which my poor Soul did groan and tremble to astonishment. Indeed I have been as one sent to them from the dead; I went myself in chains to preach to them in chains, and carried that fire in my own conscience that I persuaded them to beware of."[16]

Just as he did not set any value on ecclesiastic dignities and formalism and ritual, so while espousing the freer order of the Baptist meetings, he was not over-strict regarding their special ways. The Baptist insistence on total immersion did not impress him, nor the close communion of some of their groups. He regarded some of these forms as esteemed but not fundamental. He preached a gospel of simple and utter reliance on Christ's redeeming love as more important than any theological doctrine or ceremony or churchly order and ordinance. He did take his own son to be baptized, but he wrote against any vain reliance on the ritual itself: "Baptism makes thee no member of the Church, . . . neither if I be Baptized am I the better, neither if I be not, am I the worse before men."[17] True conversion, true Christian godliness, do not come by dogma or ritual or by works of merit, but in one way only, by Christ's grace, which is a free gift of God and nowise earned by or dependent on man's own desert.

He regarded his own conversion and his subsequent life of

Christian service as due solely to the working of Christ's grace in him. Even so he would never allow any thought of abiding holiness to enter his soul: he considered any such saintly delusions as temptations of impious pride. His opposition to these notions was his initial incentive to religious writing. Beyond his rejection of the vain pride of the Ranters, he resisted also many of the beliefs of the Quakers. As noted already, his first published work was directed against the followers of George Fox. Aside from specific doctrinal disagreements with them, Bunyan opposed mainly the Quaker declared assurance of the "Inner Light," their confidence in the abiding presence of Holy Spirit in them all. In his own experience Bunyan had suffered from the anguish of straying from the Shepherd's care; in his preaching and church services he had witnessed time and again the woeful backsliding of seemingly God-fearing men and women. Church members leading godly lives do stumble and fall. We should all watch and pray, trusting never in ourselves but only in Christ's grace to sustain us. No sinner is ever hopeless, but no saint should ever reckon himself absolutely among the blessed. Bunyan bewailed the evil straying of those backsliders, and he urged himself and others to be alert, ever hopeful but never complacent in the godly endeavor.

Appended to the autobiography *Grace Abounding to the Chief of Sinners* is another work of Bunyan's relating to his terms in jail following his arrest and trial for transgression of the Act against unauthorized preaching. This so-called *Relation of My Imprisonment* runs to about twenty-five pages, but it is a detailed account of the court procedure that led to the verdict. The reader should keep in mind some of the anti-dissident legislation which swayed to and fro in the several regimes in seventeenth-century England. During Elizabeth's reign a person who persistently refused to attend Anglican church services was subject to imprisonment. Under the Long Parliament this legislation lapsed, but after Cromwell it was again enforced. Nonconformist chapels and preachers were banned. The militant moods and tactics of some dissenters, such as the Fifth Monarchy men, were regarded as warranting the view that ecclesiastical nonconformity was bound to prove seditious in politics and a menace to the security of the state. Although the pacific spirit of the Quakers and the Baptists was well known, the more determined opponents of nonconformity would not grant them special tolerance.

It should be remembered that while dissidence was primarily that of nonconformist Protestants, the Episcopal Church of England was resisting also any Catholic resurgence. It was supposed that, during the Restoration, King Charles II's announced policy of religious tolerance and the release of persons imprisoned for transgression of ecclesiastical edicts was intended to prepare the way for return to power of the Catholic faith, to which he was believed to be devoted. During the reigns of Charles II and James II Parliament passed restrictive legislation; the degree of severity in the application of it depended on the temper of the particular courts. By the Act of Uniformity in 1662 dissident ministers and nonconformist chapels were outlawed; two years later an even more stringent Conventicle Act enforced heavy fines and jail sentences on recusants; the Five Mile Act of 1665 ruled nonconformist worship out of the cities. A still more rigorous Conventicle Act was passed in 1670. It was not until after the "Glorious Revolution" of 1688, which put William of Orange on the English throne, that religious tolerance became the adopted policy, but that was the year of Bunyan's death.

Bunyan's experiences with constables and judges showed the varying degrees of opposition to religious dissidence in England. More impressive than the firm hostility of the judges who tried him was his own firmer refusal to make any compromises with them. He most resolutely would not avail himself of the avenue of ready acquittal which was offered to him, simply to promise that he would desist from further large-scale public preaching: by implication the judges conceded that small nonconformist groups might come to hear him in houses or other nonofficial meeting places. But Bunyan used his trials to articulate fully the view of true Christian service to which he had dedicated his life. His friends were on hand to make bond for him and release him from prison, but he declared that it would be to no purpose. In all truth he could not and would not make any promise that he knew he had no intention of keeping. Whether he was in or out of prison, he was resolved to carry Christ's Gospel to all who would listen to him, be they few or many, in or out of cities or towns, in chapels or houses or outdoors.

A discussion between Bunyan and a certain Mr. Foster of Bedford provides a good sample of what went on at one of Bunyan's court trials, abridged below as follows:

> *Foster.* If you will promise to call the people no more together, you shall have your liberty to go home. . . .
> *Bunyan.* Sir (said I) pray what do you mean by calling the people together? my business is not any thing among them when they are come together, but to exhort them to look after the salvation of their souls, that they may be saved, & c. . . .
>
> .   .   .   .
>
> *Foster.* He said, that was none of my work; I must follow my calling, and if I would but leave off preaching, and follow my calling, I should have the justices' favour, and be acquitted presently.
> *Bunyan.* To whom I said, that I could follow my calling and that too, namely, preaching the word: And I did look upon it as my duty to do them both, as I had an opportunity.
> *Foster.* He said, to have any such meetings was against the law; and therefore he would have me leave off and say, I would call the people no more together.
> *Bunyan.* To whom I said, that I durst not make any

further promise: For my conscience would not suffer me to do it. And again, I did look upon it as my duty to do as much Good as I could, not only in my trade, but also in communicating to all people wheresoever I came, the best knowledge I had in the word.[18]

His trial before Justice Keeling was similar in substance and in outcome. Among their disagreements the main one concerned Bunyan's right and authority to preach. Legal authority he lacked, for his preaching was against definite English legislation. But Bunyan claimed Biblical authority and cited especially a verse from the first Epistle of Peter: "As every man hath received the gift, even so let him minister the same unto another."

> *Keeling.* If any man have received a gift of tinkering, as thou hast done, let him follow his tinkering. And so other men their trades. And the divine his calling, & c.
> *Bunyan.* Nay, sir, said I, but it is most clear, that the Apostle speaks here of preaching the word. . . .
> *Keeling.* He said, we might do it in our families, but not otherways.
> *Bunyan.* I said, if it was lawful to do good to some, it was lawful to do good to more. . . .
>
> .   .   .   .
>
> *Keeling.* Then said he, hear our judgment. You must be had back again to prison, and there lie for three months following; at three months end, if you do not submit to go to church to hear divine service, and leave off your preaching, you must be banished from the realm: And if, after such a day as shall be appointed you to be gone, you shall be found in this realm, & c., or be found to come over again without special license from the King & c. you must stretch by the neck for it. I tell you plainly; and so he bid my jailor have me away.[19]

So on and so forth. The term of imprisonment to which the judges condemned him doubled and redoubled itself until he spent more than twelve years in jail, many of them in Bedford Gaol. He was not alone in his captivity. Under the Acts of Uniformity and Conventicles all dissenters in England faced, and great multitudes of them suffered, harsh treament. Bunyan found his jail filled with them, and so he preached to them whenever they were allowed to come out of their cells and assemble in the prison courtyard.

Troubles at home aggravated his hardships in jail. His wife had a miscarriage, lost her child, and was gravely ill; erelong he became a widower worrying about his motherless children. In one of the intervals between his prison terms he remarried; his second wife not only cherished his orphans but exhausted every possible means of securing his release from prison. She even journeyed to London to plead with the king. In his *Relation* Bunyan recorded her earnest but futile appeal to the judges. Some of them treated her with cold disdain, but one of them, Judge Hales, showed genuine pity for her. When he asked her about her husband's calling and someone answered for her that he was a tinker, she exclaimed: "Yes, and because he is a Tinker and a poor man, therefore he is despised, and cannot have justice." She insisted that her husband preached nothing but the word of God, but one of the court baited her by calling it rather the doctrine of the Devil. She replied: "My Lord, when the righteous judge shall appear, it will be known, that his doctrine is not the doctrine of the Devil."[20]

Eventually Bunyan's condition in prison was somewhat relaxed. The jailers granted him considerable liberty of movement which he promptly used to spread his preaching on every opportune occasion. Prisons and jailers in England must have varied even as constables and judges. Bunyan's account of his years in Bedford Gaol included no harrowing details like George Fox's description of Doomsdale Prison. In his cell Bunyan was allowed provisions for reading and study and literary activity. The fruit of those years of captivity—enforced leisure—was abundant, alike for its religious as for its literary worth. *Grace Abounding* was written within prison walls, and also his much more universally known masterpiece, *The Pilgrim's Progress*.

Bunyan was a prolific writer. His first biographer counted sixty works by the Baptist sexagenarian, whose first pamphlet, criticizing the Quakers, was published in his twenty-eighth year. Most of these threescore writings are, like the first one, controversial discourses, or selected sermons, or edifying or theological tracts. We do not know of any edition of his Complete Works. Three books besides *Grace Abounding* are of major importance to any student of religious experience; they are the golden harvest of Puritan genius: *The Pilgrim's Progress,* first of all, and then *The Life and Death of Mr. Badman* and *The Holy War.* Any at all thorough examination, or even a running summary, of these books is quite beyond the purpose of the present study. What interests us is tracing a few of the autobiographic characteristics of these works; for Bunyan not only preached but also wrote "what he felt, what he smartingly did feel."

The Pilgrim's Progress from this World to That which is to Come is the greatest vision of English Puritanism; by common consent it has been accounted as one of the most universally read and cherished works of religious devotion in its original English version and in translations throughout the world. It has been regarded as the imaginatively objective version of *Grace Abounding* or as its allegorical pendant. It was the climax of Bunyan's self-utterance. Meditating in his prison cell on his own arduous ascent from the depths and "dumps" of worldly vanities to the blessings of Christ's grace, Bunyan imaginatively transfigured that ascent in his vision of the pilgrimage of Christian from the City of Destruction to the Gates of Heaven.

Bunyan presents this pilgrimage "in the similitude of a Dream." His epic of Christian's—that is, the Christian—life is an allegory, and he tells us in his prefatory "Apology for his Book" that he had chosen to write it metaphorically. He would express spiritual meanings in visible, tangible forms. His reader should thus start with him from his first page, always keeping in mind Bunyan's own self-portrayal in the more direct, plain speech of *Grace Abounding*. So he described his Pilgrim: "I dreamed, and behold *I saw a man cloathed in Raggs, standing in a certain place, with his face from his own House, a Book in his hand, and a great burden upon his Back*. I looked, and saw him open the Book, and Read therein; and as he read, he wept and trembled: and not being able longer to contain he brake out with a lamentable cry; saying, *what shall I do. . . . What shall I do to be saved?*"[21]

Bunyan had his dream "as he walked through the wilderness of this world."[22] Dante likewise found himself in a dark wild forest where he had lost his straight way. In Dante's vision *The Divine Comedy*, his guide through Hell and Purgatory was Virgil, "the honor and light of other poets" and of classical wisdom; for his ascent through the Ten Heavens of Paradise, Dante's guides were the mystical St. Bernard and his adored Lady Beatrice. Dante's rise was from the secular classical to the sacred Christian ideals. But the face of Bunyan's Christian was *"from his own House"*; his city which he was fleeing was the City of Destruction, and for his first step from it he needed and got the guidance of the Evangelist. Christian must leave all that he had and follow the way of salvation, to Christ. "All that he had," however, included his wife and his children; his abandonment of them is bound to perplex the reader of his holy pilgrimage. We recall a similar quandary in the Buddhist gospel: Gautama likewise left his family in their palace, to seek alone the way to salvation. In *Grace Abounding*, as we may recall, Bunyan's marriage to a godly wife was his start towards the light of Christ; and in following the course of Christian's pilgrimage, with the various companions whom he meets and whom he joins on his way, we are bound to expect that Bunyan's Christian epic could not conclude without the further pilgrimage of his wife and children. *The Pilgrim's Progress* was sure to have its Second Part. In the versified conclusion of his masterpiece Bunyan intimated that he might "dream again."

Bunyan's allegory repeatedly expresses his own groping from darkness towards the light and the truth of Christian belief to which his own religious travail had led him, by Christ's mercy. More terrible than anything to Christian was the burden upon his back, his dread weight of despair in his contrition of sin. All the soothing arguments of Worldly-Wiseman were of no final avail, however plausible they might at first appear. Morality cannot take precedence over the Straight Gate; reformed conduct alone does not suffice for salvation, which requires a thorough regeneration, a new heart. Mr. Legality proved to be a misleading guide and a cheat. Bunyan found no salvation in the doctrine of good works; the inner spirit alone availed; it was the grave person Good-will that answered Christian's knock and opened the Wicket Gate to him.

In other ways *The Pilgrim's Progress* expresses in allegorical vision, and by a similarity of imagery, Bunyan's own religious struggles as recorded in *Grace Abounding*. A notable instance is Christian's wallowing travails through the Slough of Despond. Bunyan, assailed by doubts whether he was among the elect— "Whether I had any Faith or no"—wrote: "I found myself in a miry bog that shook as I did but stir."[23] Likewise Christian, after he had begun to "sink in the mire," and had been led by Help towards the steps and reached sound ground, was told that this "Miry slow . . . is the descent whither the scum and filth that attends conviction of sin doth continually run, and therefore is called the *Slough of Dispond;* for still as the sinner is awakened about his lost condition, there ariseth in his soul many fears, and doubts, and discouraging apprehensions, which all of them get together, and settle in this place."[24]

The pilgrim sought sound ground, and higher ground. He could find no resting place until he could see his way clearly. This he began to perceive in "the Interpreter's House": there in a variety of exhibits was shown the difference between the right way and the wrong way. In a succession of allegorical images he learned to set Patience above Passion; he was admonished not to follow the ruinous course of the man in the iron cage who had sinned against the light, hardened his heart, and yielded to the lures of Lusts and Pleasures and Profits. One of the men whom Christian saw was just rising out of bed and shook and trembled as he put on his raiment; he related a dream from which he had awakened, a dream similar to one of Bunyan's own dreams, a dream of the Day of Judgment, and he not ready for it. But there also were the damsels, Piety, Charity, and Prudence, who visualized those virtues which Christian must endeavor to attain.

The pilgrimage was resumed, with growing reassurance and sustaining hope, but also with further trials and conflicts. The Devil had set his obstacles and deputies all along the way to deter Christian and lead him astray. In those episodes of the allegory Bunyan defends his view of the Christian life of striving and devotion against wrong doctrines. In the Valley of Humiliation Christian's pilgrimage was challenged by a foul fiend, Apollyon, whom Bunyan described in words of a horrible nightmare. The demon tried all his wiles to dissuade Christian from his holy quest and, failing in this, challenged his further step in a rage. Their fight was frightful; Christian was wounded in his head, hand, foot, but in the end he smote his foe stoutly and set him to flight. The pilgrim proceeded thenceforth with drawn sword in hand, and well he might, for now he entered the Valley of the Shadow of Death, in which was the mouth of

Hell, where Christian thought well to take another weapon, All-prayer. Fiends were all about him, trying to lure him with hints of grievous blasphemies. In his plodding way forward he met good companions and bad: Faithful, whose firm endeavors stirred him to redoubled zeal; but also Talkative, who discoursed glibly of holy things, but notwithstanding his fine tongue was in fact but a sorry fellow and a vain companion.

Christian and Faithful were next embroiled in the corrupting Vanity Fair, a foul tangle of worldliness through which they strove to work their way unflecked. But when they refused to be lured by any of the vendors' booths, saying firmly "We buy the Truth," they aroused mockery and insults, and then riotous hostility, so that they themselves were charged with starting a disturbance and were haled before a tainted trial court. Faithful was condemned to die by horrible torture and fire; but even as he was burned to ashes, a chariot of horses took him up to Heaven.[25] Christian was jailed but escaped and went on his way. Before long he gained another good companion, Hopeful. They stumbled and retraced their steps and fell prisoners of the Giant Despair in the dungeons of his Doubting Castle; assailed by threats of hopelessness and torture, they were about to be torn to pieces. Then by good grace Christian remembered that he had in his bosom a key called Promise that could open any lock. So it did and set them free on their holy pilgrimage. This dark episode recalls Bunyan's own devastating doubt when he, assailed by atheistic notions, was harrowed by the idea that he was himself, like Judas, a betrayer of his Lord. And, like Christian, he was freed from his shackles. "The Scriptures now also were wonderful things unto me; I saw that the truth and verity of them were the Keys to the Kingdom of Heaven."[26]

Christian's sorest hardships were then largely behind him. He and Hopeful reached the Delectable Mountains of Immanuel's Land, and so on to the Country of Beulah. These holy idyls were not without their discordant undertones, for the two pilgrims came across "a brisk lad," Ignorance, a misleading Flatterer, and a derisive Atheist who even at their very approach to their blessed goal tried to swerve them away from it. Christian's pilgrimage was seen by Bunyan as a continual struggle. Before the very Gate of Heaven he and Hopeful had to cross a deep river without a bridge. It is the river that all mortals sooner or later must cross. Christian was almost swamped by the deep waters; a great darkness and horror fell upon him; but with the help of Hopeful who kept his head above water, he finally stepped on solid ground and reached the other bank. The two pilgrims trod now to the Holy Gates which were opened to receive them, which, as Bunyan wrote, "when I had seen, I wished myself among them."[27]

The Second Part of *The Pilgrim's Progress* does not have much interest for our autobiographical study. Bunyan recounted his second dream, about the pilgrimage of Christiana and her children, who followed in Christian's footsteps on a similar quest. In the felicitous comment by Bunyan's recent biographer, the atmosphere of this second holy journey is "more like a peacetime tour of the battlefields than of a new campaign."[28] For all that, reports of Christian's perilous adventures had been brought back to the City of Destruction, and Christiana is worried about her impending dangers. Her fears are solaced at the Interpreter's House, where a guide and champion is provided for her. The portrayal of this Greatheart in his valiant mastery over all obstacles gives this second part of Bunyan's epic of salvation a heroic tone.

Two major works by Bunyan have some features of mastery, though not on the level of genius. They are *The Life and Death of Mr. Badman* and *The Holy War*. The former work is a novel in the Puritan manner, tracing the way to Hell: the life and death of an ungodly reprobate. The latter book is of especial interest to us in its imaginative account of the strife of good and evil powers in human life: an ongoing contention which had embroiled Bunyan's own career as portrayed in *Grace Abounding*.

Mr. Badman's wicked life is recounted in the form of "a familiar dialogue between Mr. Wiseman and Mr. Attentive." This novel is an edifying tract by a master in the perception of the devious and callous and ruthless ways of the evildoer. In reciting the sins of Badman's early years Bunyan brought in some personal recollections; the reader is reminded of pages in *Grace Abounding*.

> When he was but a Child, he was so addicted to Lying that his Parents scarce knew when to believe he spake true; yea, he would invent, tell, and stand to the Lyes that he invented and told, and that with such an audacious face, that one might even read in his very countenance the symptoms of an hard and desperate heart this way. . . . He was also much given to *pilfer* and steal, so that what he could, as we say, handsomly lay his hands on, that was counted his own; . . . you must understand me of *Trifles;* for being yet but a Child he attempted no great matter, especially at first. . . . He could not endure the Lord's Day because of the Holiness that did attend it. . . . He counted it a glory to Swear and Curse, and it was as natural to him, as to eat and drink and sleep.[29]

It is as if Bunyan had asked himself: What would I have become, had it not been for my compunction and the misery in sinfulness which I felt through the working of Christ's saving grace in my soul? The ruinous harvest of the early sowing of sin as described by Bunyan is an exposure of the great variety of vices and deceits and corruptions and callous wickedness of the society in which he lived. It is a black biography throughout with no relieving note of genuine remorse.

The vices of Badman's childhood were multiplied in youth

and in later years. He cheated his master and wasted his own time and substance in drunkenness and profligacy. His father, trying his best to reclaim a wayward son, was persuaded to set him up in business; but young Badman rioted through all his capital. Then the reprobate concocted a scheme to marry a rich orphan, a pious young heiress. To win her to his plans, he played the hypocrite; but his pretended repentance was forgotten, once he had won her and clutched her fortune. He ran through his newfound profits, added new debts to the old, deceived his creditors by a fraudulent bankruptcy, proceeded from one wickedness to another, and wrecked himself by dissolute excesses.

Riding one day drunk as a madman, he was thrown down with a broken leg by his horse and was carried helpless to his home. Swearing foully at first, he became frightened by the gravity of his accident and burst out in prayers for God's mercy. But when his misery subsided he was again his old vicious self. After the healing of his leg he came down with a dangerous fit of sickness. His wife was torn between hopes of his recovery to some virtue as well as to health, and despair of his ever abandoning his wickedness. He for his part abused her with empty protestations and vile mistreatment and finally drove her wretched to her death.

Badman's career had its ups and downs. By his wiles he managed eventually to amass great wealth and the power that goes with it. After his good wife's death he preferred random profligacy to remarriage, but one of his harlots outwitted him into marrying her and then gave him curse for curse and full measure all around.

Thus Mr. Wiseman continued the tale of Mr. Badman, wicked to the core and to the very end. As Mr. Attentive, listening to it, remarked, "This is a dreadful Story," and the most dreadful part of it was that Badman died as he had lived, a thoroughly wicked and bad man. Bunyan did not have much confidence in deathbed repentance, and his novel did not close on a note of pious relief. Badman died "as quietly as a Lamb." But his quiet death was a death in utter unbelief and evil. "Mr. Badman was naught, his life was evil, his *wayes* were evil, evil to his end: he therefore went to Hell and to the Devil, how quietly soever he died."[30]

Bunyan's fourth major work has a long descriptive title: *The Holy War, made by Shaddai upon Diabolus, for the Regaining of the Metropolis of the World. Or the Losing and Taking Again of the Town of Mansoul.* The dominant theme of the work is Bunyan's view of human life as an unremitting struggle between the powers of good and evil. The theme is plain to the reader of *Grace Abounding;* in both parts of *The Pilgrim's Progress* the pilgrimage of Christian and later of his wife and children is marked throughout by obstacles to be surmounted and fierce enemies to be overcome. *The Holy War* is a dramatic reenact-ment of this basic conviction: The Christian hope is the hope of the Lord's peace, but this peace is not one of placidity; it is a peace of heroic readiness to resist and persist. We should re-call again that Bunyan's first published work was his criticism of the confident notion of an "inner light" of native godliness and assured divine presence in a man's soul. Bunyan's militant view of the good life was not only a theological doctrine but also the plain daily evidence of his own experience. The auto-biographical note in *The Holy War* is pronounced clearly by him in his poetical preface "To the Reader":

> Then lend thine ear to what I do relate
> Touching the Town of Mansoul and her state,
> How she was lost, took captive, made a slave,
> And how against him set that should her save.
> Yea, how by hostile ways, she did oppose
> Her Lord, and with his enemy did close.
> For they are true, he that will them deny,

Must needs the best of records vilifie.
For my part I (myself) was in the *Town,*
Both when 'twas set up, and when pulling down,
I saw *Diabolus* in his possession,
And *Mansoul* also under his oppression.
Yea, I was there when she own'd him for Lord,
And to him did submit with one accord. . . .

Let no man then count me a Fable-maker,
Nor make my name a credit or partaker
Of their derision: what is here in view
Of my own knowledge, I dare say is true.
I saw the *Princes* armed men come down
By troops, by thousands, to besiege the Town.
I saw the *Captains,* heard the *Trumpets* sound
And how his forces cover'd all the ground.
Yea, how they set themselves in battel-ray,
I shall remember to my dying day.[31]

As we read the motto on the title page, "I have used similitudes," we can understand Bunyan's guiding idea in his book.

The Holy War has been called a people's version of *Paradise Lost.* The extent of Bunyan's knowledge of Milton, if any, is uncertain. He does begin with an account of the fall of Satan, whom he calls Diabolus, and with the Satanic plan of a campaign against Shaddai, God the Father. Shaddai had built the town of Mansoul as the goodliest in his whole creation, for his own delight. Diabolus with his demonic cohorts proposed to seize and possess this choice city and thus avenge themselves on God. After a long conference by the Pandemonium the details of strategy were worked out. On Lucifer's motion, applauded by all the fallen angels, Diabolus assumed the form of a dragon. Led by him, the evil legions approached their intended prize. Mansoul had five gates: Ear-gate, Eye-gate, Mouth-gate, Nose-gate, and Feel-gate. The invaders chose the first of these, for the plan was to try the stratagem of wily eloquence. Diabolus and his chief orator Ill-pause advanced to the Ear-gate and with subtle cunning persuaded the townsmen of Mansoul that they should no longer submit slavishly to Shaddai's restriction but should eat of the forbidden tree. The ruse succeeded: Diabolus entered Mansoul not as conquerer but as liberator. He established his power in its central Castle and reorganized the entire rule of the town.

By this double "use of similitudes," the siege metaphor and that of the forbidden fruit in the Genesis story of original sin, Bunyan began his tale of man's fall. For just as in Biblical tradition Adam signified both the first man and mankind entire, so Mansoul in Bunyan's view was to stand both for the individual soul and for human society. *The Holy War* was meant to recount the warfare of good and evil in each man and also in world history. It invites comparison with St. Augustine's *City of God,* in its portrayal of the contrast of the worldly and the holy social order. Victorious Diabolus by devious and gradual devices removed from office the former good rulers and officials of Mansoul and put in his own bureaucrats. The roster of these burgesses and aldermen is self-descriptive of the new way of life that was established in corrupted Mansoul: "Mr. Incredulity, Mr. Haughty, Mr. Swearing, Mr. Whoreing, Mr. Hardheart, Mr. Pitiless, Mr. Fury, Mr. No-Truth, Mr. Stand-to-lies, Mr. False Peace, Mr. Drunkenness, Mr. Cheating, Mr. Atheism."[32] The allegory here is perhaps too transparent, of the variety of evil motives and powers that debase and taint human nature.

The second part of Bunyan's story related the delivery of Mansoul from the bondage of sin. Shaddai, resolved to deliver his beloved town, accepted the loyal offer of his son Emmanuel to lead the army of liberation, with his four deputy commanders, Captain Boanerges of the challenging voice, Captain Conviction, Captain Judgment and Captain Execution. They assailed the walls of Mansoul, and much fierce fighting ensued, but without decisive success until the King's Son Emmanuel himself came forth and took direct charge of the troops. He first caused the white flag of pardon to be set upon Mount Gracious, but when this offer was spurned by his foes, Mansoul was attacked in full force; its gates were broken, its strongholds reduced, and likewise the gates of the Castle in which Diabolus was entrenched. The evil beast was forced out, shrunk and cringing, and was stripped of his armor and bound fast in chains. The townsmen's humble pleas for forgiveness were granted, but the Diabolonians who led them astray were condemned by a jury whose names are as self-descriptive as the former roster of burgesses and aldermen appointed by Diabolus: "Mr. Belief, Mr. Trueheart, Mr. Upright, Mr. Hatebad, Mr. Lovegood, Mr. Seetruth, Mr. Heavenlimind, Mr. Moderate, Mr. Thankful, Mr. Humble, Mr. Goodwork, and Mr. Zealforgood."[33]

Prince Emmanuel established a new form of government in Mansoul and admonished the citizens to pursue the way of righteousness: "Observe therefore, Oh my *Mansoul,* to be punctual in all things that I have given in charge unto you, and that not only as a Town corporate, and so to your officers and guard, and guides in chief, but to you as you are a people whose well-being, as single persons, depends on the observation of the Orders and Commandments of their Lord."[34] This struggle and liberation and reorganization of Mansoul would correspond to the remorse and repentance and conversion of the sinful soul. In Bunyan's story it was in its way a climax, but we should not mistakenly regard it as a blessed conclusion, for the evil forces of Diabolus, though conquered, were not utterly rooted out. The banished Fiend planned new assaults from without, and from within treacherous Diabolonians conspired to regain possession of Mansoul, notably one Mr. Carnal-Security. Raiding parties threatened Mansoul's defenses, some of them Doubters under Mr. Incredulity, others like Mr. Profane carrying subversive messages from Diabolus. Rioters stormed through the streets, coaxing and blandishing and menacing by turns, until once more Prince Emmanuel arrived with a relieving army. Thus, on one side of the allegory, the backsliding convert is once more reclaimed to contrite repentance. The warfare of counterforces for the possession of Mansoul, for the direction of man's soul, swayed back and forth. Yet there was to be a climax, for "Great is truth, and will prevail."[35] But the conclusive victory is in the Lord's keeping; Mansoul must ever be on the alert; the repentant soul must be a vigilant sentinel at the post of duty. The conclusion of the book is a divine challenge: "O my Mansoul, how have I set my heart, my love upon thee, watch. Behold, I lay none other burden upon thee, than what thou hast already, hold fast till I come."[36]

After his doubled and redoubled terms of imprisonment, Bunyan lived for sixteen years of fruitful activity, tireless preaching and writing: six works in the last year of his life! He, the author of *The Holy War,* was ever militant, but his warfare was in the spiritual life. He did not engage in political conflicts, and his battles were ever for the relief and reclaiming of souls. He died in his sixtieth year, his last words were: "Take me, for I come to thee."[37]

We have noted in *Grace Abounding* and also in Bunyan's other books the evidence of an intensely and arduously devout spirit, but also of a genius for penetrating expression. The reader of Bunyan's writings is bound to be impressed by their high quality of substance and style; impressed, but also astonished, for they are all the works of an uneducated mind. Bunyan wrote slightingly of his schooling, in which he barely learned to read and write and soon forgot the little he had learned. But then we have to acknowledge his mastery of style, tutored or untutored, which has justified a biographer in calling him "the greatest representative of the common people to find a place in English literature."[38] Some critics may decry him as "a philistine genius," but others cite the "surprising fact that one of the most famous books in the world was written by a tinker of very slight education."[39] This is the same kind of paradox of genius that, on a much higher scale, has puzzled students of Shakespeare, with his "little Latin and less Greek," and has led some of his readers with much leisure for dubious speculation to sponsor their supposed learned authors of the great dramas. In Bunyan's lifetime some hostile critics who could not deny the mastery of his best works refused to acknowledge his full claim to them and belittled him as a borrower or even a plagiarist. It has been pointed out that Bunyan had his predecessors; so did Shakespeare; but Bunyan did stamp his work with genuine originality of treatment and style. So he wrote about *The Pilgrim's Progress:* "The whole and every whit is mine. . . . I am for drinking water out of my own cistern."[40] As to his style, we should remember how deeply he drank throughout his life out of the purest fountain: his pages are full of quoted or suggested Scriptural passages, and in his own sentences "the prose of the translation of the English Bible, faultless as it is, loses nothing in Bunyan's hands."[41] His stylistic cultivation was in his daily reading of the Bible.

CHAPTER V

JOHN WESLEY

In the general history of ideas the eighteenth century is regarded as a period of secular-critical thinking, the Age of Enlightenment. It was also a period of brewing and then raging revolution against social corruption and injustice. It was marked by a radical shift from optimistic theories in the early part of the century (Leibniz, Shaftesbury, Pope) towards pessimism and vehement negation. Voltaire's swerving life-outlook before and after the Lisbon earthquake (1755) signalized a characteristic of the epoch; the years 1776 and 1789 punctuate another aspect of the sharp deviation.

Turning to Great Britain in particular, the social historian records the political and social-economic injustices of the age, its moral decay, and spiritual-religious degradation. The so-called parliamentary government was not really representative; aristocrats and landed gentry controlled elections to Parliament in many "rotten boroughs." Old Sarum, for instance, without inhabitants, still sent two members to the House of Commons, while large cities had no representation. The penal code was shocking in its unreasonable severity, without regard to real justice. A person could be hanged for a theft of over five shillings. Where penalties were imposed in this manner, robbers sought safety from capture by murdering their victims; and the land was unsafe for travel, as the word "highwayman" indicated. The multitudes of common folk, exploited and lacking social prospect, were

105

themselves sodden in drunkenness and vice, coarse copies of their profligate masters. Hogarth's drawings present a shocking array of that dissolute society along its dismal range. The clergy of the established Church of England owed their so-called "livings" to the pleasure of landed proprietors and often left the actual divine service to the care of servile curates. Their congregations, to be sure, included many upright and genuinely pious worshipers, but there were also many perfunctory rectors in the pulpits, and outright scoffing unbelievers outside. If one is to trust a comment by a bishop of the period, "there never was an age since the death of Christ, never once since the commencement of the world, in which atheism and infidelity have been more generally confessed."[1] Another dismal comment has been cited, castigating the moral decay of the age: "Vice and wickedness abound in every place, drunkenness and lewdness escape unpunished; our ears in most companies are filled with imprecations of damnation; and the corners of our streets everywhere . . . the horrible sounds of oaths, curses, and blasphemous execrations."[2]

Students of the history of philosophy will remember George Berkeley's lifelong opposition to the spiritual decay of the age; as indicated on his title pages, his books were directed against skeptics and atheists. This general picture should not be blackened overmuch, but we should keep in mind its dark features if we are to understand and appreciate the religious and social reform which is recorded in John Wesley's *Journal*. Our main interest here is in Wesley's variety of religious experience, but his religion had social purport and involvement. Wesley was ever bent on the saving of souls, but in his way of saving souls he was also engaged in reforming the entire social order. The judgment of the historian Lecky has been cited, that Wesley's lifework preserved England from a revolution like the French.[3]

The Wesleys, John and Charles, were two of nineteen children born in twenty-one years to a poor, devoted, but also rigid and likewise very ill-used rector of Epworth and his patient but also resolute wife. The younger son, Charles, is best known for his composition of church hymns; he wrote over six thousand of them, and many were of high poetical merit and enduring appeal. While he collaborated with his brother John, he remained until his death in 1788 a confirmed Anglican priest: he left definite instructions that his funeral service was to be conducted by a rector of the Church of England. We are dealing here with the beginnings of the Methodist Church, and we shall note that John Wesley's own attitude towards its separate establishment was a very slow and wavering and arduous process.

Our passing reference to Wesley's parents needs some further comment. Both Samuel Wesley and his wife Susannah had been brought up in the homes of nonconformist clergymen. Samuel joined the Anglican Church when he went to Oxford; Susannah's shift in church allegiance came earlier in her youth and was due to her objection to the Calvinist doctrine of predestination held by the Puritans. She was of an aristocratic lineage, well educated, a lady of great loyalty and also of very well-reasoned and firm convictions. She showed lifelong devotion to her family through grinding poverty and recurrent grief; nine of her nineteen children died in infancy. She loved and respected her husband, but her convictions were her own. Intellectual acquiescence was not to be expected; political differences would start frictions. A story persisted that when Samuel prayed for the King, Susannah did not respond with an "Amen," for, as she said, she was a Jacobite and did not recognize William of Orange as king. Then, said the rector, we should part, for if we have two kings in England, you and I must have two beds. And he betook himself to London and did not return to Epworth until after his King William's death, on March 8, 1702; for they were both agreed about his successor, Queen Anne. The tale had flaws: There is no such long gap in Samuel's correspondence from Epworth, and besides, Anne Wesley was born some three months after the death of King William.⁴ But the story persisted, like the apocryphal one about Galileo's dropping weights from the leaning tower of Pisa. What is significant in this Wesley tale is that it was told and gained credence and was believed by John Wesley himself, for it must have described one aspect of the Wesley household.

Samuel Wesley has not received his due regard from posterity to compensate for his hardships in life. He was an obstinate convert to Anglicanism and rigid in his theology and church-manship. He married Susannah Annesley the year he was ordained; they lived from hand to mouth in poor "livings" until they came to Epworth, when he was thirty-five, to live out their lives there on his pitiful stipend. He had to borrow money which he had no way of duly repaying: that he served a three month's sentence in jail for his debts was not a blot on his character but a deplorable result of his penury of which his malicious enemies took advantage. But debt-ridden or not, he would and he did see all his three sons through Oxford and his Jack a Fellow there!

Life at Epworth was not only one of indigence but also full of annoyances and worse. The town, in northern Lincolnshire, northeast of Sheffield, accessible now by well-traveled roads, was in Wesley's days situated on a strip of land, in the "Isle of Axholme," amidst the fens. Long-postponed plans to drain the marshes were being resisted by the "Islonians" who were churlish and hostile to any outside meddling in their affairs and especially to Tory politicians and tax collectors and straightlaced divines. The year before Samuel and Susannah Wesley came to Epworth, the surly natives had burned the house of the tax gatherer, Nathaniel Reading. They had no understanding or appreciation of their new rector. That he was an Oxford man, a literary editor of quite some distinction, a poet notable enough to be satirized if not respected by Alexander Pope, and immersed in his lifelong commentary on the Book of Job—all this meant nothing to them any more than his learned sermons. What they did know and resented was that he was a surpliced Tory, a friend of the hated Reading, a rector meddling in their own affairs, and a promoter of the plans to drain their fens and bring outsiders to lord it over them. They could not oust him, for he had the grant of his living; but they pestered him, damaged his crops, killed his livestock, and finally set his rectory afire.

That fire was a momentous event in Methodist history, for it caught little John in his bedroom, from which he was rescued as "a brand plucked from the burning" only minutes before roof and wall collapsed. The rectory was rebuilt but remained long unfurnished, and the Wesleys had to live in the nearby thatched parsonage of Wroote, separated from Epworth by the flooded fens through which the rector had to wade or go by boat. Defying all hardships, Samuel Wesley stuck to his parish, respectable though harassed and destitute. He did have high patrons, the Archbishop of York and the Duke of Buckingham; the latter provided for John's going to Charterhouse School. One should always remember Susannah's role in this family travail. When the great Archbishop asked her once whether she had ever actually lacked bread, she replied that strictly speaking she had not, but it had been such care to get it and to pay for it that it was the next degree of wretchedness to being without any bread whatever. As a sort of comic relief, to our minds, a story was kept alive that the Epworth rectory was haunted for a season by a ghost; "old Jeffrey" they called him, whose escapades included the usual tapping on walls and windows, shaking of furniture and pushing of doors, but with the specialty of stirring up noisily whenever the rector prayed for the King—

a Jacobite specter! Many theories were proposed to account for his reported doings; it is of interest to mention that John considered a supernatural explanation.

Of the nineteen children that were born to them, Samuel and Susannah Wesley brought up seven daughters and three sons. The girls found good or indifferent husbands, most of them; only one, Hetty, in the stern judgment of her father, brought shame to the family, from which her brother John sought to protect her in a spirit of Christian forgiveness and charity. The main concern of the parents seems to have been with their boys' education and careers, to which they applied themselves with early care and discipline. Little John—he was born in 1703, their fifteenth child but only the second boy—was started reading the Book of Genesis on the morning after his fifth birthday; it was the year before the rectory fire almost finished him. His first teacher was his mother, who had a full classroom in her own house. Keeping our eyes on John, we find him being directed to read graspingly and to write simply and clearly and forcefully, a lesson which he never forgot, even though he might depart from it on occasion in later years, in his correspondence with young ladies. Regarding his religious upbringing he wrote later: "I believe till I was about ten years old, I had not sinned away that 'washing of the Holy Ghost' which was given me in baptism; having been strictly educated and carefully taught that I could only be saved 'by unusual obedience, by keeping all the commandments of God.' . . . But all that was said to me of inward obedience or holiness I neither understood nor remembered."[5]

In 1714 John Wesley left his home to go to London to Charterhouse School, where he studied for about seven years, mostly ancient languages and mathematics, living on a diet chiefly of bread, sprinting each morning for exercise, being sorely fagged by the older boys and very likely doing some of it in his turn.

His reminiscing statement, that he entered Charterhouse in a state of grace and left it a sinner, probably meant nothing very serious; he said that his sins were not scandalous. Very likely he was referring to a certain youthful negligence, but no grave remissness; as he stated, he kept his regular church attendance and Bible reading and morning and evening prayers.⁶ His spiritual attitude seems to have been somewhere between George Fox's "purity and innocency" and John Bunyan's devastating conviction of radical guilt.

From Charterhouse seventeen-year-old Wesley proceeded to Christ Church College, Oxford. Quite unlike the later intellectual glory of its colleges, of Newman's Oriel and of the Balliol of Thomas Hill Green, eighteenth-century Oxford education was generally lax. Five years before Wesley, Joseph Butler had found Oriel disappointing, and thirty years later Edward Gibbon was to record a most damning account of a university career: utterly negligent tutors, quite irregular lectures, perfunctory standards all around: "I spent fourteen months at Magdalen College; they proved to be the fourteen months the most idle and unprofitable of my whole life."⁷ Christ Church College scarcely warranted such utter disdain, although it had declined from its earlier eminence. A zealous student could, and John Wesley did, gain a good classical education there; that is, after his season of random college life. He seems to have done considerable rowing and tennis, some translating from Latin poets and versifying on his own, and living beyond his means. The letters of his father, himself groaning under unpaid debts, express double paternal care, both affection and anxiety.

Eventually the young collegian must have done some good study, especially of the classics, for when his brother Charles followed him to Oxford, they conversed readily in Latin. And in English speech likewise he was gaining a degree of distinction as leader of a debating society; it would serve him well later in his sermons and other discourses. Had he earned the high regard of his masters, or was it merely due to his being from Lincolnshire that he gained election to the fellowship at Lincoln College? Be it as it may, it marked a milestone in his young career. It gratified his family—"Dear Mr. Fellow-Elect of Lincoln!"—it gave him assured financial stability; it also led him to set some high standards for his future, both intellectual and religious. He had taken holy orders, had been ordained deacon, and had decided that his life as a college Fellow was not to be the usual one of academic idleness and eating, drinking, and sleeping: "Leisure and I have taken leave of one another." A record of his adopted weekly schedule of studies confirmed his general decision: Mondays and Tuesdays were to be devoted to Greek and Latin; Wednesdays, to logic and ethics; Thursdays, to Hebrew and Arabic; Fridays, to metaphysics and natural philosophy; Saturdays, to oratory and poetry; Sundays, to divinity.[8] This timetable was probably not controlling his entire time strictly, for there were also social diversions, and not only social. He formed friendships and carried on correspondence especially with two ladies, one of them a brilliant widow, the other a deeply religious young woman who had helped confirm his decision to enter into holy orders.

Oxford Fellowships allowed considerable latitude in their residence requirements, and John Wesley decided to help his father as his curate, first for a summer and then for a longer term, toiling in the desolate fen-girded village of Wroote, trying somehow to reach the surly ignorant wights, who gave him no more attention and goodwill than they had given his father. Aside from the duties of his curacy, he was assisting his father with his long manuscript on the Book of Job and doing a great deal of reading on his own. Three works especially engrossed him: *The Imitation of Christ* (or *The Christian Pattern*), Jeremy Taylor's *Holy Living and Holy Dying,* and William Law's *Christian*

Perfection. The meditations aroused by these readings marked a deepening of religious emphasis in his youth. Being recalled by his college rector, he returned to Oxford to teach Greek and philosophy at Lincoln, and soon became involved in one of the most important spiritual relations of his life.

The new engagement was shared with his younger brother Charles, who had followed him to Christ Church and who, like himself, had passed through a season of college diversion to a more serious and devout life-outlook. When John Wesley returned to Lincoln College, he found that Charles and a friend were starting a group for serious studies several times weekly. John joined them and became their leading spirit. Before long half-a-dozen other Oxonians were meeting together in his rooms, to read the Greek New Testament and other devotional and serious works. They attended church services and Holy Communion as a group, and in Oxford and London they undertook to translate their piety into Christian social service, visiting the poor, using their own means to free debtors from jails, bringing Christ's gospel to the weary and the heavy-laden. This "Holy Club" commanded the profound devotion of its members. One of them, Charles Morgan, practiced rigorous fasting and other austerities which were reported to have aggravated his ill health and hastened his death. In a letter which John Wesley wrote to Charles's father, he undertook to disprove this report by well-chosen evidence, and he gave a valuable account of the activities of the group. Of especial interest is the list of questions which the members considered in their pursuit of the true directions of Christian piety. The questions and the answers to them outlined some of the characteristic features of the life-design of "Oxford Methodism" which Wesley's later lifelong mission was to articulate more fully.[9]

The report of these devout activities soon got around, and it aroused widely divergent reactions. From Epworth John and

Charles received warm parental encouragement. The Anglican rector had spoken words to John that seemed to anticipate the son's later Methodist conviction: "The inward witness, son, the inward witness—this is the proof, the strongest proof, of Christianity."[10] But the general run of Oxford collegians, and many dons also, turned upon the group with hostile derision. To the most common name of Holy Club, other nicknames were applied to the members: Sacramentarians, Bible Moths, Godly Club, The Reforming Club, Supererogation Men, Bible Bigots, Enthusiasts, and, what turned out to be the most important eventually, Methodists. This last derisively intended epithet called attention to the methodical religiosity of the group, their common intense convictions and practices.[11]

During these years at Lincoln College John Wesley was seeking and very gradually finding his own way to his purpose in life. He had set down Saturdays, first scheduled for oratory and poetry, for his weekly self-examinations, and some of his questions reveal both his ideal aims and his embroiling problems and obstacles: "Have I loved women and company more than God?" Similar questions about pride, or lewd thoughts, or idleness were followed by resolutions. He would ever keep in mind death, God's immediate presence; he would spend six hours daily on study; he would rise each morning at five. He advanced the hour later in life to four o'clock, and preached at five to those he found ready to listen.

His own studies were of an impressive range and variety, if we are to judge from a six months' list of them:

Drake and LeClerc's Physics, Burnet on the Reformation, Dennis against Pope, Salmon's Review, Welstead's Poems, Lee against Locke, Hickes on Schism, The Great Atlas, Dr. Halley on Magnetism and Gravity, Ditton on Matter's Thinking, The Souls of Brutes, Watts, Keil's Principia, Cowley, Locke, Norris, Heautontimorumenos,

Cheyne of Fevers, Ezra in Hebrew, Horace's Odes, Horace's Epodes and Satires, Life of Whiteways, Horace's De Arte Poetica and Epistles, St. Matthew, part of the fifteenth chapter of Proverbs [which he translated into Latin verse], Virgil's Eclogues, Logic, Virgil's Georgics, St. Mark, St. Luke, the Aeneid, Life of Plutarch, Epictetus, the Acts, the Iliad, Romans, Xenophon, Colossians and Thessalonians, Proverbs and Ecclesiastes, Cornelius Nepos, Jackson, Cowley and Watts, On the Case of Subscribing, Prior on Berkeley, Satires of Juvenal, Vertot's Revolutions of Rome, Synge on Toleration, Clarendon, Milton, Rapin on Eloquence, Ephesians, and twelve Odes of Anacreon.[12]

Does the reader find the list of titles insufferably tedious? Think of the young Fellow of Lincoln who read all those works on his six months' schedule!

Up North at Epworth his father felt that he was nearing the end of his career. He plodded through towards the conclusion of his Job Commentary and, concerned both about the continuance of his church work and the assurance of his wife's residence at the rectory, urged his son to make his plans for succeeding him at Epworth. Wesley would not return to the fens of Lincolnshire; he wrote out his reasons in argumentative detail. The discussion of them continued for so long that finally when he felt bound to accede to his father's urging, he was too late; the Epworth living was already preserved for another applicant. As it happened, about that time another alternative was presented to John and also to Charles—an alternative which found such active support from the old rector that it helped console him for his disappointment about the Epworth succession. This was the Christian mission of the Wesleys to Georgia.

The Georgia colony was started by Colonel James Oglethorpe, with a London Board of Trustees, having a philanthropic aim: to provide a new start in life for men who in various ways had failed or gone astray in England, especially for imprisoned debtors. Oglethorpe's attention had been called to the Oxford "Holy Club," and he welcomed the offer of some of them to join in a missionary colonial endeavor overseas. Thus, as we may read in the beginning of Wesley's *Journal,* he and Charles and some others sailed for Georgia in October, 1735. It turned out to be a tempestuous voyage which upset most of them, John Wesley excepted; he was frightened but not seasick. Between storms he and Charles ministered to the English voyagers. A group of devout Moravian Brethren on board had their own clergymen. The Wesleys practiced an austere diet (no flesh or wine) and tireless piety, as their common schedule may indicate:

> From four in the morning till five, each of us used private prayer. From five to seven we read the Bible together, carefully comparing it (that we might not lean to our own understanding) with the writings of the earliest ages. At seven we breakfasted. At eight were the public prayers, at which were present usually between thirty and forty of our eighty passengers. From nine to twelve I commonly learned German, and Mr. Delamotte Greek. My brother writ sermons, and Mr. Ingram read some treatise on divinity or instructed the children. At twelve we met to give an account to one another of what we had done since our last meeting, and what we designed to do before our next. At one we dined. . . .

And so forth until bedtime between nine and ten.[13] Besides prayers private and public and Bible and other readings, John Wesley's priestly duties involved him in endeavors to preserve Christian goodwill on board. He tried to reconcile two quarrelsome ladies, one of whom pretended amity and then turned against him, also later in Georgia in a scandalous violent outbreak which he described in ugly detail.

His own missionary plans on arrival in Georgia had included as a major interest Christian work among the Indians. One of them, Tomo-Chachi, met him on board, with his suite, and expressed an earnest hope that his own proposed work would be really religious, unlike that of the French and the Spaniards. Wesley's later experience altered his early views of the Indian natives. He had come to them with romantic notions about uncorrupted primitive life, similar to those which Rousseau was to expound in his *Discourses* at the middle of the century. But within two years' dealing with them he found them corrupt in their own way: "All, except perhaps the Choctaws, gluttons, drunkards, thieves, dissemblers, liars. They are implacable, unmerciful, murderers of fathers, murderers of mothers, murderers of their own children. . . . Whoredom they account no crime, and few instances appear of a young Indian woman refusing any one."[14]

His experience with the English settlers was not much less disappointing. He was a strictly formal Anglican priest, and he was dealing with a random lot of men and women of undisciplined standards. He would bring them to Christ, through the proper gate of the Church ordinances as he understood them. Wesley in Georgia was a strict High Churchman. "His ritualism, his severe literalism, and his perfectly conscientious yet overstrained adhesion to rubrics and canons brought him into conflict with the people, few of whom were members of the Church of England or of any other Church."[15] Many of those settlers resented his pulpit admonitions as meddling aimed at them personally; they spurned his strict administering of the service ritual as priestly arrogance. He came to grief through lapses of tact, especially in dealing with irascible women's tempers.

Most distressing of all his woes in Georgia was his involvement with Sophy Hopkey, the niece of the chief magistrate of Savannah. The young lady had given up a suitor whom she judged unworthy; she was enchanted with the charming and distinguished Oxford priest and responded for a while to his religious appeal to her. But, infatuated with her as Wesley became, and

even avowing it to her on one intimate occasion, he was torn
between "the weight of an unholy desire" and his still undecided
priestly plans for his career. Sophy, for her part, became im-
patient with her pious but inconclusive wooer and reached her
own decision in accepting another suitor's proposal. The Reverend John Wesley was asked to publish their banns of marriage on Sunday, but on Saturday she and her William Williamson were married. Lapse number one. Then she, Mrs. Williamson,
presented herself for communion without informing him, her
priest, of her intention to do so. Lapse number two. Wesley
refused her communion; whereupon her new husband sued him
for defamation, assessing damages at one thousand pounds. Wesley's enemies drew a long bill of particular grievances against
him. The upshot of the miserable affair was that Wesley decided
to return to England, where he cleared himself substantially with
the Georgia Trustees and had only his own wretched memory
of it all.[16]

Far more important than all these Georgia misadventures
was Wesley's contact with the Moravian Brethren settlers in the
colony. They were actually Germans and Austrians, followers of
the Bohemian reformer John Huss and more directly of Count
Zinzendorf, who had built for his disciples the village Herrnhut. During his voyage to Georgia Wesley had observed their
pious serenity in the deadliest storms, not so much courage as
complete devout calm. In Georgia he had been impressed by
the evidence of the simple joy and grace in their Christian
worship. That inner confidence in the Lord he did not possess.
On his return voyage, nearing the English coast, he wrote down
his dismal sense of his spiritual want. "I went to America to
convert the Indians; but oh, who shall convert me? who, what
is he that will deliver me from this evil heart of unbelief? I have
a fair summer religion. I can talk well; nay, and believe myself, when no danger is near. But let death look me in the face,

and my spirit is troubled."[17] The Moravian Brethren seemed to have that faith which he felt that he lacked: "that faith which none can have without knowing that he hath it, . . . 'having peace with Christ and rejoicing in hope of the glory of God.' "—"that faith which enables every one that hath it to cry out, 'I live not; but Christ liveth in me; and the life which I now live, I live by faith in the Son of God who loved me, and gave Himself for me.' "[18]

In London and Oxford and elsewhere he met and had repeated long conversations with one of the Moravian leaders, Peter Böhler, which convinced him that their Moravian Church had what he most needed. Unlike Böhler, he was torn in his inmost spirit. He could not live without preaching, but within him was a deadly quandary and protest. "Leave off preaching. How can you preach to others, who have not faith yourself?" Böhler encouraged him earnestly: "Preach faith *till* you have it; and then, *because* you have it, you *will* preach faith."[19] The gradual solution of this crucial problem in Wesley's life was a major part of his advance towards his basic understanding of the Christian religion.

Actually during the four months prior to his own climactic experience he is reported to have preached about eighty sermons. He was moving towards his day of light, but arduously, in "continual sorrow and heaviness" in his heart, praying "for this very thing, justifying, saving faith, a full reliance on the blood of Christ shed for *me;* a trust in Him, as *my* Christ, as *my* sole justification, sanctification, and redemption."[20] Thus he had at last his life-consummate experience, on a May day in 1738, in London, which he has recorded in words that recall a supreme page in St. Augustine's *Confessions:*

> I think it was about five in the morning, that I opened my Testament on those words, . . . "There are given unto us exceeding great and precious promises, even that ye should be partakers of the divine nature." . . .

Just as I went out, I opened it again on those words, "Thou are not far from the kingdom of God." In the afternoon I was asked to go to St. Paul's. The anthem was, "Out of the deep have I called unto Thee, O Lord; Lord, hear my voice. O let Thine ears consider well the voice of my complaint. If Thou, Lord, will be extreme to mark what is done amiss, O Lord, who may abide it? For there is mercy with Thee; therefore shalt Thou be feared. O Israel, trust in the Lord: for with the Lord there is mercy, and with Him is plenteous redemption. And he shall redeem Israel from all his sins." In the evening I went very unwillingly to a society in Aldersgate Street, where one was reading Luther's preface to the *Epistle to the Romans*. About a quarter before nine, while he was describing the change which God works in the heart through faith in Christ, I felt my heart strangely warmed. I felt I did trust in Christ, Christ alone for salvation; and an assurance was given me that He had taken away *my* sins, and saved *me* from the law of sin and death.

And he added later: "I have constant peace; not one uneasy thought. And I have freedom from sin; not one unholy desire." He was still "much buffeted with temptations, but cried out and they fled away."[21] This experience, climactic at the time, could hardly be regarded as wholly analogous to those of Saul of Tarsus on his road to Damascus, or of Augustine in the garden. It was perhaps more properly his dramatic confirmation in Christian faith than his conversion from sin to piety. Wesley had experienced an earlier spiritual quickening, in his Oxford days. But the Aldersgate arousal of living faith came at the right time in his career.

His brother Charles had experienced a similarly decisive hour; the two of them were full of their message and proclaimed it abroad in burning words which disturbed less intense devotees. Remembering his discussions with the Moravian Brethren, especially with Peter Böhler, though he disagreed with some of his convictions, Wesley resolved to go directly to Herrnhut, the center of the Moravian activities, and to meet with their chief leader, Count Zinzendorf. He was entertained hospitably by Moravian groups at several stops on his way and was welcomed at Herrnhut, where he had extended conferences with several of the leaders, whose accounts of their experiences and beliefs he recorded in detail. But while he valued deeply their doctrine that "the free grace of God [is] the cause, and faith the condition of justification," and the Moravian trampling under foot "the lust of the flesh, the lust of the eye, and the pride of life," and their true Christian love of each other,[22] he was realizing more and more clearly his radical divergence from some of their beliefs. These differences had already been shown in his discussions with Peter Böhler; they became accentuated in his relations with some of the English Moravian groups. Eventually the reaction of the Moravian Brethren to him became definitely negative, as he recorded it in the Fourth Part of his *Journal,* and their separation from each other was imperative.

Wesley objected to the Moravian belief that "there are no degrees of faith, and that no man has any degree of it before all things in him are become new, before he has the full assurance of faith, the abiding witness of the Spirit, or the clear perception that Christ dwelleth in him." Furthermore, he definitely rejected their idea of "stillness"; that is, that, while waiting for Christ, one should not go to church, or communicate, or fast or use so much private prayer, or read the Scripture, or pursue any temporal or spiritual good. Wesley, on the contrary, believed that the way to divine Grace is gradual; while awaiting the blessed climax, we should use and practice all the ways and means to Christian righteousness. He "earnestly exhorted those who had believed to beware of two opposite extremes—the one, the thinking while they were in light and joy, that the work was ended when it was just begun; the other, the thinking when they were in heaviness, that it was not begun because they found it was not ended."[23] In his letters to the Moravian Church, one started in 1738 and laid aside for further reflection and the other sent to Herrnhut two years later, Wesley outlined his specific agreements and disagreements with Moravianism in a generous but candid spirit. His own pursuit of the holy life was one of humble endeavor towards an ideal always above him. He could not share the Moravian confidence that their church was "so led by the Spirit that it was not possible for it to err in anything."[24] One may recognize in Wesley's objections to Moravianism a basic criticism similar to that expressed by Bunyan in his controversies with the Quakers.

Wesley was approaching the middle of his life-course, but, unlike Dante who at that point found himself in a dark forest, having lost the right way, he, Wesley, was actually getting out of the woods and starting on a preaching career scarcely matched in church history. It engaged him for some time in collaboration with George Whitefield, at first in the Bristol region—a collaboration which, at its beginning, required of him a hard decision about a radical change in preaching methods. Whitefield, born in a tavern and growing up as a barkeep, had been a poor servitor at Oxford, poor also in his intemperance. Charles Wesley had turned him towards higher things, and he had joined the Holy Club, with his social superiors. The genteel formalism of the Church of England had alienated him; he had been drawn to Moravianism and then to his own free-lance unconventional preaching outdoors to groups that grew into crowds and multitudes. Wesley's own popular appeal had repeatedly forced him to step out of houses and chapels into the open air; but he also was driven to preaching outdoors because church after church was closed to him by clergy and public officials who regarded his sermons and the conduct of his services as unsound. The *Journal* records a long series of these ejections. So a surpliced divine of Exeter forbade Wesley to preach in his church. "Not," said he, "that you preach any false doctrine. I allow all that you have said is true. And it is the doctrine of the Church of England. But it is not guarded. It is dangerous. It may lead people into enthusiasm or despair."[25]

Wesley found this ostracism by his church hard to endure, for he had grown up in the Anglican tradition, and during his mission to Georgia had even aroused resentment by his strict High Church formalism. The experiences which had led to his climax at the meeting on Aldersgate Street had not wiped out entirely his accustomed pulpit procedure. He wrote explicitly: "I could scarce reconcile myself at first to this strange way of preaching in the fields, . . . having been all my life (till very lately) so tenacious of every point of decency and order, that I should have thought the saving of souls almost a sin if it had not been done in a church."[26]

His consuming zeal to bring his Christian message to the people, and his astounding success in that endeavor soon outweighed his initial reluctance. In obedience to his call to bring the Gospel to the people he overcame his priestly dignity and "submitted to be more vile, and proclaim in the highways the glad tidings of salvation."[27] Before long he was preaching abroad to large audiences, recorded in the *Journal* as running up to fifteen thousand. From the Bristol countryside his territory spread in every direction, to Wales and Cornwall, to North Britain and Ireland, and of course to London. There could scarcely be any reckoning of the countless miles he covered on horseback over roads of all description, carrying the message of the Gospel to his multitudes. But be it remembered, he was ever ready to speak the words of grace to odd passersby and chance acquaintances. His mare had lost a shoe; while it was being replaced he talked "closely, for near half an hour, both to the smith and his servant.

. . . How easy it is to ransom every fragment of time . . . when we feel any love to those souls for whom Christ died."[28] His preaching schedule was as unconventional in the timing as in the location of his sermons. His people knew the schedule he kept, rising at four, starting to preach at five. A large company of tinners, fearing "they should be late," woke him up between two and four, "singing and praising God. At five I preached once more. . . ." That was in West Britain. Another time, in the North, "I preached at five . . . to a large congregation, part of whom had sat up all night, for fear they should not wake in the morning. Many of them I found, either were or had been Papists. Oh how wise are the ways of God! How am I brought, without any care or thought of mine, into the center of the Papists in Yorkshire!"[29]

Wesley's preaching thenceforth was marked by increasingly strong emotional appeal, increasingly strong for him whose sermons had formerly been distinguished by their reasoned and dignified tone. His new fervor stirred or occasioned many morbid excesses familiar in religious revivals. In the large congregations which he drew he met repeatedly with men and more often with women who went into hysterical outbursts, as they appeared to some, or demonic seizures, as they were regarded by others, or yet again as divine raptures. We are reluctant to cite the lurid instances. Close reading of the passages in the *Journal* which record these excesses, which Wesley described again and again in their shocking details, indicate his reasonable ways of dealing with many of them, but also his uncertain interpretation of some of those cases of seeming strife by the devil with the saving work of divine Grace.

A secular mind would judge that Wesley often veered towards superstition; a more positively religious thinker of a reasonable temper would note that Wesley succeeded in skirting credulity. Sometimes his comment is as revealing as his actual report: "I made it my business to inquire concerning the truth of a strange relation which had been given me, and I found there was no possibility of doubting it. The plain fact was this": An Anglican priest had preached in two or three churches against the Dissenters and "inveighed very much against the novel sect, the upstart Methodists (as he termed them). . . ." calling them ravening wolves and hypocrites. When, shortly after, he had started another sermon on the same topic, "he was suddenly seized with a rattling in his throat, attended with a hideous groaning. He fell backward against the door of the pulpit, burst it open, and would have fallen down the stairs, but that some people caught him and carried him away, as it seemed dead, into the vestry. In two or three days he recovered his senses and the Sunday following died." If that was a case of direct divine punishment, another one seems to have been a grace vouchsafed to man and beast alike. One day, leaving Newcastle, Wesley and his horse were both ailing: "He would scarce set his foot to the ground. By riding thus seven miles I was thoroughly tired, and my head ached more than it had done for several months. (What I here aver is the naked fact; let every man account for it as he sees good.) I then thought, Cannot God heal either man or beast, by any means, or without any? Immediately my weariness and headache ceased, and my horse's lameness in the same instant. Nor did he halt any more either that day or the next. A very odd accident, this also!"[30]

Not at all exceptional in his day but yet significant for a person with Wesley's standard of intelligence was his habit through the years, when deliberating about a difficult decision, to consult God's will for him by opening the Bible and reading the first verse that caught his eye or the one at the top of the page. The reader who recalls young John's reaction towards the antics of the ghost "old Jeffery" in the Epworth rectory would be bound to consider his more mature adherence to the belief in specters and apparitions, recorded especially in the later volumes of his *Journal*. A Mr. P. told him that one night at one o'clock he rang for his servant to say that Mrs. Prior had just died; he had seen her ghost entering his room. One hour later his nurse came to inform him of the lady's death at that very hour. Wesley preserved an eight-page report of some two dozen cases of apparitions: "The reader may believe it if he pleases or may disbelieve it, without any offence to me. Meanwhile, let him not be offended if I believe it, till I see better reason to the contrary."[31] More disturbing to modern thinking minds is Wesley's belief in witchcraft, and for systematic reasons: "Giving up witchcraft is, in effect, giving up the Bible; . . . if but one account of the intercourse of men with separate spirits be admitted, their whole castle in the air (Deism, Atheism, Materialism) falls to the ground. I know no reason, therefore, why we should suffer even this weapon to be wrested out of our hands."[32]

Relevant in this connection, however, is the evidence given in the *Journal* of Wesley's aversion to mystical accounts of supernatural experiences. On his way riding to Epworth, where he preached from his father's tombstone to a large multitude, he finished his reading of two of Mme. Guyon's mystical works. He recognized in them the quietism which had disturbed him in the Moravian Church and in other dissenting sects: "Ah, my brethren! I can answer your riddle, for I have ploughed with your heifer. The very words I have so often heard some of you use are not your own, no more than they are God's. . . . Oh that you knew how much God is wiser than Man! Then would you drop Quietists and Mystics together, and at all hazards keep to the plain, practical Word of God." Even more contemptuous was his judgment of Jacob Behmen (Boehme), whose mystical *Mysterium Magnum* he rejected as "most sublime nonsense, inimitable bombast, fustian not to be paralleled."[33] He "sat down to read and seriously consider some of the writings of Baron Swedenborg. I began with huge prejudice in his favor, . . . but I could not

hold out long. . . . He is one of the most ingenious, lively, enter-
taining madmen that ever set pen on paper."[34]

His collaboration with Whitefield was and remained personally
friendly, but a doctrinal divergence between them became unavoidable, much as they both regretted it for its threat to split the
Methodist movement. The issue was over the Calvinist trend in
some Methodist preaching, towards which Whitefield and others
inclined and which the Wesleys strongly resisted. John and Charles
had learned their opposition to the doctrine of predestination at
their mother's knee; as a girl she had turned to the Church of
England because of her disagreement with the Calvinism of so
many Puritans. Charles Wesley satirized predestination in verses;
John, in long reasoned arguments, but also in terse condemnation, as in this one which outraged the Reverend Augustus Toplady, he of the "Rock of Ages" hymn: "The sum of all is this:
One in twenty (suppose) of mankind are elected; nineteen in
twenty are reprobated. The elect shall be saved, do what they
will. The reprobate shall be damned, do what they can. Reader,
believe this, or be damned. Witness my hand, A— T—."[35] With
more fervor than irony Wesley rejected the Calvinist doctrine, as
in his sermon of "Free Grace": "This is the blasphemy clearly
contained in *the horrible decree* of predestination. And here I fix
my foot. On this I join issue with every assertor of it. You represent God as worse than the devil; more false, more cruel, more
unjust."[36]

One of his radical objections to the doctrine of predestination
was due to the "antinomian" temper which it induced in those who
felt assured of being among the elect. Dispensing with the long
theological term and using simpler words, Wesley was shocked by
their serene or even complacent feeling of an unassailable holiness—"do what they will"—as he put it in his devout slap at
Toplady. This placid confidence he had noted with disapproval in
the Moravian Brethren; it impressed him more grievously in some

of his own Methodist ranks; he opposed it root and branch. Against both predestination and self-assured holiness he advocated the arduous, humble, but hopeful pursuit of Christian righteousness, ever trusting in Christ's grace: "Let none pity or spare one limb of either speculative or practical Antinomianism, or of any doctrine that naturally tends thereto."[37]

Wesley's spreading countrywide arousal of religious interest, a literal revival, was countered by equally widespread opposition to the tenor and the manner of his preaching, which grew in intensity from criticism and controversy to active repression and flagrant persecution.[38] Much of the controversy is now dust-covered in dull volumes of churchly argument. The Wesley brothers and their associates in growing numbers were confronted with vigorous resistance by clergy and populace.

Not all of their antagonism was benighted and vicious. Wesley's revival started in the Bristol countryside, and the Bishop of Bristol was the most reasonable Anglican of the century, Joseph Butler, known to critical theologians for his *Analogy of Religion* and to philosophical students as an outstanding master of ethical theory. Wesley wrote down a record of his stiff session with the eminent Bishop. After a discussion about the Anglican warrant for his doctrine of faith and justification, in which Wesley did not surrender to Butler's judgment, and Wesley's refusal to be drawn into a discussion of his own involvement in Whitefield's ideas and pretentions, he had to face the Bishop's censure: "Well, sir, since you ask my advice, I will give it to you very freely. You have no business here; you are not commissioned to preach in this diocese. Therefore I advise you to go hence." Wesley replied forthrightly: "My lord, my business on earth is to do what good I can. Wherever, therefore, I think I can do most good, there I must stay, so long as I think so." He reminded Butler what doubtless the Bishop knew full well, that in his ordination as Fellow of a College, he was not limited to any diocese, but had "an indeterminate commission to preach the word of God in any part of the Church of England." And so they parted, Butler in his Bristol bishopric and Wesley in the countryside of the diocese and elsewhere abroad.[39] In a letter written earlier the same year Wesley had expressed his view of his broad Christian mission in a striking phrase: "I look upon *all the world* as *my parish*—Thus far I mean, that in whatever part of it I am, I judge it meet, right and my bounden duty to declare unto all that are willing to hear me the glad tidings of salvation."[40]

The opposition to Wesley's work assumed very violent forms, not only of denunciation and calumny but also of literal stoning and bodily assault. Scurrilous tracts and flyleaf attacks spread the rumor that both he and Charles had been expelled from Oxford, that they were both hypocritical mountebanks, that in fact they were Papists, Jesuits out of Rome bent on undermining the Church of England—and many other false gossips. The populace was not content with vilification but turned from their rectors' pulpit harangues against the Methodists to outright riots and mudslinging and to public violence. The *Journal* recounts the repeated mob outbreaks with which John and Charles Wesley and a number of their allied preachers had to contend throughout the land. In the Staffordshire riots the unruly crowd "dragged me along till we came to the town, where, seeing the door of a large house open, I attempted to go in; but a man, catching me by the hair, pulled me back into the middle of the mob. They made no more stop till they had carried me through the main street, from one end of the town to the other. . . . Many cried out: . . . 'knock his brains out; down with him; kill him at once.' " The index to the Standard Edition of the *Journal* lists over threescore cases of mobs and riots. During one assault with clods and stones a gentlewoman offered Wesley and his wife refuge in her crowded coach, which was so packed that "a large gentlewoman who sat in my lap screened me, so that nothing came near me."[41]

Facing ugly mobs was not Wesley's only tribulation on his preaching journeys. He had to contend with recurring ill health; drastic digestive ills aggravated most painfully his cross-country riding over rough roads and made his public appearance an unmanageable predicament. Severe colds which settled in his lungs and threatened him, as he feared, with consumption choked his formerly strong voice and left him scarcely audible. He did not spurn altogether the warnings of his physician, but he would not stop preaching and give himself the respite he needed for recovery. He wrote his own epitaph, as it turned out, thirty-seven years before he died:

Here Lieth the Body
of
John Wesley
A Brand Plucked out of the Burning;
Who Died of a Consumption, in the Fifty-first year of his Age,
Not Leaving, after his Debts are Paid
Ten Pounds behind him:
Praying
God, be Merciful to me, an Unprofitable Servant.[42]

The incidental reference to Wesley's wife raises a topic which calls for some further notice. His experience with women was not a pleasant part of his life. A general report of the Wesley brothers recounted their strong personal appeal, especially to women. Charles's marriage to Sarah Gwynne, in his early forties, settled him to happy domesticity in his composition of hymns and peaceful adherence to the Church of England. John Wesley's love affairs were quite another matter. The three women who gained his deep affection had all been his nurses during illnesses. His infatuation with Sophy Hopkey, as was noted, was complicated by his resolution to follow priestly preaching journeys; his two other loves were also affected, in different ways, by the same problem. Fourteen years after the Hopkey affair, Grace Murray won Wesley's love not only by her almost ecstatic acceptance of his proposal but also by her evident enjoyment of the prospect of sharing with him in the adventures of his cross-country preaching, with all its hardships. But Charles Wesley disapproved strongly of his brother's marrying one whom he deemed John's social inferior. Charles therefore promoted strongly and successfully Grace's marriage to another wooer, John Bennet. This disappointment left John Wesley desolate and almost tore apart the two brothers.

The name of Wesley's third lady, whom he did marry, was Mrs. Vazeille, a merchant's widow. Their troubles began immediately after the wedding. Wesley started his honeymoon with a sermon, and before the end of his first month was off on a preaching trip, returning for a few days only in order to start on another journey. His wife could not see it at all; she would not go with him and would not be left alone. She was moreover jealous of Wesley's popularity with his Methodist ladies; she was suspicious of him and rifled his correspondence; she wore him out, and herself, with her harangues and finally left him, after twenty years of marital distress and ten more years of some temporary reconciliations, before she died in 1781. It was a pitiable matter altogether.

Over against the hardships without and within, Wesley's life-long work was bearing abundant fruit. In 1785 he wrote: "I was now considering how strangely the grain of mustard seed, planted about fifty years ago, has grown up. It has spread through all of Great Britain and Ireland; the Isle of Wight and the Isle of Man; then to America from the Leeward Islands, through the whole continent, to Canada and Newfoundland. And the societies, in all these parts, walk by one rule, knowing religion is holy tempers; and striving to worship God, not in form only, but likewise 'in spirit and in truth.' "[48] The rule of the societies, as the

Methodist groups were called, was not only one of fundamental guiding spirit. Wesley spelled it out in many specific regulations. They applied not so much to matters of belief as to practical conduct, individual and social. They listed definite evils and ways of doing harm which were to be shunned, and counter ways of doing good, a positive Methodist ethics of Christian piety. They were stringent rules, for they condemned not only flagrant wickedness but common worldly conduct. Wesley's admonitions against wearing of gold and jewelry, or velvet and silks, or any showy apparel of glaring color, remind the reader of Savonarola's sweeping reform of Medicean Florence.

Rigorous as he was in disciplining Christian conduct, Wesley was emphatic on his doctrinal freedom always within definite limits, as has been noted already. In his eighty-fifth year he proclaimed the Methodist platform of spiritual liberty: "The Methodists alone do not insist on your holding this or that opinion; but they think and let think. Neither do they impose any particular mode of worship; but you may continue to worship in your former manner, be it what it may. Now, I do not know any other religious society, either ancient or modern, wherein such liberty of conscience is now allowed, or has been allowed, since the age of the apostles. Here is our glorying and a glorying peculiar to us. What society shares it with us?"[44]

Although he was not so strict as his brother Charles about his definitely Anglican priesthood, John Wesley had no design on starting another church. The unsectarian tone of the just-quoted passage written near the close of his life expressed what had become his steady hope through the years, of remaining within the Church of England while spreading the Gospel according to his convictions. But as so many of the Anglican churches, as also the Presbyterian ones in Scotland, were closed to him, so that he had to preach outdoors, he and his followers were obliged to build chapels for their meetings, first in wintry and otherwise inclement weather and later for all their work. The direction of these under-takings engaged Wesley's energies and also raised the problems of administration and general policy. Actually before his eyes a new church was emerging, definitely headed towards separation from the Church of England in which he had been ordained. Many of the members of his societies had come from the Presbyterian Church and also from various nonconformist groups. The Meth-odist societies in America felt especially drawn towards a sep-arate denominational status, and this attitude was accentuated definitely during the tensions preceding the Revolution. Wesley had written unsympathetically concerning the insurgence of the colonies; it is significant that one finds scarcely any extensive comment on American affairs during the revolutionary years. For the American Methodists, independence from England meant separation from the Church of England.

So Wesley through the years had to face gradually and then conclusively the issue of a Methodist Church. In his earlier com-ments he had written of "Methodism so-called" or "the new name of Methodism" (not so new, since the early Oxford days of the Holy Club); later he used the term himself to describe the so-cieties which he had started, and towards the end of his life he adopted it earnestly. But he never lost altogether his spirit of Anglican loyalty.

The reader of the *Journal* is bound to be impressed by Wes-ley's enduring vitality, astounding in view of his periodic inva-lidism. He outlived his own epitaph almost forty years, and his old age was marked by sturdy vigor almost until the very end. In 1788, as he entered upon his eighty-fifth year, he reviewed his continuing good health with gratitude "to the power of God, fitting me for the work to which I am called," but also noted some of the "inferior means": his constant exercise and change of air; his never having lost a night's sleep, sick or well; his ever having sleep at his command; his having constantly, for above sixty years, risen at four in the morning, and for over fifty years preached at five; and so forth.[45] But at New Year's, 1790, at long last, he recognized his impending collapse, yet reaffirmed his resolve to carry on: "I am now an old man, decayed from head to foot. My eyes are dim; my right hand shakes much; my mouth is hot and dry every morning; I have a lingering fever almost every day; my motion is weak and slow. However, blessed be God, I do not slacken my labor. I can preach and write still." He "writ sermon" about two months later, almost on his deathbed. Two days later his *Diary* ended. His last letter was a final protest against slavery, "that execrable villany which is the scandal of religion, of England, and of human nature."[46] He died on the second of March, 1791, near the end of his eighty-eighth year.

This account has been centered on Wesley's lifelong devoted Christian ministry, for this was the dominant concern of his life. Nevertheless, for a full view of his personality, we should note also that he was a consuming reader and a prolific writer. Most of his studies were religious, but not altogether. The titles of books mentioned in his *Journal* cover the span of literature, history, philosophy, science, medicine. He commented on Xenophon's *Memorabilia* of Socrates and paid a high tribute to the *Meditations* of Marcus Aurelius. He criticized Pascal's *Thoughts,* wrote a French grammar, and labored on a Hebrew grammar. His literary and artistic judgment was not impeccable: he regarded "Ossian" as not inferior to Homer or Virgil; "in some respects, superior to both."[47] He recognized few striking pictures in the collection of the Marquis of Rockingham, which is said to have included some of Van Dyck's finest works.[48]

Regarding his career as an author, he remarked that the publication of his works had not covered his expenses: in about seventy years he had lost some six hundred pounds. Yet we are told that his royalties from his *Primitive Physic* brought him thirty thousand pounds which he used in distributing free copies of the book. He urged his readers and hearers to work hard, earn much, and give away to all in need, and he practiced his precepts. The money he received from his *History of England* was given away within a week.[49]

Despite his unresponsiveness to Van Dyck, Wesley was ever commenting on natural and artistic beauty. He had very definite critical ideas about music; he defended the simple devotional quality of English hymnology against the operatic adventures of Continental church singing. For all his Christian humility, he was proud of his church choir in Bolton: "such trebles, boys and girls, . . . are not to be found together in any chapel, cathedral, or music-room within the four seas."[50] And by way of a closing word, a point which is not quite out of place in considering a devoutly consecrated man. Wesley showed on some occasions a keen sense of humor: "An odd circumstance occurred during the morning preaching. It was well that only serious persons were present. An ass walked gravely in at the gate, came up to the door of the house, lifted up his head and stood stock still, in a posture of deep attention. Might not 'the dumb beast reprove' many who have far less decency, and not much more understanding?"[51]

CHAPTER VI

JOHN HENRY CARDINAL NEWMAN

A prominent trend in Western religious activity has been the search for some basis of unity among the various Christian bodies, the so-called ecumenical movement. It started first among the Protestant churches, and, as we know, it has led to several denominational unions. It was a motivating influence in the assembling of world conferences, in which representatives of Eastern Orthodox Churches have participated; but, as it has been expressed, all these activities have been "outside of Rome." The official position of the Vatican has been that all non-Catholic communions are always welcome—welcome to return to Mother Church, to Rome. It cannot be said, not quite yet, that the Roman Catholic hierarchy has abandoned this view, but certainly within it some more liberal attitudes have found expression, with the view that a reconsideration and a reappraisal of both sides is needed before real Christian unity can be approached.

On the Roman Catholic side three main positions may be distinguished. There are many laymen and clergy, and also high prelates in the hierarchy, who take a definitely liberal position and maintain that the Church of Rome must rethink thoroughly its ideas and policies in the light of modern ascertained knowledge. Against any such accommodation to modern thought, a hard core of conservative churchmen, especially in the Roman Curia, cleave firmly to the old established traditions and forms and resist any change whatever. Between these two may be noted theologians and ecclesiastics who, themselves loyal conservatives and wary of any radical modernism, yet realize the strength and also the spiritual integrity of their liberal colleagues and feel strongly the need of a fair and productive dialogue with them. This third attitude marked the thought and the policy of Pope John XXIII, whose hope for better mutual understanding inspired his convocation of the Vatican Council, as we shall consider it in our concluding chapter. This hope led to the election of Pope John's successor, the Archbishop Montini of Milan who, as Pope Paul VI, has continued vigorously the movement for a reexamination of the whole position of achieving Christian unity, in the extended sessions of the Vatican Council and in his more recent pontifical activities.

From the other side of the ecumenical dialogue, the trend toward a return to Rome, on Roman Catholic terms, is not apparent in most Protestant churches, and certainly not among those of Eastern Orthodoxy, which regard themselves as in some ways more ancient and more authentically Christian than Rome. One important Christian communion, the Church of England, however, while renouncing the ecclesiastical dominance of the Vatican, has yet felt its continued participation in the Catholic orthodox tradition and has distinguished itself from the other Reformed denominations. Within it there have been demands for a closer cooperation with Rome; they have been expressed with various degrees of emphasis by the so-called Anglo-Catholics.

A very noteworthy form of these motives in Anglican-Episcopal circles was the Oxford or Tractarian Movement in the nineteenth century, in which a number of leading Anglican churchmen actually turned to Roman Catholicism. Chief among them was John Henry Newman (1801-1890), whose autobiography is not only a most intimately self-revealing account of religious experience but also a masterpiece of English literature. Newman entitled his work *Apologia pro Vita Sua, Apology for My Life*

(1864), really a self-defense through a progressive history of his religious opinions, which led him from the position of a firm Anglican and a critic and opponent of Rome to that of a Roman convert and eventually to devout activity within the Catholic fold. In our studies we have examined the autobiographies of Catholic saints and of dissident Protestant reformers, always endeavoring to avoid partisan attitudes and only seeking to explore and understand the varieties of religious experience. In the same spirit we shall follow Newman's confession as he traced his religious travails and his journey from Anglican Oxford to Catholic Rome. Our Episcopal colleagues are plainly aware of the different trends in their church which distinguish the so-called high churchmen, clergy and laity alike, from their fellow members who would not omit but would rather emphasize the adjective *Protestant* Episcopal in the name of their church. Many of the rest of us should find interest in understanding better the varying trends in religious opinion and alignment.

John Henry Newman was led to write his *Apologia* as a result of a controversy in which he was involved with the liberal churchman Charles Kingsley. In a book review of J. A. Froude's *History of England* Kingsley had expressed his view that the Roman Catholic clergy had not been noted for an unqualified devotion to the truth, and had cited Newman as an example. In a series of letters between the two men, which were eventually published, Newman endeavored to uphold his integrity forthrightly. Kingsley, nevertheless, issued a long pamphlet in which he renewed and amplified his attack. Newman then felt in honor bound, as he stated, to defend himself against any charge of untruthfulness. He would lay bare his entire life.

> Whatever judgment my readers may eventually form of me from these pages, I am confident that they will believe me in what I shall say in the course of them. I

have no misgiving at all, that they will be ungenerous or harsh with a man who has been so long before the eyes of the world, who has so many to speak of him from personal knowledge; whose natural impulse it has ever been to speak out; who has ever spoken too much rather than too little; who would have saved himself many a scrape, if he had been wise enough to hold his tongue; who has ever been fair to the doctrines and arguments of his opponents; who has never slurred over facts and reasonings which told against himself; who has never given his name or authority to proofs which he thought unsound, or to testimony which he did not think at least plausible; who has never shrunk from confessing a fault when he felt that he had committed one; who has ever consulted for others more than for himself; who has given up much that he loved and prized and could have retained, but that he loved honesty better than name, and Truth better than dear friends.[1]

Newman was very resolute in his biographical report of himself.

I mean to be simply personal and historical. I am not expounding Catholic doctrine, I am doing no more than explaining myself, and my opinions and actions. I wish, as far as I am able, simply to state facts, whether they are ultimately determined to be for me or against me. Of course there will be room enough for contrariety of judgment among my readers, as to the necessity, or appositeness, or value, or good taste, or religious prudence of the details which I shall introduce. I may be accused of laying stress on little things, or being beside the mark, of going into impertinent or ridiculous details, of sounding my own praise, of giving scandal, but this is a case above all others, in which I am bound to follow my own lights and to speak my own heart. It is not at all pleasant for me to be egotistical, nor to be criticized for being so. It is not pleasant to reveal to high and low, young and old, what has gone on within me from my early years. It is not pleasant to be giving to every shallow and flippant disputant the advantage over me of knowing my most private thoughts, I might say even the intercourse between me and my Maker. But I do not like to be called to my face a liar and a knave; nor should I be doing my duty to my faith and to my name, if I were to suffer it. I know I have done nothing to deserve such an insult; and if I prove this, as I hope to do, I must not care for such incidental annoyances as are involved in the process.[2]

These two extended passages should show at the outset the spirit in which Newman wrote his autobiography, and also the literary mastery of his intimate utterance. In chapter after chapter he recounts the history of his religious opinions, and first of all, his spiritual temper in childhood and youth, his early thoughts and feelings and experiences.

Newman's life spanned the nineteenth century, as Wesley's did the eighteenth. He was born in 1801, in London, the first of three boys and three girls. His two younger brothers went different ways. Francis William, after a brilliant student career at Oxford, turned out to be a crochety mind of numberless specialties and heterodox inclinations. Charles Robert grew up a recluse of atheistic convictions. Both of them caused anxiety and then distress to their distinguished brother. The father, son of a family of landed gentry in Cambridgeshire, who was engaged in banking in London, combined with his business career a strong taste for music and Shakespearean drama. He was supposed to have had a distant Dutch ancestry, but the surmise that it had a Jewish strain, which has found its way into an encyclopedia article, has been held by the most searching of Newman's biographers as being without any sound basis.[3] Newman's mother, Jemima Fourdrinier, was of Huguenot descent, a pious lady of Calvinist slant, who held and imparted to her children the belief that they should realize their need of God's grace for redemption from their sinfulness.

From earliest childhood John Henry was raised on daily reading of King James's Bible: its themes and the divine harmonies of its style possessed his thought and his imagination and roused him to early self-utterance. But he also remembered listening in rapt attention to his mother and aunt as they read aloud Walter Scott's *Lay of the Last Minstrel*. On his own he pored over the Waverley novels. He burst into prose and verse, kept a diary during his early adolescence, and started two or three periodicals. He had learned his catechism, but, as he wrote, he did not have "any formed religious convictions," not in his boyhood.

A strong imaginative temper contended in him with some wayward critical reactions: "I recollect copying out some French verses, perhaps Voltaire's, against the immortality of the soul, and saying to myself something like 'How dreadful, but how plausible!' " He also "read some of Hume's Essays; perhaps that on Miracles. So at least I gave my father to understand, but perhaps it was a brag." On the other hand, this free-thinking youth was roaming in fairy lands of fancy. "I used to wish the Arabian Tales were true; my imagination ran on unknown influences, on magical powers, and talismans. . . . I thought life might be a dream, or I an Angel, and all this world a deception, my fellow-angels by a playful device concealing themselves from me, and deceiving me with the semblance of a material world." This dream-world outlook made him "very superstitious. . . . I used constantly to cross myself on going into the dark."[4]

Banker Newman's enthusiasm for music and literature was shared in an emphatic way by his son. John took part in string quartet-playing of Mozart and Beethoven; one enthusiastic biographer praised him as a violin virtuoso that might have rivaled Paganini. His schooling led him from the Bible and English literature to the masters of classical antiquity. At the private school of Ealing he took no part in athletics or youthful frolics;

he impressed his masters and schoolfellows as a studious, pensive boy of quiet, sensitive dignity.

Towards the close of his schooling at Ealing in the autumn of 1816, when he was fifteen, as he wrote, "a great change of thought took place in me. I fell under the influence of a definite Creed, and receiving into my intellect impressions of dogma, which, through God's mercy, have never been effaced or obscured." We should scarcely understand these words to mean that the schoolboy of fifteen grasped and accepted certain specific doctrines which he never outgrew. His classical master, described by Newman as "the excellent man . . . who was the human means of the beginning of divine faith in me," put into his hand several books, "all of the school of Calvin." Reading them confirmed him in mistrust of an indifference to "the reality of material phenomena" and in concentration on what became his dominant conviction: "the thought of two and two only supreme and luminously self-evident beings, myself and my Creator." Various religious writings engrossed his mind; the Calvinist doctrine underwent modification in his thought; he contended with the terrible aspects of the doctrine of eternal damnation. Other problems of the Christian tradition perplexed him, but the basic certitude of his spiritual life in communion with God, the essence of this his first conversion, was not lost.[5] More than fourteen centuries before him, St. Augustine had declared: "God and the soul, that is what I want to know. Nothing more? nothing whatever."[6] So Newman from his early youth was and remained firm in his citadel of faith, in the unassailable reality of his own being with God. Through the long years ahead his intellect would be spelling out the further implications of this inmost faith, and the road of his spiritual destiny would point him to directions of which he was yet unaware.

The schoolboy was about to go to the university: whether Oxford or Cambridge was left uncertain until the very hour of his departure, when, with his father, he finally turned towards Oxford. He was accepted at Trinity College, where he did well, for within a year he earned a scholarship there—a stipend of sixty pounds for nine years. His masters thought highly of him— "Oh, Mr. Newman, what have you given us in your son!"[7] His own estimate of them, and of Oxford education generally, was quite different from Gibbon's condemnation in the previous century. Oxford was experiencing an intellectual renaissance affecting all its colleges from its radiating center, Oriel, where the Provost Eveleigh had instituted genuine high standards of instruction, examinations, conditions for appointment to fellowships, all the way through.

At Trinity young Newman was working hard to earn his degree with honors. Concern for his career urged him on as well as intellectual zeal, for his father's banking firm had come on evil days and had had to suspend payments for some weeks; young Newman was considering the likely need of self-support. His self-reliance had to be also in his own studies, to a considerable extent; he rose early and worked late, averaging twelve hours daily. He overstrained in his preparation for his final examinations, suffered from the confusion of extreme fatigue; his nerves "quite forsook him," and he failed in his aim: "got a common pass, but of honours nothing."[8]

This academic disaster would have crushed an ordinary youth in any further intellectual plans, but not Newman. His reaction to his failure to get an honors degree was to settle down to renewed endeavor to win what was regarded as one of the highest honors in Oxford, a Fellowship at Oriel College. The examination for it was a gruelling affair which lasted four days. To the astonishment of those who remembered his earlier breakdown, he won the election. Dr. Copleston, the Principal of Oriel, stated that, while in many points of classical scholarship Newman was inferior to other candidates, "yet in mind and power of composition, and in taste and knowledge he was decidedly superior to some competitors who were of a class above him in the schools."⁹

In terms of his life-career Newman's election to the Oriel Fellowship was as important as his first conversion, at Ealing, had been in his religious life. As a Fellow of Oriel he had academic prestige, an assured income, and who knows what high prospects in life. Could his own ambition look any further than to live and die a Fellow of Oriel? He had not been long in his new college before his influence on student life and on Oxford policy began to be very apparent. His mind was dominated not by secular interests in the technical mastery of academic, mainly classical, scholarship, but by the moral and religious problems of the university community in which he now had a recognized role. He concerned himself with checking student excesses in drinking and loose conduct. He felt that it was a chief duty of his position as Fellow to guide his students spiritually. Keenly distressed by the common indifference about the supreme values of life, he held fast to the divine truths of Christian orthodoxy and resisted the loose liberalism that self-confidently passed for critical thinking.

Newman's orthodoxy went deeper than formal ecclesiastic conformity. It had to rest on solid theological ground; he demanded of his mind mastery of the basic principles and early foundations of Christian doctrine, and to this end he undertook a thorough systematic reading of the Fathers of the Church, the Patristic writings, chronologically. As his heart and spirit were dominated by his felt inmost communion with God, so his intellect was becoming increasingly theological, and to him the religious complexion of English society was a matter of grave anxiety. The liberalism and the religious indifference which he resisted were common in fact, if competent judgment and some not much later statistics are to be trusted. Two thirds of the nation had ceased to attend church, and barely one third were Anglicans; the rest were various nonconformists. The Bishop of London and the Prime Minister agreed that the Church of England faced a crisis. Two tendencies contended within it, the so-called High Church and Low Church: the former characterized by its emphasis on traditional adherence and stricter theological formalism; the latter by evangelical informality, extempore praying, emotional preaching, quasi-Methodist practices regarded with disfavor by the High Churchmen. And always, of course, there was the tension between all the churches derived from the Protestant Reformation and the Church of Rome.

Newman faced squarely the problem of defining clearly to himself and convincingly to others his position as a priest of the Church of England, in distinction not only from the Roman Catholic position but also from that of the Presbyterians, Baptists, Methodists, and other Protestant confessions. The settlement of this problem was to him a daily necessity. The various ways in which he had gained recognition at Oxford involved their respective duties. He was serving as vice-principal of a small college and as one of the four public tutors and was on the Board of Examiners for honors degrees (despite his own failure!). But he was also vicar of the Oxford parish Church of St. Mary's, a university preacher. What doctrine was he to communicate to his Oxford congregation, and on what grounds was he to make it truly convincing?

To many modern minds of a secular turn, theology is abstruse and wearisome: to others who in their way are genuinely religious in their sympathies, theological mastery seems quite subordinate to pious devotion. But to Newman theology was the very citadel of religion, indispensable and all-decisive. The Anglican faith to which he was committed had to be demonstrated as theologically sound. Dogmatic theology was Newman's central concern as a Christian and a priest. So he wrote: "From the age of fifteen, dogma has been the fundamental principle of my religion: I know no other religion; I cannot enter into the idea of any other sort of religion; religion as a mere sentiment, is to me a dream and a mockery."[10]

This very important point needs some careful clarification. Newman's dismissal of religion as a mere sentiment did not signify his initial and ultimate reliance on reason for the complete possession of Christian truth. He is not to be described offhand as a theological rationalist. The very beginning of faith is in the soul's self-surrendering response to the divine voice of truth, and its fullness in the saintly life transcends any rational formulation and proof. But as this maturing spiritual process is not one of mere sentiment, so it is not one of mere reason. The whole being of the soul is lifted up to God, in thought and feeling alike. Reason must seek out and find evidence towards compelling verity, yet that verity can be only incomplete, "in part," "as in a mirror, darkly." It points towards a consummation which faith contemplates but which surpasses our rational mastery and cannot be held bound by it. As it is faith that must urge reason to express and formulate it in doctrine, so it is faith that must keep reason from misguided overconfidence. "The greatest risk will result from attempting to be wiser than God has made us, and to outstep in the least degree the circle which is prescribed as the limit of our range."[11] Newman pursued the course between mere sentiment, an emotional or mystical certitude, and a strictly rationalistic position in religion. In that course of seeking God's truth, he was bound not to stop short of the utmost degree of assurance that reason could wrest. But realizing all along that even our best reason must look beyond its last step to the still higher reaches of eternal consummation, in faith, Newman who was a poet as well as a dogmatic theologian, had his mystical flights of the saintly imagination.

His exploration of the foundations of Christian orthodoxy

had expanded his historical outlook. He had declined an invitation to collaborate in a planned work on church history along popular lines; what was needed, in his judgment, was thorough inquiry into the original source materials, especially those of the Patristic period. As truth is revealed through the clearance of error, so the formation of Christian orthodoxy required the exposure and refutation of various heresies. Newman directed his study to the outstanding heresy of Arianism, in a work which, as he wrote, opened a grand and most interesting field to him, but involved ramified research which taxed his energies and the final accomplishment of which left him in a state of utter exhaustion.

His long labor on *The Arians of the Fourth Century* coincided with a choice experience, his intimate friendship with Hurrell Froude, like himself a Fellow of Oriel. Froude, ailing in health but most active and aggressive in spirit, was urging an Anglican orthodoxy of an increasingly Catholic slant. He abhorred Puritanism; he resisted any evangelical informality in the Church of England or any latitudinarian concessions to alleged private judgment and self-reliant criticism; against them all he advocated the unyielding authority of the Holy See. Newman, not yet able to follow his dear friend in this Romanist tenor, shared in the directions of his antagonisms; their intimate friendship was to Newman a compelling self-exploration of his own religious position and likely outlook.

On many points of church organization and church order, Newman's attitude was definitely Protestant. Ecclesiastically he was not a Romanist or a Papist. He considered the self-arrogation of dominion by the Roman Catholic clergy as presumptuous in the sight of God. In his boyhood he had regarded the Pope, not as Holy Father and Vicar of Christ, but rather as Antichrist; even so, in his early days as Fellow of Oriel, he had preached a Christmas sermon to that effect. But, as he wrote, "from the

time that I knew Froude I got less and less bitter on the subject.
I spoke . . . of the Roman Church as being bound up with
'the *cause* of Antichrist,' as being *one* of the *'many* antichrists'
foretold by St. John, as being influenced by 'the *spirit* of Antichrist,' and as having something 'very antichristian' or 'unchristian' about her."[12] He modified and expanded that stigma to
mean that Rome had corrupted the early and true Christian faith
with its own many unchristian beliefs and ritualistic and ecclesiastic practices. While he was thus tempering his condemnation,
for long years he did not abandon his judgment of Romanism
as an institution. In these respects he was in the main Protestant
in his interpretation of Christianity.

But it was quite otherwise when it came to many theological
fundamentals. Had not the Protestant reformers, in their resistance to the ritualistic and churchly corruptions of Rome, gone
quite too far in their neglect and even dismissal of the formal
and dogmatic kernels of ritual and doctrine, both essential to
true Christianity? By insisting on their conviction of justification by faith alone and on personal devotion in sentiment and
fervent emotion, had not the Evangelicals, Anglicans and even
more nonconformists minimized the holy importance of the
priestly office and its many sacramental instruments in the operation of divine Grace and ministration in men's lives? These
questions, and the developing answers to them, which would be
deciding Newman's later course and spiritual career, were engrossing him when he decided to join the ailing Froude and
Froude's father on a journey to the Mediterranean lands.

That journey was fruitful and critical in several ways. Fruitful it was in its arousal of Newman's genius to poetic utterance.
A great number of his finest religious poems were written during those months, including "Lead, Kindly Light." But in Sicily
he came down with a critical illness which menaced his life,
brought him to the very face of death, and through eventual

recovery confirmed his conviction of his unfulfilled bounden duty
to God. His Mediterranean voyages roused him to a vivid sense
of the early Christian Church in its westward expansion. His
travels in Roman Catholic lands, both city and countryside,
impressed on his mind the Romanist issue which he could not
evade. His feelings about Rome were profound but discordant: "the most wonderful place in the world, . . . the first
of cities, . . . grows more wonderful every day, . . . but a
city under a curse." His letters reveal this contending veneration and revulsion that Rome aroused in him: "As to the *Roman*
Catholic system, I have ever detested it so much that I cannot
detest it more by seeing it; but to the Catholic system I am
more attached than ever. . . . Rome," he wrote, "has stolen
away half my heart"; yet "Oh that Rome was not Rome!" for
the religion it harbors is a "wretched perversion of the truth. . . .
I seem to see as clear as the day that union with her is impossible." Two lines of a poem are poignant with this ambivalent
emotion:

> O that thy creed were sound!
> For thou dost soothe the heart, thou Church of Rome![18]

The second line sounds prophetic, or ominous, of the future.

His return to Oxford marked the beginning of a most vigorous and earnest undertaking, far reaching in its influence on
others but finally self-reversing in its bearing on his own religious course. He joined several colleagues—chiefly Froude and
Pusey and John Keble, the religious poet—in a common pledge
to write and collaborate in defense of the Church. This was the
beginning of the Anglican Oxford Movement, which advocated
a more positively sacramental Christianity than that which characterized nonconformist chapel services or, what seemed more
important, that towards which evangelical Low Churchmen in
the Church of England tended. In greater detail, Newman and

his associates laid emphasis on the importance of fasting during Lent and also on Fridays and before partaking of the Eucharist; on a more sacramental interpretation of the liturgy, and on many other rituals: priestly confessionals, priestly mediation in divine ministration. It would, however, be a misinterpretation if the Oxford Movement were to be described as merely a revival of ritualism in the Church of England. Nor was it simply an exaltation of the priestly office, with its accent on the Apostolic Succession of the clergy, deriving sanction and authority from the early Fathers of the Church and the disciples of Christ himself. This Apostolic Succession was itself regarded as an instrument of the divine charge, to preserve the true faith of Christ through the ages. The immemorial sacramentalism was cherished as itself the holy symbol of Christian orthodoxy, God's truth in Christian minds and hearts.

Imperatively Newman was brought to the all-important theological issue regarding the one genuine orthodoxy. What is the substance and the core of this true Christian faith? In this theological examination we must trace Newman's steps very carefully and fairly, if we are to understand and appreciate his final decision to leave the Church of England and proceed to Rome. The immemorial Apostle's Creed binds the worshiper to faith in "the Holy Catholic Church." If this "Holy Catholic Church" is to be distinguished from the present Roman Catholic institutional system, how are we to recover the true venerable Apostolic doctrine, clear it from unwarranted accretions and corruptions, but remain loyal to the true ancient foundations, without proceeding in the manner of many dissenters who act as though they were as good apostles as St. Peter and St. Paul?

Newman called the position which he advocated for the Church of England the right middle course, the *Via Media,* between Roman Catholicism and Protestant nonconformity. With the

Romanists he held that whatever doctrine had been accepted as orthodox by the early Church was to be received by us as coming from the Apostles and authoritative. He was aiming to regain for his belief and commitment the earliest and most nearly Apostolic statement of Christian doctrine, most directly derived from the teachings of the New Testament. But while firmly declaring this range of agreement with Rome, he was one with all Protestants in rejecting later accretions and corruptions, be they ecclesiastic or doctrinal. As a devout Christian he would be loyal to the divine source of truth; so as an historical scholar he aimed at a thorough exploration of his sources, Biblical and Patristic. He used Scripture as divinely inspired and inerrant; he had no thorough understanding or appreciation of the modern literary-historical or "higher" criticism of the Bible, achieved largely by German scholars. As Dean Stanley is reported to have said: "How different the fortunes of the Church of England if Newman had been able to read German!"[14] In his sermons Newman deplored the preoccupation of men with modern winds of doctrine, the neglect of the ancient masters of Christian truth. He was advocating the spirit of classicism in theology. What solidity in Christian belief could be expected, if every man was to rely on his own exegesis?

This general policy in theology needed implementation: the substance and the tenets of the early Apostolic Christian faith required thorough investigation. Newman had already been engaged precisely in those studies, in his chronological reading of the Patristic writings; he had mastered at the original sources the controversies roused by the Arian heresy. He took the leading part, in collaboration with others, in the preparation and publishing of translations of the early Church Fathers. He collaborated similarly in the issuance of a large number of "Tracts for the Times," which expounded the views of those active in the Oxford Movement, who thus came to be generally known as Tractarians. They advanced especially the authority of Church tradition and the Prayer Book, Apostolic Succession of the clergy, and opposed the Erastian heresy of the supremacy of the State in ecclesiastical matters. As might be surmised, some of these tracts aroused much discussion and dispute. Besides disagreement with the doctrinal and ecclesiastic views held by the members of the Oxford Movement, there was a more general attitude of impatience with the devout earnestness of the Tractarians on the part of many university men who were formally Anglicans but went about mostly concerned with their daily affairs. Even before the publication of the *History of the Arians,* the Provost of Oriel, Dr. Hawkins, had been disturbed by what he regarded as Newman's undue preoccupation with theological and ecclesiastic issues and with the religious and pastoral guidance of his students, rather than, as befitted a college tutor, with their university education. Differences between them could not be adjusted; the Provost then assigned fewer and eventually no pupils to Newman.

In all this discussion Newman was not maintaining a Papist attitude, but still he was not, either doctrinally or in general tone, quite so negative towards Rome as he had been. Was he ambiguous in his own mind, or perhaps diplomatic in the bad sense? Against the latter imputation, on the score of sincerity and honesty, Newman defended himself in the *Apologia,* but with the recognition that for some time he had wavered in indecision.

> Alas! [he wrote] it was my portion for whole years to remain without any satisfactory basis for my religious profession, a state of moral sickness, neither able to acquiesce in Anglicanism, nor able to go to Rome. But I bore it, till in the course of time my way was made clear to me. If it be objected to me, that as time went on, I often in my writings hinted at things which I did

> not fully bring out, I submit for consideration whether
> this occurred except when I was in great difficulties, how
> to speak, or how to be silent, with due regard for the
> position of mind or the feelings of others.[15]

Newman demanded a firm hold of basic positive orthodoxy; his objection to a mainly negative status was the reason for his dislike of the term "Protestant." And he was concerned lest the doctrine of the *Via Media* as applied to the Anglican system suffer from the same defect. He required a religious profession that could be shown to be "one, intelligible, and consistent." But was the Anglican *Via Media* really "a substantive religion"? Was it more than "a mere modification or transition-state of either Romanism or popular Protestantism"?[16] The position which Newman was seeking to maintain as the sound alternative for the Church of England was tenuous and, as he increasingly felt, unstable.

For some time he sought reassurance by a redefinition of the term "Catholic." Catholic Christianity, he reasoned, has three branches: the Latin, the Greek, and the Anglican. "Each of these inherited the early undivided Church *in solido* as its own possession. Each branch was identical with that early undivided Church, and in the unity of that Church it had unity with the other branches. The three branches agree in *all but* their later accidental errors."[17] In doctrinal interpretation, when dealing with Rome, we should distinguish the Catholic teaching of the early centuries, the formal Roman doctrine as formulated by the later Councils (especially that of Trent, 1545 ff.), and the actual popular beliefs and usages of Roman Catholics through the centuries. Protestants commonly set aside Romanism in all these three senses. Newman for his part would readily condemn much of that third kind of popular beliefs and practices, and also some of the later conciliar formulations, but not the original Catholic orthodoxy.

In this spirit he endeavored to redefine the Anglican position as between Popery and Protestantism: the Articles of the Church of England "do not oppose Catholic teaching; they but partially oppose Roman dogma; they for the most part oppose the dominant errors of Rome. And the problem was to draw the line as to what they allowed and what they condemned."[18] Despite all his efforts to maintain his own position within the Anglican confession, Newman felt himself insecure and actually tending towards Rome. The issue between Romanism and Anglicanism which he kept reformulating was also an issue of his own self-division, the contention within his own spirit. Increasingly poignant and compelling eventual decision one way or the other, it went far beyond any insecure mediation. "The Anglican said to the Roman: 'There is but One Faith, the Ancient, and you have not kept it'; the Roman retorted: 'There is but One Church, the Catholic, and you are out of it.' . . . The course lay thus, Apostolicity *versus* Catholicity."[19] Which one was to prevail?

Two strong blasts of criticism upset his transitional stand, for the study of controversies in the ancient Church modified his presumably clear conception of "Apostolicity" and raised the dreary question as to whether the Anglican position might not itself be a heretical alternative in a modern setting. Newman's Patristic studies had led him, beyond his work on the Arian heresy of the fourth century, to a careful examination of the so-called Monophysite dispute, which had given rise to a number of alternative doctrines. As theologians know, it was a very abstruse topic. It was concerned with the interpretation of the relation of Christ's divine essence to his human nature, and also of Mary as the Mother of Jesus of Nazareth. Was Mary to be worshipped as literally the Mother of God, *Theotokos?* Thus she was signalized on Byzantine icons; thus she was adored by many priests and bishops and theologians. But others, notably the Patriarch Nestorius of Constantinople, rejected this sort of adoration as impious idolatry. Was the Godhead of Christ Jesus to be affirmed all the way through, even in the cradle, even in his nursing and diapers? God forbid! they said. Mary bore Jesus of Nazareth, that is, his human nature; but the divine nature of Christ was distinct and God-incarnate. In the ensuing controversy both of these opposite views were rejected by the Church as heretical. According to the true Catholic doctrine, as it had been authoritatively declared in the Nicene Creed, Christ was consubstantial, one in substance, with the Father, *homoousios*. Christ Jesus was true God and true man; his human nature was united with the divine nature to form one Person. But although the Catholic Church condemned both extreme teachings as heretical, they continued on their own, schismatically, Monophysite and Nestorian. As Newman proceeded with his studies of those early issues in the Church, he was shocked by the thought that his own Anglican Church, in separating itself from its Roman home, might be in the same way repeating the recalcitrancy of old heretics.

On top of those quandaries came another blast, in an article written by Cardinal Wiseman, about the so-called Donatist heresy. During the persecution of the Christians by the Roman Emperor Diocletian, some bishops in North Africa had surrendered supinely to the pagan oppressor. After the period of persecution had ended they wished to resume their offices and their authority in ordaining priests. But a certain Donatus and his followers declared that their faithless submission to Diocletian rendered them unworthy and without sanction and authority in the Church. This Donatist position was condemned by a Church Council, which gave its verdict that the *priestly* role and office of a consecrated bishop was not nullified by his individual *personal* taint. St. Augustine held that position against the Donatists, who were stigmatized as heretics.

The specific details and involvements of these theological and ecclesiastic controversies need not confuse our perception of the main points which disturbed Newman. Had he not declared that whatever doctrine and other principle was authorized by the Church Councils and prevailed generally was to be held as true Christian doctrine? Even though doctrines condemned as heretical might persist tenaciously, yet "the palmary words of St. Augustine" kept ringing in his ears: *Securus judicat orbis terrarum,* secure in its judgment is the Church Universal. On the crucial issue which he had defined as "Apostolicity *versus* Catholicity," the balance was swaying decidedly toward Catholicity. For heretical error was as ancient as orthodox truth. "Apostolicity" itself could not qualify all Patristic doctrines, but only those judged to be the true ones by the Church Universal—Catholic orthodoxy. Against Rome separate churches could have no orthodox standing: " *'Securus judicat orbis terrarum!'* By those great words of the ancient Father, the theory of the *Via Media* was absolutely pulverized."[20]

"Absolutely pulverized!"—so Newman wrote more than twenty years later in his *Apologia.* But at the time when his mind was struggling with the Monophysites and the Donatists, he was still endeavoring to show that the Anglican essential doctrines were not at radical variance with Catholic Rome. We should note the important shift in his dialectic: Newman was undertaking to hold on to the Anglican position by maintaining that it was in substantial agreement with Roman Catholic doctrine. For in his mind already Rome had the authoritative standard. To achieve this readjustment was his purpose in his *Tract Ninety: Remarks on Certain Passages in the Thirty-Nine Articles,* which was issued in February, 1841. That tract dealt critically with, among other problems, the doctrine of Justification by Faith Only, the General Church Councils, and with the Papal hierarchy. Newman argued that Article XI—"That we are justified by Faith only, is a most wholesome doctrine"—does not imply a denial of baptism, or good works as also being instrumental in salvation. He maintained that Church Councils may require royal or princely sanction, and being human, may err; but he also recognized that, meeting in the name of Christ and Catholic-ecumenical in convocation, a Council may also be a "thing of heaven," and its decrees authoritative. As to Article XXXVIII, that "the Bishop of Rome has not jurisdiction in the realm of England," Newman held that Papal supremacy was attained historically in the course of time in Rome, and that also in the course of time could be, and in the case of the Church of England was abrogated, without in any way affecting the unity of that Church with the essence of Christian-Catholic communion. "There is nothing in the Apostolic system which gives an authority to the Pope over the Church, such as it does not give to a bishop. It is altogether an ecclesiastical arrangement, not a point *de fide,* but of expedience, custom or piety."[21]

Despite all these proposed adjustments, Newman was finding his position as Anglican priest no longer tenable. He could no longer preach in full sincerity from the Anglican pulpit of St. Mary's, Oxford, and he would retire from it without, however, resigning. But still he "could not go to Rome; she suffered honours to be paid to the Blessed Virgin and the saints which I thought incompatible with the Supreme and Incommunicable Glory of the One Infinite and Eternal."[22] It was not long, however, before these and other objections to Rome were one by one swept away. "In 1843, I took two very important and significant steps. 1. In February, I made a formal Retraction of all the hard things I had said against the Church of Rome. 2. In September, I resigned the Living of St. Mary's, Littlemore inclusive."[23] Two years later, on October 8, 1845, Newman recorded his formal conversion to Roman Catholicism.

He had hoped to live and die a Fellow of Oriel, and now he was to leave his university, never to return: "I have never seen Oxford since, excepting its spires, as they are seen from the railway."[24] In his novel *Loss and Gain: The Story of a Convert*, published anonymously three years after his own conversion, Newman recalled imaginatively that last day of parting with his whole past life, in describing Charles Reding's departure from Oxford: "He crossed the Meadow, and walked steadily down to the junction of the Cherwell with the Isis; he then turned back. What thoughts came upon him! for the last time! There was no one to see him; he threw his arms round the willows so dear to him, and kissed them; he tore off some of their black leaves and put them in his bosom. . . ."[25] The poignant emotional tone of it recalls some of Turgenev's pages.

During the following period of his life—it was to last forty-five years—Newman lived and moved for a while as a simple humble convert to the Ancient Faith. But the Roman Catholic leadership was fully aware of the importance of gaining a person like himself, an outstanding Anglican churchman and leader of the Oxford Movement. After being sent to Rome and for some time serving in Birmingham, he rose high in the Church. He was asked to direct a newly established Catholic University in Dublin, a position which he held for only four years. His writings spread his high renown as a master of English prose. In poetry also, his *Dream of Gerontius* confirmed the mastery of his earlier religious poems; it has been praised as "the happiest effort to represent the unseen world that has been made since the time of Dante."[26] In 1878 Pope Leo XIII made him a Cardinal of the Church.

An examination of the very numerous works by Newman, however brief, is quite beyond the scope of this study, which is centered on his autobiography, the *Apologia*. As he himself wrote, "from the time that I became a Catholic, of course, I have no further history of my religious opinions to narrate. In saying this," he added, "I do not mean to say that my mind has been idle or that I have given up thinking on theological subjects; but that I have had no changes to record, and have had no anxiety of heart whatever. I have been in perfect peace and contentment. I have never had one doubt."[27] One of the main writings of his later years, however, requires attention: his *Discourses On the Scope of University Education.*

The educational *Discourses* were the chief fruit of Newman's work as Rector of the Catholic University of Ireland, a project strongly urged by the Pope, which failed to gain the adequate support of the Irish episcopate and leading laity, and which Newman had finally to relinquish. Aside from the various ecclesiastical obstructions which compromised the success of the undertaking from the outset, the enduring worth of the *Discourses* was in their masterly statement of Newman's ideals for a university in which a dominant concern for the spiritual welfare of the students would find expression in a truly catholic program of studies—catholic in its recognition of the sovereign importance of theology, and catholic also in its attention to the ascertained modern knowledge in the various sciences. This dual emphasis was urged by Newman in his first university sermon in Dublin: "I want the intellectual layman to be religious and the devout ecclesiastic to be intellectual."[28]

Newman was aiming at a university which would be neither a strictly priestly seminary nor a merely secular institution. In his conception of liberal education he was urging upon the laity his conviction that "a University, as the name implies, is the seat of universal knowledge,"[29] and therefore cannot exclude theology; but for the same reason—addressing now the clerics, the Irish episcopate—it cannot be indifferent to modern scientific knowledge. He was a theologian; in discourse after discourse he would secure for theology its due, major place in university education; but his recognition of the due place of scientific instruction was equally emphatic, and it found expression in the establishment of the medical school, which proved to be one of the main fruits of the project for a Catholic university in Ireland.

Of especial interest in Newman's educational program was his distinction between universities and academies or other institutions of research. The latter are concerned with the discovery of facts and the expansion of knowledge; but the main purpose of universities must be the imparting of knowledge for the cultivation of wisdom. We are reminded of his own view of his relation, as tutor, to his students at Oxford, his main care for their spiritual guidance and welfare. The emphasis on spiritual integrity motivated his advocacy of liberal spirit in university teaching, beyond narrow specialization and beyond a merely professional outlook. He was wary of experts who "breaking up their subject into details, destroy its life, and defraud us of the whole by their anxiety about the parts." As to professionalism, Newman was very clear. A university, to be sure, should teach law and medicine, but a genuine university professor in these or other similarly special fields should not be a merely professional practitioner in his approach to his subject. He "has taken a survey of all knowledge, he is kept from extravagance by the very rivalry of other studies, he has gained from them a special illumination and largeness of mind and freedom and self-possession, and he treats his own in consequence with a philosophy and a resource, which belongs, not to the study itself, but to his liberal education." Newman advocated with power and eloquence this ideal of the higher culture of young minds and its wider civilizing mission. "A university training . . . aims at raising the intellectual tone of society, at cultivating the public mind, at purifying the national taste, at supplying true principles to popular enthusiasm and fixed aims to popular aspiration, at giving enlargement and sobriety to the ideas of the age, of facilitating the exercise of political power, and refining the intercourse of private life."[30]

Some years after Newman's resignation as University Rector in Dublin and at the time of his writing the *Apologia,* he became interested in the offer of five acres of land in Oxford suitable for the establishment of a Catholic Center there, a college or hall or oratory. The plan in some form had the support of his Bishop Ullathorne of Birmingham, and if successful would have reconciled him somewhat to his disappointment in Dublin. His purpose was to help protect students from heretical and irreligious influences, the "importation of scepticism and infidelity" in the university. But after considerable initial support, opposition to the project developed, against a Catholic Center at Oxford and in favor of a definitely Catholic university elsewhere, a sort of English Louvain. One of the chief and firmest opponents of Newman's Oxford plan was Henry Edward Manning, himself a convert, a former Anglican archdeacon and one-time Tractarian, later converted to Rome, who was appointed Archbishop of Westminster following the death of Cardinal Wiseman. His disagreements with Newman were aggravated by increasing mutual distrust, and worsened into antagonisms. It was an increasingly distressing story, and it has been interpreted in different keys: criticisms of Newman's lack of due ecclesiastical and doctrinal discipline, notwithstanding his piety as a convert; countercriticisms of Manning's intransigent Romanism— "more papist than the Pope"[31]—and of his ruthless ultramontane diplomacy. While the recorded facts, including extant correspondence, would scarcely warrant appeal to the adage, to understand it all is to forgive all, perhaps a fair appraisal of the grave tension between the two converted former Tractarians would lay its emphasis on their wholly different conceptions of the essence of religious loyal devotion.

In the closing part of his *Apologia* Newman returned to his controversy with Charles Kingsley, whose criticism had compelled him to write his autobiography. He gave a general answer to Kingsley and then in a long appendix replied in detail to his critic's accusations.

Newman's general answer to the criticisms is a plain appeal to the certitude of the Catholic believer. He readily acknowledged the many intellectual difficulties with which the Christian Creed, Catholic and Protestant, is beset: "it is a simple fact, that, for myself, I cannot answer those difficulties . . . but I have never been able to see a connexion between apprehending those difficulties, however keenly, and multiplying them to any extent, and doubting the doctrines to which they are attached. . . . Difficulty and doubt are incommensurable."[32] The essential condition for dispelling any doubt about any Catholic doctrine was the commitment of his mind, at his conversion, to the belief that "the Catholic Roman Church was the oracle of God, and that she had declared that doctrine to be part of the original revelation."[33] Be it the doctrine of Transubstantiation, or of the Trinity in Unity, or of the Immaculate Conception of the Blessed Virgin, or any other, Newman maintained the certitude of Catholic believers as Catholics, without any of the alleged superstition or hypocrisy imputed by their critics.

For himself, he declared his total acceptance of "the universally received traditions of the Church," past, present, and future, "till the end of time."[34] He went further. He pointed out that "the Catholic Church claims, not only to judge infallibly on religious questions, but to animadvert in secular matters which bear upon religion, on matters of philosophy, of science, of literature, of history, and it demands our submission to her claim. It claims to censure books, to silence authors, and to forbid discussions. In all this it does not so much speak doctrinally, as enforce measures of discipline. It must of course be obeyed without a word, and perhaps in process of time it will tacitly recede from its own injunctions."[35] That is, as we may say, as obedient children we conform implicitly to the verdicts and prohibitions of Mother Church, and if or when she decides otherwise, we again conform accordingly. All the way, we conform.

The non-Catholic reader, nowise aggressively hostile but still trying to understand, may inquire beyond this account of the believing Catholic's attitude towards the infallible authority of his church doctrines, regarding the process by which the Church herself has been led to select and adopt the doctrines which she has declared as authoritative. Newman had considered carefully Doctrinal Development, but, as he had pointed out almost twenty years earlier and never ceased to maintain, that development may be one of truth or of error. That precisely is the difference between orthodoxy and heresy: "The maxims and first principles of religion in a perfectly logical mind lead to Rome; their denial to religious negation."[36]

Kingsley in his criticism had cited a long series of passages in Newman's writings in which Newman seemed to him to be evasive and "economizing" in matters of truthfulness. A few of those charges may be noted here. Newman, as a convert to Roman Catholicism and therefore committed to the Catholic doctrines and traditions, felt bound to defend as acceptable many reported miracles and similar events which surely lack sufficient evidence to make them credible or which run plainly counter to sound reason. For all we know to the contrary, portions of the True Cross may be treasured in Rome, and likewise the Crib of Bethlehem, and the bodies of St. Peter and St. Paul—for all we know to the contrary. But, urged Kingsley, can Newman really believe that from the tomb of St. Walburga medicinal oil has been flowing, and still flows, after almost a thousand years?—or that the blood of St. Januarius, in Naples, really liquefies?—or that the eyes of Madonna in the Roman States really move? If Newman should answer in the affirmative, would we judge him to be quibbling or not? Are we to question his intellectual capacity or his moral integrity in matters of this kind, of which there are so many examples in Roman Catholic tradition?

Kingsley's charges cut deep, for he was not dealing with the believing minds of ignorant medieval peasants, but with that of an educated Oxford Fellow, a thorough historical scholar and a systematic theologian. Newman's answers, given in greatest detail seriatim to more than thirty of Kingsley's charges, were and are sure to produce radically different impressions on different readers. What is one to think when one reads his reply to some of them? "I think it impossible to *withstand the evidence* which is brought for the liquefaction of the blood of St. Januarius at Naples, and for the motion of the eyes of the Madonna in the Roman States"; or, regarding St. Walburga's medicinal oil: "The oil still flows; I have had some of it in my possession; it is medicinal; some think it is so by a natural quality, others by divine gift. Perhaps it is on the confines of both."[37]

We may repeat in general comment that Newman's fundamental and all-decisive step was his initial one at his conversion: to accept without any reservation the authority of the Roman Catholic Church in all matters of religious belief and practice; past, present, or future. *After* his conversion, he shared the Catholic's acceptance of matters which Anglicans and other Protestants and unbelievers have found unacceptable.

In our study we have endeavored to report Newman's self-searching autobiography objectively, without too critical intrusions either overt or implicit. The *Apologia* is a highly important human document, not only of a significant period of English social history but also of a certain basic aspect of religious thought and experience. For centuries the Roman Catholic position has been that of unyielding traditional authoritarianism in upholding its doctrines and beliefs as true and unchanging, always and everywhere. That view still characterizes the more conservative Catholic priesthood and hierarchy; but of more recent date there have been liberal stirrings in Roman Catholicism, and they have been spreading. A whole generation of so-called Modernists have endeavored to gain a hearing from their Catholic brethren for a thorough reexamination of the old traditions, without much success but with a greater likelihood lately of some basic changes in attitude and policy. That is one significant aspect of the long discussions at the Vatican Council convocated by Pope John XXIII and reassembled by Pope Paul VI. The conservatives in the Roman Curia and elsewhere have seemed to be in the minority and on the defensive, though very tenacious. Bishops and Cardinals have spoken in liberal terms, and their views have prevailed in some of the voting. How far this felt need for a reconsideration of the entire relation of Rome to other Christian faiths will go, is a question for the future. Will it lead to an altered attitude and a real realignment, or else to firm adherence to a new version of traditional authority, a new formulation of unchanging doctrine?

One may speculate what Newman's attitude would have been in the present Catholic situation. Some Modernists have seemed to find in his writings initial impulses to their own movement; but the acceptance of this appraisal of Newman's thought would require very considerable reinterpretation of the Modernist spirit. His biographers record that when the question of Papal Infallibility was being debated, Newman was against the adoption of the doctrine. But after it had been proclaimed by the Vatican Council of 1870, Newman felt bound to adhere to the words of St. Augustine, which, as he wrote, had pulverized his confidence in his Anglican *Via Media:* "As to faith," he declared, "my great principle was *'Securus judicat orbis terrarum.'* "[38] Secure in its judgment is the Church Universal: when that Church proclaimed Papal Infallibility, Newman's opposition to that doctrine ceased. Indeed, he was reported to have described his earlier resistance to it as due to his anxiety that its promulgation might have a deterrent effect on the conversion of many to the Catholic faith.

John Henry Newman renounced his Anglican faith and was received into the Roman Catholic communion on October 8, 1845. Two days earlier, on October 6, Ernest Renan, having finally reached his conclusion of disbelief in the Roman Catholic dogmatic theology and having decided that he could no longer honestly remain in the priestly calling to which he had been brought up, left his seminary of St. Sulpice and joined the secular world. We shall turn next to Renan's account of his spiritual pilgrimage.

CHAPTER VII

ERNEST RENAN

In his Weimar garden Goethe had planted an oriental tree, *gingo biloba*. He wrote a lyric about its two-lobed foliage, which seemed to him to be a symbol of his own personality:

> In my poems, don't you feel it?
> I am both twofold and one.

Ernest Renan's character and career would serve as a confirming comment on Goethe's poetic mood. "Nearly all of us are double," Renan wrote. "The more a person develops intellectually, the stronger is his attraction to the opposite pole: that is to say, to the irrational, to the repose of the mind in absolute ignorance."[1] This reflection, confessional in Renan's case, should be kept in mind steadily, if we are to understand and to do justice to the record of his spiritual pilgrimage which is given in his *Recollections of My Youth, Souvenirs d'enfance et de jeunesse,* and which is also revealed in his other works. He has been called "the most learned of all the great autobiographers,"[2] and his learning was rigorously critical and rational; but always, alongside his reason and his logic and his historical grasp of the facts, another demand of his spirit was straining for recognition.

He started the preface to his *Recollections* with an account of one of the most popular legends of his native Brittany, about an imaginary city called Is, which was supposed to have been swallowed up by the sea. Mariners might see the spires of its

169

churches in the deep hollows of the waves when the sea was very rough, and in calm weather they might hear its bells chiming immemorial piety. (Did not Claude Debussy compose a tone-poem entitled *La cathédrale engloutie, The Submerged Cathedral*?) Renan, recalling at the age of sixty his own spiritual voyages, learned and critical and historical, wrote: "I often fancy that I have at the bottom of my heart a city of Is with its bells calling to prayer a recalcitrant congregation. At times I halt to listen to these gentle vibrations which seem as if they came from immeasurable depths, like voices from another world."[3] His formal education had been in Catholic dogmatic theology, but his scholarly studies had made it increasingly hard, and finally impossible, to persist in his orthodox commitments, and he had to leave the seminary. This factual rupture was irrevocable for him; on no condition would he return to his Catholic allegiance. His philosophical studies and reflections, his search for the historical facts, his critical inquiries and judgments ruled out any submission to orthodox theology, but his rigorous reason did not quite silence his priestly temperament. The ancient cathedral, submerged, was still there, to his nostalgic vision. As he told us, "man writes . . . to transmit to others the theory of the universe which he carries within himself."[4] Renan's universe, the world of his lifelong experience, was in many ways dual. The contending strains in his heritage and thought and commitments and career: they are in many ways characteristic of our modern temper and of the problems we have to face. We shall find Renan's autobiographic recollections a most revealing window on the troubled scene of our modern culture.

The duality of interplaying and also contending strains may be traced in various aspects of his life and character. On his father's side he was the descendant of Breton farmers and tradesmen and fisher folk. The first Renans were supposed to have crossed the Channel from Cardigan in the late fifth century. His grandfather had settled in the town of Tréguier, the seat of a diocese, and had added to the income from his fishing the proceeds from a grocery. Renan's father, Philibert, had studied navigation and the English language, attained the rank of captain, served in the Napoleonic wars, and returned to Tréguier a man of an independent spirit and fiery republican convictions. But his chosen bride was of a staunchly royalist family and was besides half-Gascon, of old Bordeaux ancestry. From the outset Renan was under these two influences, and each of them was strangely compounded. His local environment and his father's impression on his homelife doubled the traditional Breton mystical devotion with the likewise Breton immemorial protesting individuality. His mother, half-Breton, half-Gascon, had outgoing élan and irrepressible good spirit, without blustering gasconade, and intense Breton piety without submissive humility. She recognized her boy's gifted mind and had priestly ambitions for him. Under the protecting guidance of Holy Church he would be guarded from the modern heresies, religious and political; he would serve the Lord; and who could tell what high station the Lord had in mind for him!

Although herself half-Gascon, Renan's mother possessed a mind more than half-Breton; she was perfect in the native Breton speech and thoroughly versed in the proverbs and folklore of Breton tradition. Ernest Renan throughout his life felt himself one with the Bretons: "I can feel that I think for them and that they live again in me."[5] He recognized in himself significant traits which have marked many distinguished Bretons through the ages on both sides of the Channel, in French Britanny, in Cornwall, in Wales and the Scottish Highlands, in Ireland. He pointed out how the Breton-Celtic imagination enriched the treasury of medieval romance: the Welsh *Mabinogion,* the Arthurian romances, the legends of Merlin and Tristan and the Holy Grail.

In the field of religious thought the Breton-Celtic strain through the ages has been marked by a forthright spirit ready for dissent: some students have called it the Celtic revolt. In its expression acute thinking and dream revery interplay and contend in subtle duality, keen logic and fiery vision, and always spirit unbound. The gifted Breton of ages past and of modern times has been a soul of saintly devotion doubled with a mind of unyielding independence. In the early Christian centuries, in medieval Scholasticism, and in our modern age, Bretons have stirred controversies over radical issues and bases of assurance. During the time of St. Augustine, as was noted in our first chapter, the British (probably Irish) theologian Pelagius aroused the Church with his doctrine that man has the freedom of will to choose between right and wrong, that he is not wholly passive in the process of his soul's salvation, and is therefore justly punishable if he chooses the ways of sin. In the Scholastic revival of learning, the central Problem of Universals was raised by Roscelin, a native of Lower Britanny, in his advocacy of Nominalism, the doctrine that the only real objects of thought are those of particular things, and that Universals are mere names by which we refer to classes or qualities of the real particular objects: a doctrine which anticipated modern empiricism but which had heretical implications for medieval theology, especially with regard to the orthodox doctrine of the Trinity, and which was condemned by the Church. One of Roscelin's students, the Breton nobleman Peter Abelard, resisting both that master and also his opposite extreme, William of Champeaux, advanced to a critical revision of the Problem of Universals. In his lectures which raised him to the summit of fame he gave a profound interpretation of the doctrine of the Atonement, and also of the basic nature of sin. But in his personality fervent passion for his beloved Heloise contended with the keenest dialectic and unstrung his life-career tragically.

Two of Renan's countrymen, with him, present a modern trio that parallels the one just mentioned. Lamennais and Chateaubriand were both natives of St. Malo, not a long distance from Renan's Tréguier. Lamennais (1782-1854) sprang to renown and honor in the Catholic world with his *Essay on Indifference in Religious Matters,* in which he championed established orthodoxy against self-confident freethinking. Religious truth requires universal sanction which only the social mind of abiding tradition can possess. But his Catholic ideal, a bulwark of divine truth and social well-being, was an ideal of a church genuinely Christ-like in its concern for the weary and the heavy-laden. Against ecclesiastic pride and emoluments, he preached and practiced the social gospel of the Master, and he died disowned by the Catholic hierarchy. Chateaubriand (1768-1848) combined in a romantic-poetic temperament aristocratic loftiness and humanitarian zeal, reverence for tradition and Rousseauistic dreams of return to primitive innocence. Disillusioned in his early radicalism by the bloody course of the Revolution and the Terror, he sought spiritual reassurance in the Christian tradition: not, however, in adherence to dogmatic theology, which had left him unconvinced and skeptical, but rather in his romantic vision of the Christian pageant in Western civilization. His *Génie du Christianisme* glorified the beauty of Christianity, in its mysticism, sacraments, doctrines, scriptures, cathedrals; the Christian epic in the arts, in eloquence, and poetry; Christian missions, Christian chivalry, Christianity as the light of spiritual beauty in the course of history.[6] His memoirs, in worldly and in spiritual concerns, revealed the contending motives in his personality: skeptical disillusion seeking escape in sentimental-romantic devotion.

Even this brief review should justify the recognition of the term "Breton genius" as signifying a genuine fountainhead of ideal values, devout and radical in subtle duality. The overemphasis on hereditary-racial factors in the determination of individual mind and character is liable to prove a precarious speculation. It is important, however, to recognize Renan's own insistence on explaining the origins of personality in its racial inheritance. He applied this theory in interpreting others as well as himself. "We Bretons believe that a man owes more to his blood than to himself."[7] In his essay on Lamennais he wrote explicitly: "Britanny and the seminary: they were his origins and, I dare say, all his explication."[8] In a passage of devout rhetoric he expressed his spirit of Breton ancestor worship: "God is my witness, ancient fathers, that my only joy is in meditating at times that I am your conscience, and that it is through me that you gain life and utterance."[9] He wrote to a friend: "You will find me all Breton in everything."[10]

His interpretation of the Breton-Celtic spirit is significant autobiographically, because he regarded whatever was good in his character and aspiration as due to his Breton strain. This is the importance, for our study, of his famous essay, "The Poetry of the Celtic Races." In his account of the Celtic epos he was also exploring and revealing his own self. Thus, while recognizing the fair criticism of his strong commitment to the hereditary-racial explanation of personality,[11] we should not miss the autobiographic relevance and significance of it for our understanding of his self-portrayal. Note his tribute to the characteristics of the Breton spirit: its sincerity and impetuous forthrightness, its zeal for the ultimate, its devout piety, and its unyielding independence in thought and in consecration, its dreamy and nostalgic melancholy. Were not these and other tributes to the Breton-Celtic spirit also Renan's own expressions of, or aspirations for, his own soul? We should not neglect them in pursuing Renan's more directly personal account of his spiritual pilgrimage. Always he maintained that "the characteristic feature of all degrees of the Breton race is its idealism—the endeavor to attain a moral and intellectual aim, which is often erroneous but always disinterested."[12] It is his own dedication.

The life-career of our Breton started with a tragic shock in his childhood; at the age of five he lost his father. Philibert Renan's fishing ship returned to Tréguier without its captain; he had left it at Saint-Malo and vanished without a trace. A month later his body was recovered on the Breton coast. His death left his family in a very precarious condition. The grocery store which he had operated along with his fishing trade was scarcely solvent and had to be given up. His widow had to lease her home to meet the demands of creditors; for some time she had to go to her mother in Lannion. Renan in later years recalled those indigent days when he had learned to "hide his misery," cheered in his poverty by his adored mother's ever-buoyant good spirit and by his sister Henriette, twelve years older than he, who had recognized in his mind the promise of a great future and, moved by sisterly faith and love, gave him her full material and moral support. After the family's return to Tréguier, she tried to direct a school there, without success, and then pursued a teaching career in Paris and later in the family of the Polish Count Zamoyski. The intimate record of her noble generosity to her brother at all times is evident in their long correspondence.

Young Renan's schooling was started in the church seminary of his native Tréguier. His accounts of his priestly teachers, written after the span of almost half a century, combine ironical but nowise malign comments on their simpleminded theology with profound veneration for their upright character and intense piety. Their faith was unquestioning; in his later years as a student in Paris seminaries he had teachers of far greater learning, but none more convincingly possessed of the truth. So he wrote at the age of sixty:

> These worthy men were my first spiritual guides, and I
> have them to thank for whatever was good in me. Their
> every word was my law, and I had so much respect for
> them that I never thought to doubt anything they told
> me until I was sixteen years of age, when I came to

Paris. Since that time I have studied under teachers far
more brilliant and learned, but none have inspired such
feelings of veneration. . . . It has been my good fortune to know what absolute virtue is. I know what faith
is, and though I have discovered how deep a fund of
irony there is in the most sacred of our illusions, yet
the experience derived from the days of old is very
precious to me.[18]

How deep a fund of irony! Renan cited one instance of it. On
the eve of the annual May festival of the Breton St. Yves, congregations from many parishes assembled in the Tréguier church
to do him homage, firmly believing that on the stroke of midnight the saint's statue would stretch forth its arms to bless the
kneeling worshipers: but only on the condition of their absolute belief without exception. If even only one among them
doubted that the miracle would actually take place, the saint,
offended by any such suspicion, would refuse them all his bene-
diction. Did Renan's pious teachers themselves believe this? They
were "disinterested and honest to the core," he wrote, and "contrived to steer a middle course between not doing anything to
weaken these ideas and not compromising themselves."[14] (We
should keep this story in mind, for we shall meet its match in
Count Tolstoy's reminiscences of his childhood, in our next
chapter.)

At the age of fifteen Ernest had won all the prizes for excellence at the Tréguier school. His sister Henriette, teaching in Paris
and eager to advance her brilliant young brother's education, reported his fine record to her school physician who by good chance
was a close friend of Abbé Dupanloup, the director of the small
seminary of Saint-Nicolas-du-Chardonnet. Dupanloup's aim was
to bring together sons of the Parisian aristocracy and the most
gifted lads of provinicial seminaries. Thus, as he purposed, the
nobility and the priesthood of France would be joined more

intimately. The young Breton wonder was just the sort he was looking for; and so Henriette Renan was able to write her brother that he had been offered a full scholarship good for ten years, to be accepted without delay. It would change his entire future! With the blessings of his mother and his Breton priests Ernest left his native town for Paris.

It was his first journey from his countryside. Even though he seldom left the seminary, he felt the impact of the immense new world of the metropolis all around him, overwhelming. For the first time he came to realize that there was learning, knowledge, wisdom too, quite outside the Church: secular knowledge and insight—scientific, philosophical, literary, much of it critical and rational; historical learning, much of it disturbing to his simple faith. The cherished link with his treasured homelife, Henriette, came to see him every week; as he later realized, she knew this larger world of thought. He should explore it on his own. His letters to his mother, intimate and deeply affectionate but also hesitant in their halting sincerity on certain topics, record the first steps outward and forward of the young searching mind that was bound before long to leave the seminary gates behind and proceed on its critical way.

The young Breton's first experiences at the Paris seminary were those of nostalgic alienation. Initially in his classes he found himself rather disappointing to his teachers, but later also disappointed in them. The Tréguier valedictorian was not anywhere near the top in his classwork at Saint-Nicolas. That sharp challenge, however, did not demoralize him; it spurred him to more intensive study, and he started up the ladder with steady resolution and eventual success. But as he thus proved his own capacity for mastery, he was also finding the intellectual standards of Abbé Dupanloup's faculty urbane and interesting, yet not really satisfying to his more rigorous reflection.

Exciting to his mind was his exposure to the larger world all about him. In their talks after dinner or in the walks of an evening the young Parisian aristocrats discussed the topics of the writers of the day—Lamartine, Victor Hugo. Dupanloup's idea of a Christian life was that of a mellow culture responsive to all the spiritual values, alert and engaging and withal genial. His piety was engaging and eloquent and very broadly humane, quite different from that of the simple but utter consecration of the Breton priests of Tréguier. "Saint-Nicolas was at that period the most brilliant and worldly house in Paris."[15] This religious outlook—may we call it quite secular spirituality—expanded Renan's views of life, aroused his imagination; but this very expansion and arousal raised problems for his critical reason, problems which the most eloquent pulpit oratory could not meet and which required a more rigorous method of examination. He had come right up to the standards of his masters, but they could not meet his own more exacting intellectual demands. He had been brought out of the simple unquestioning Catholic orthodoxy of his Breton priests into the broad urbane assurance of a humane and eloquent piety. He had and he always retained very high regard for the Christian generosity of Abbé Dupanloup, which manifested itself later in very difficult circumstances, but as a student of Christian theology he could not remain satisfied with the oratorical approach to the Christian verities.

His more cultivated intelligence was probing at deeper levels the grounds of his earlier implicit orthodoxy, with very precarious prospects. Still committed to theology as he was, he required more solid foundations. Philosophical reading and reflection were beginning to unsettle his young conformity. "I came to realities from words and I set seriously to study and analyse in its smallest details the Christian Faith which I more than ever regarded as the centre of all truth." Before long he would find himself in disagreement with the conclusions of his theological professors at St. Sulpice, but he never lost his respect for their chosen methods of thorough research and analysis of doctrine rather than the eloquent profession of it. So he wrote: *"Malheur au vague!* There is nothing so mischievous as the vague; it is even worse than the false."[16]

In accordance with the general order of Parisian clerical education, after his two years at Saint-Nicolas-du-Chardonnet, Renan proceeded to Issy, the preparatory branch of the great seminary of St. Sulpice. He had had his full measure of oratory and the mastery of style; what he needed now was more logic, solid training in the mastery of systematic doctrine. The Sulpician theologians emphasized rational procedure, philosophical competence along with private and communal devotional service. Significant to note, Renan found the daily schedule at Issy rather heavy on the devotional side; but still there was time enough for philosophy and other studies, and these seemed to have claimed his real devotion. This increasingly clear shift in his spiritual center and emphasis was in fact a gradual dissipation of his faith; his exacting intellect was on the ascendant. As yet he had no definite set of arguments against his erstwhile orthodoxy; but his absorption in critical studies was sure to lead him to heterodox and quite negative conclusions.

At Issy and, two years later, at St. Sulpice, he found the philosophical approach strongly influenced by Cartesian rationalism. The Sulpician foundation had to be rational grounds. These theological masters were suspicious of any fideism, the reliance for faith on faith alone. That sort of reliance ran the hazards of eroding skepticism. Renan studied the Cartesians; Malebranche impressed him preeminently, but thinking and logic, in Renan's mind, did not proceed straightforwardly to the verities of faith. Had not St. Thomas Aquinas counselled us to go with reason as far as it can ever take us, resting assured that faith would take us, beyond reason but not counter to reason, to our ultimate certitude? But Renan could not see this further course of rational direction as pointing towards the finalities of faith. For a while he ventured along with the will to believe. His reading of Pascal's *Pensées* seemed to be drawing him towards full orthodox reliance; but it gave him no permanent reassurance: the rational skepticism which had induced him to try Pascal's wager reasserted itself despite the wager. After all, the St. Sulpicians were right in their opposition to Pascal: the truths of orthodoxy were not to be possessed by wagering affirmations.

Along with his theology and Malebranche, Renan was branching afield in philosophy, reading Kant, Herder, Hegel. His mind was disturbed by discrepancies which he could not dismiss, between the metaphysics of the philosophers and of the theologians, and the former simple faith which he still demanded but which he no longer held with firm conviction. His Christian faith, he declared to himself, must somehow be the center of all truth: but how? Assuredly there could be no more important study for him than the study of the divinely revealed record. Is theology based on Holy Writ?—then he must master it, his Bible; and for that purpose he needed mastery of its original versions. Indispensable to him were Greek and Hebrew; he must heed the words of the evangelist Philip: "Understandest thou what thou readest?"[17] New Testament Greek he did possess as a matter of course; but before long by gruelling study he was gaining such a grasp of Hebrew that his Semitic professor, Le Hir, entrusted him with the seminary course in elementary Hebrew. In order to perfect himself further in his Semitic studies he was authorized to attend the lectures of Professor Quatremère at the Collège de France. But these studies, and the entire atmosphere of the Collège de France, so different from the Seminary of St. Sulpice, while they perfected his philological competence, weakened still further his orthodox foundations. His notebooks of those years show not only his growing mastery of Hebrew but also his repeated disclosures of flaws in the traditional understanding of the Old Testament.[18]

The Semitic studies, Biblical philology and history alike, naturally led Renan into the modern literary-historical or so-called "higher" criticism of the Old Testament, in which German scholarship was expert. Renan had to add to his attainments knowledge of German. We should not mistake the motivation in these researches. Unlike the negative *philosophes* of eighteenth-century France, most of the German "higher critics" were men of positive religious purposes, of constructive intentions. Like many other Biblical students Renan was engaged in forthright pursuit of his truth; he was exploring the Biblical foundations of the Christian faith. But that faith, so he felt bound to demand in his Christian insistence, that faith, if it was to be the center of all truth, had to be true and infallible throughout. Was it indeed based on God's own word?—then it could not contain a single error, a single pair of contradictory statements. One flaw, one untruth anywhere would unhinge it altogether.

It was not long before he realized beyond the possibility of dispute that the Biblical texts could not sustain the august theological claims for them. Renan was compelled to renounce his belief in Scriptural infallibility, in the traditional interpretations. These ill-founded convictions were upset by the more reliable understanding of the Hebrew texts and by more thorough study of the Biblical record. The conclusions of the "higher criticism," quite familiar to most Biblical scholars today, were shattering in their first impact on traditional orthodoxy. The Mosaic authorship of the entire Pentateuch could not be sustained by scholarly examination; nor could the common view of the Psalms as Davidic, nor the single authorship of the Book of Isaiah, nor the whole traditional doctrine of the ancient religion of Israel. Competent study of the New Testament texts would lead the mind to similar though not so extensive conclusions.

The challenging modern Biblical criticism of traditional Catholic orthodoxy was a different sort from that presented by earlier skeptical attacks on the belief in miracles. The Church could always appeal to the unbeliever's incapacity to establish absolutely his negative conclusions. But here Renan was confronted with patent inconsistencies in a Scripture which in orthodox terms was bound to be considered as infallible. Admit a single fissure in the orthodox structure, and it could no longer stand. It had to be errorless or nothing. Had not his Sulpician masters taught him the Cartesian test of truth, as free of contradictions?

Renan could not follow the sinuous ways of the so-called Catholic liberals, loose in their theology and exegesis, picking and choosing, thinking that they could admit one dogma and reject another and keep on believing in the balance. Liberals they could be, but not liberals and Catholics. "No one who has studied theology can be guilty of such inconsistency, . . . everything rests upon the infallibility of the Scripture and the Church. . . . In a church founded upon divine authority, it is as much an act of heresy to deny a single point as to deny the whole." Renan could not be reconciled to or content with a truncated Scripture, with half a Gospel. St. Sulpice was his fourth seminary in which he had been prepared for his priestly Catholic ministration. He could remain loyal to it only on its own august terms, but on no other. "The Catholicism which was taught me is not the insipid compromise, suitable only for laymen, which has led to so many misunderstandings in the present day. My Catholicism is that of Scripture, of the councils, and of the theologians. This Catholicism I loved, and I still respect it; having found it inadmissible, I separated myself from it."[19]

His separation was an unavoidable but a tragic experience. He was in a quandary about his future course and career. He had gone through three seminaries before coming to St. Sulpice; he was almost twenty-one years of age. While he could sign himself in his letters to his mother as tonsured cleric, he was still not finally committed to the priestly calling for which his entire education had been preparing him. Was he now to break with his religious past and pursue a literary or other secular career? But was it not only his youthful devotion to his Catholic faith that had attached him to his seminary priests, rather than any strictly clerical commitment? As the time approached, at St. Sulpice, for his expected priestly decision, he felt his increasing reluctance and resistance to it. More and more he felt himself a scholar, not a cleric. And as a scholar he cherished unbounded inquiry, with no surrender of his mind to dogmatic authority. He was finding himself incapable of starting with prescribed conclusions. But despite all reluctance and resistance, the actual step of withdrawal, how could he take it? His sister Henriette, to whom he could unburden his mind and heart in perfect candor, had herself quite disowned orthodox commitments. While she had for some years worried about his priestly inclinations, yet refrained from intruding upon his conscience, now that she began to learn about his growing alienation from orthodoxy, she urged him to leave St. Sulpice.[20] Their correspondence through his years at the Paris seminaries provides an intimate record of the gradual process of his disturbed but resistant faith, invading doubts, forthright critical study and tireless self-probing, and the tragic but resolute conclusion. Already at Issy he was turning to serious reflection about himself and his future course. More and more he would rely on reason. His career must be that of study and meditation. He could not share his hesitations with *maman* so long as he had not reached any decision. Despite his "terrible doubts," he had accepted tonsure; in all honesty with himself, he could not refuse it, for his refusal would have been a more final commitment than his acceptance. Likewise regarding the next step, to the minor orders; but as to the subdeaconship, that would be really irrevocable; he could not take it, in the state of mind in which he found himself.[21]

Henriette's letters, for her part, show her deep concern lest her cherished brother should choose the ecclesiastical course, but also the most scrupulous respect for his own spiritual freedom of decision. She would not urge or persuade him, but as she felt his mind coming towards her own views, she was ready with her forthright response. He should preserve his mind's initiative, his personal integrity; above all, he should avoid any surrender of his thought or will to someone else, be it a person or an institution. Important alone is the demand and the approval of one's own conscience. Renan had urged her, in her travels to Poland, to make a pilgrimage to Kant's tomb in Königsberg. She recalled to him Kant's noble tribute to the sovereign principle of Duty.[22]

But there was his mother, who in her simple faith had ever looked forward to her beloved Ernest's service in the Church, who could not possibly understand his religious problems and difficulties, to whom he could not write in any sincere spirit. Yet, loving her deeply, he scorned himself for his imposed evasions and almost hypocrisy and deceit. Ever since his departure for Saint-Nicolas Seminary her love for him had been beset with anxieties. He had to reassure her that he ran no danger in riding on railroad trains. In reporting to her his ups and downs in his class standing, he cited the similar records of his best rivals for the top. When he decided to receive the tonsure he did state that it was no irrevocable obligation but declared that he regarded it as a solemnly assumed engagement.[23] His mother was impressed by his appointment to teach the course in elementary Hebrew at St. Sulpice but was alarmed by the report that he was to attend the advanced courses in the subject at the Collège de France. He had to calm her fears: only two of the professors there, Quinet and Michelet, attacked religion in their lectures, and "God preserve me from sullying my ears in listening to such calumnies and such blasphemies!"[24] This is very disturbing when we recall the utter absorption with which young Renan read Michelet's medieval history. But it was not as misleading as it might appear; for Renan stated explicitly later his aversion to hearing words against Christianity: he may not have believed any longer, but he never ceased to respect his former faith, his "old friend," as he called it.[25]

In the summer of his year of decision, 1845, he paid a visit to Tréguier; his hard, unendurable emotions while at his mother's side are recorded in a letter to his intimate friend, Abbé Cognat. How is he to pierce with his own hand the heart of his mother with the true words about himself which would leave her desolate? "There she is, two steps from me as I write. Ah, if she only knew! . . . I tremble sometimes at the seeming hypocrisy of my conduct. . . . I should sacrifice everything to her, except my conscience and my duty."[26]

More distressing than all else was his own self-rending indecision. What alternatives were open to him? Could he follow the course of the German Biblical critics, many of whom were active Christian liberals? His Catholic conscience was too strong to accept any such compromise, even though, as he wrote, he was for some time rather Protestant in his outlook. Could he possibly, somehow, despite his Biblical criticisms, regain his former ardor in the Christian faith? The answer of his reason was an unqualified denial: "Outside rigid orthodoxy, there was nothing, so far as I could see, except free thought in the manner of the French school of the eighteenth century."[27] Reason was unyielding, but his heart was in desperate straits at the very thought of disowning his faith. "For four years a terrible struggle went on within me, until at last the phrase, which I had long put away from me as a temptation of the devil, 'It is not true!' could not be denied."[28] His only resistance to Catholic orthodoxy, but it proved to be all-decisive for him in the end, was intellectual: "Catholicism satisfies all my faculties, except my critical reason."[29] His notebooks of the time record some of the tragic stages of this struggle within himself. He pored over the Old Testament prophets, seeking some verse of indisputable Messianic-Christian significance. He sought assurance through the most persistent prayer: "Oh, tell me then what Thou art.—My God, am I in good faith? Purify me, . . . tell me yes or no! Here I have been in the chapel praying to Jesus, and he has told me nothing."[30]

"Such then were these two years of inward labour, which I cannot compare to anything better than to a violent attack of encephalitis, during which all my other functions of life were suspended. . . . My inward feelings were not changed, but each day a stitch in the tissue of my faith was broken." On one point he was becoming more and more convinced: whatever his future course in life and thought might be, he could not continue in his former plans of a priestly Catholic career. Try hard as he might to avoid it, he had to acknowledge the truth, devastating to his hopes but indisputable, which already at Issy but more finally at St. Sulpice had come to dominate his mind, that he was no longer orthodox, and that he must abandon his priestly prospects. "An inward voice told me: 'Thou are no longer Catholic; thy robe is a lie; cast it off.' "[31] He had to walk out of the seminary. Hard as it was to declare this decision to his priestly professors, whom he loved despite his inability to agree with their orthodoxy; doubly hard as it would be to impart his resolve to his mother, it had to be done; there was no other way open to him. On the sixth of October, 1845, Ernest Renan closed the seminary gates behind him, crossed the street over to a hotel and changed into a layman's attire.[32] (We may recall again that two days later John Henry Newman renounced his Anglican faith and was received into the Roman Catholic communion.)

To the great credit of his teachers, they were sorely grieved but showed Christian grace and benignity in their reactions to his withdrawal. His Semitic professor Le Hir kindly and "without offense" offered him financial help to tide him over his first steps. Renan declined his master's kindness with thanks. As it was, Henriette had sent him twelve hundred francs, which, as he wrote, he scarcely touched, but which relieved him of any immediate anxiety. Before him was the large secular world in which he was to work out his new career and his spiritual destiny. Henceforth he was to have only one commitment, his consecration to the pursuit of truth: "Take me whither thou wilt; I am ready."[33]

His life-redirecting decision involved and imposed others, some of them of more distant importance for his career, to be considered in their due season, but others of immediate concern, unavoidable, and one in particular taxing his powers of candid avowal. He had, somehow, to explain to his mother his departure from the seminary. "Judge how I suffered," he wrote to Henriette. "She has only the vaguest suspicions of my condition. . . . I fear to let her perceive it, and yet I ought to. . . . One of these days, at a certain hour that I should never forget, I shall have to be more explicit. What I have told her is that it is doubtful, . . . that we should wait. . . ."[34]

One of his tentative plans, to proceed to Germany for further study, alarmed her simple piety; as it happened, he was able to solace her with better news. On the recommendation of his good priests he had been offered a position at the Collège Stanislas, a lay school of the Oratorians, good Catholics. His actual teaching duties would be minor; he would have much time for his own studies. His mother was overjoyed by this prospect, but another letter told her that her Ernest was leaving Stanislas to devote himself entirely to research. In January, 1846, three and a half months after leaving St. Sulpice, he had passed "with full success" his examination for the bachelor's degree; two weeks later he informed her that he had accepted a new tutorial position which would assure him of self-support and leave most of his time free for his further preparation to take the university examination for the licentiate.[35] What had actually taken place he reported in his more intimate correspondence with Henriette. He had understood that his position at the Collège Stanislas was to be that of a layman; but the authorities insisted that he appear before his classes in ecclesiastical habit. This he refused to do and left. Further evasion in informing his mother was unendurable to Renan, yet he could not bring himself to write her plainly. Henriette assumed this duty for him, in a letter of admirable candor and sympathy.[36]

He was crossing one by one the academic gates towards a learned career. In October, 1846, one year after leaving St. Sulpice, he passed his examinations for the licentiate with honors. He was attending courses at the Sorbonne and at the Collège de France and at the same time was tirelessly pursuing his own scholarly researches: and in both directions his advance was immediate and amazing. In his Semitic researches he was expanding his knowledge to include Arabic, Syriac. Of all this his letters to Henriette have preserved a truly remarkable record. To Professor Garnier at the Sorbonne he had ventured to write some comments about one of his lectures in philosophy. In his very next session Garnier had read his letter to his class and commented on it in a most obliging manner. Furthermore, he invited young Renan to call on him, conversed with him most generously, encouraged him to write further and visit him, and later devoted two whole sessions to a discussion of another critical comment of Renan's. He urged him to pursue philosophical studies; it was all most extraordinary at the Sorbonne.

His Semitic studies were attracting the attention of distinguished savants. He was encouraged to compete for an academic prize in the field of comparative philology; by dint of the most intensive work he completed and submitted his *Historical and Critical Essay on the Semitic Languages in General and on the Hebrew Language in Particular*. His work was unanimously awarded the prize. What was more important for Renan's career, the president of the Academy of Inscriptions told Renan that in view of the not far distant retirement of Professor Quatremère, he, Renan, should look forward to succeeding him in the Chair of Hebrew at the Collège de France, for which he had higher qualifications than anyone else in France. All this presented itself to a young man of barely twenty-four, only sixteen months out of the seminary and without any university prestige. It left Renan breathless. He was to learn later that Professor Quatremère had some other favorite candidate in mind as his successor. Actually other official appointments came his way more immediately as Renan received his higher diplomas. The French Government sent him on a research assignment to Italy and later to the territory of ancient Phoenicia. Of the latter, and also of his eventual appointment to the professorship of Hebrew at the Collège de France, with its repercussions, we shall take further note.[37]

His long correspondence with his beloved sister was to terminate at the middle of the century, happily for both, by Henriette's decision to accept her brother's urgent appeals to her to return to Paris and share his scholarly life. Renan paid the highest tribute to her incomparable help to him as literary secretary, adviser, and virtual editor. Besides his ancient Biblical and more broadly Semitic studies, he was engaged in literary and historical writing on a ramified scope, and in modern history and literature he acknowledged her superior knowledge in many fields. For her part she found her joy and happiness in being by his side in his progress. No one was more overjoyed than she when he was elected a member of the *Institut,* in the *Académie des Inscriptions et Belles Lettres,* and he not quite thirty-four years old! (The election to the *Académie Française* came later.) She was besides a most competent manager in their little ménage of high thinking and plain living.

There was to be a hard shock to this family idyl, when Ernest Renan met and loved and married Cornélie Scheffer. Henriette who, long years earlier, during her brother's boyhood, had refused a proposal of marriage in her devoted care for her family and for him in particular; who even as late as 1850 had declined another marriage proposal because he plainly needed her daily help, found the imminent entry of another woman into their midst most painful to confront. (Yet Renan stated that when she first joined him in Paris Henriette had urged him to marry.)[38] Her eventual mastery over herself, her generous and wholehearted, though tearful, acceptance of the new situation manifested selfless nobility of character above praise. The like tribute can scarcely be accorded to her brother. In his self-analysis he noted his practice of poverty, modesty, politeness, and conscientious morality;[39] but neither he nor those who knew him noted in his personality the capacity for utter self-denial.

Renan's astonishing progress in his secular learned career had nowise left behind him the deeper currents of his religious experience. He had definitely terminated any priestly plans for his life, although for a while he had not rejected his Catholic communion in every way. He still went to confessional and, as it seems, even to Eucharist, but only for a while. The complete severance came hard, but it did come. Although the Protestant alternative did not attract him, as a somewhat substitute orthodoxy, he did consider it critically, to do it justice. Kant, Fichte, Herder did regard themselves as Christians. Was it really an irreducible choice: either Roman Catholic orthodoxy or unbelief in the manner of the eighteenth-century *philosophes*?

He found among his papers, in a copy of a letter he had written one month before leaving St. Sulpice, his search for a third alternative: "Will not some one found amongst us a rational and critical Christianity" unlike "the Catholic faith which is like a bar of iron?" "May I live to see this Christianity assuming a form capable of satisfying all the requirements of our age? May I cooperate in the great work?" He declared earnestly: "I cannot be an orthodox Catholic; but at whatever cost, I am resolved to be a Christian."[40] Only he wrote it in the reverse order.

What he had abandoned was a traditional and, in his firm judgment, untenable system of doctrines and beliefs; but that system also included devotion to ideals and principles of living which had never relaxed their sovereignty over his highest nature. He cleaved to them even more firmly than before, and for the sake of them he would never abandon his respect for the moral strain in the Catholic spirit. "The Gospel will ever be my moral law; the Church has given me my education, and I love her." Rejection of the traditional teachings which his reason and his Biblical research had shown to be unsound, and dismissal of the miraculous and supernatural strain in orthodox religion and so much of the dogmatic theology about Christ could not affect the sublimity of the gospel *of* Jesus, the eternal truths of the Sermon on the Mount. He would be a true disciple of Jesus. So after almost forty years of reflection and productive critical work, Renan could write: "Jesus has in reality ever been my master. In following out the truth at the cost of any sacrifice I was convinced that I was following Him and obeying the most imperative of His precepts."[41]

What he had lost and what he often regretted that he could not recover was his capacity for unqualified adoration: "Ah! when shall I kneel down?" In his meditations, recorded in his notebooks, his thought of Jesus waivers between admiration, supreme respect, and a sort of moral adoration. Jesus was the only man before whom he would bow in homage. His meditation was a prayer to Jesus: "Thou art my master in morals, . . . thou are a God beside me. . . ." There is always science, which likewise has its rights, . . ."but, God, how Thou hast surpassed me in the great vital science! . . . If Thou art God, make me know it. . . . My God, why canst Thou not answer me?" Right alongside of this page Renan wrote his "profession of faith." It is not a statement of doctrine but an utterance of aspiration: "I believe in a God, superior to humanity; but no anthropomorphism, neither material nor psychological. God is not a man in body or in spirit. . . . Religion: sublime word, immensely comprehensive in its full meaning, when we do not stunt to only some branches this great tree which has its roots in the spirit of man."[42]

In the duality of his spirit, of which he was ever conscious, he was wary of the adoration to which he aspired; he would not turn his steps towards St. Sulpice. Does religion, in its essence and kernel, does it require adoration? On the one hand he criticized the secularists of his day who admired and revered Plato, Socrates, but had no word for Jesus? "I imagine what that imbecile, Garnier, would say if one spoke to him of Jesus Christ. Oh Jesus, thou surpassest them all, and I will demonstrate it." But still—must we really adore the Lord? "Why not call oneself a disciple of Jesus without adoring him, regarding him as the greatest of men, as the moralist *par excellence,* and cleaving to him? In this sense, every man should be a Christian." He had been quite disillusioned about the supreme assurance of faith, but he reflected: Is not the ever uncertain but yet loyal aspiration towards the ideal the true course for our human spirit? There is a sublimity in the right kind of skepticism: "Doubt is so beautiful that I have been praying to God never to deliver me from it; for then I should be less beautiful, even though happier."[43] About the same time Tennyson was writing in *In Memoriam:*

There lives more faith in honest doubt,
Believe me, than in half the creeds.

Renan's meditation on the moral sublimity of Jesus was shared
with a counter-devotion to science. In its broadest sense, as the
critical-rational study of reality, the scientific method dominated
his intelligence; it had also engaged his deep interest in its more
limited significance, as physical science. This interest was stim-
ulated by his close friendship with the chemist Berthelot, who later
rose high in his specialty to a professorship at the Collège de
France and membership in the Academy of Sciences. Berthelot's
extensive correspondence with Renan, and also with Henriette, for
whom he had the highest regard, reveal in a fine way the mutual
inspiration in intimate personal relations. When Renan came to
know Berthelot, he had just closed behind him the gates of St.
Sulpice, but his whole education had been priestly. In the young
chemist Renan came to recognize a plainly secular devotion, devotion to the scientific research of nature. Nowise abandoning his
one supreme loyalty to spirit, Renan was drawn in close kinship
to the physical world around him. Years later he wrote: "I have
a keen liking for the universe."[44]

This inclination—we could hardly call it a definite shift—in
Renan's outlook may be noted in his work, *The Future of Science*.
He expected from the advancement of modern science, with
deeper insight into the basic principles of physical nature, also
a more fully warranted understanding of human nature and more
intelligent reorganization of human relations. The advance of
culture, as he thought, requires a considerably privileged social
position for the competent and the gifted; but the guiding moral
purpose of the right social order must be the promotion of the
greatest common welfare. The events of 1848, as he stated, turned
his mind towards the social problems, and he recognized not
only the force but also the merit of the socialist protest. But he

also perceived the misdirections of the socialist emphasis. The pressing demand for economic reform should not neglect the deeper spiritual needs of men. This issue engaged Renan's social philosophy; in dealing with it through the years he seemed to be moving from a democratic emphasis towards an aristocratic spirituality disdaining any philistinism. Men's efforts should not aim at prosperity, be it individual or communal, but at the greater realization of the higher cultural values.[45]

As on the one hand he was urging a less dogmatic and more secular and scientific approach to human problems, so on the other hand he pointed out, beyond the demand for political and social-economic reform, the deeper need of moral regeneration. *The Future of Science* was Renan's reaction to the year of revolutions, 1848. But he respected the counsel of his elder friends, who advised the young man of twenty-five to publish some selected portions of his book as articles but to let the rest of it season awhile. It actually seasoned some twoscore years and was not published until the close of his life, without revisions, but with much basic disavowal in the preface. He acknowledged the "naiveté" and the "exaggerated optimism" of his social philosophy of 1848; he renounced the ideas of an egalitarian society as a utopian dream; the social problem did not allow of short-shrift solution. But he reaffirmed his "favorite thesis" and method of inquiry: the science of man requires a historical outlook, to be explored in a patient and philological study of the works produced by the different epochs.[46]

One result of his scientific reflections was confirmed emphasis on intellectual integrity: thoroughness of research, readiness to accept its findings and conclusions, be they what they may. It is this spirit which he respected in his friend Berthelot's science. Valid and fruitful as it was in the study of nature, it was also august in the higher inquiries of morals and religion. Surely dogmatism would be idle in scientific work; in religious reflection it would be impious. Not only Old Testament scholarship but also deeper spiritual loyalty to the pursuit of truth directed him to the study of the *Book of Job,* of which he made a translation from the Hebrew, with a commentary. (We are told that Rome put it on the *Index* of prohibited books.) In reading Renan's own writings, we are reminded of Job's words to his friends who were endeavoring to twist the tragical facts of his life into conformity with their dogmatic beliefs: "Will ye speak unrighteously for God, and talk deceitfully for him?" For what could be holier or more genuinely pious than unwavering respect for the facts and thorough integrity in the pursuit of truth? Spinoza who wrote of "God or Nature" also wrote "God or Truth, *Deus seu Veritas.*" And St. Augustine declared, in terms which Renan could have accepted for his own: "Let every good and true Christian understand that truth, wherever he finds it, belongs to *his* Lord."[47]

The many achievements of Renan's career expressed his steady commitment to the quest of truth, no matter where it might lead. The imposing list of his twoscore volumes which faces the title page of his collected works is as it were a large-scale map of his mind's far-flung domains. Should the reader glance even at the table of contents of some of those tomes, he would be astonished by Renan's detailed charting of his territories. In the field of his studies which especially concerns us, Biblical research and Semitics, he gained outstanding rank. Eventually he was recognized as the premier French master of Hebrew and was appointed to the respective professorship at the Collège de France, to which he had long been entitled by right. That appointment was bound to stir criticism by the established orthodoxy, which Renan roused to strong aggression with a phrase in which he spoke of Jesus as "the incomparable man." It simply and conclusively would not do: his course of lectures was suspended, and two years later was terminated outright. He refused the substitute offer of appointment as sublibrarian of the National Library and preferred to retain his independence and self-reliance. (In 1870 his professorship was restored to him; the Gascon strain of ironic humor expressed itself in his declared intention to begin his lecture-course at the Collège de France with the words: "As I was remarking at our last meeting"—eight years earlier!)[48]

Renan's most widely read book was written during his travels in Bible lands while on his official mission in the region of ancient Phoenicia, a mission of very gratifying results to him as a scholar, but of the most tragic termination personally. His sister and later his wife accompanied him on his exploration. Later Cornèlie had to return home, but Henriette was ever an aide at his side, in Syria and Lebanon and Galilee. By ill chance, however, both of them were laid low by marsh fever. Their first physician did not cope with the disease competently, and when at last the right treatment was given to the delirious sufferers, it came too late for Henriette. Renan himself was carried half-conscious to his ship and had a precarious and slow recovery. So Henriette would not see the book which she had urged her brother to write and which was to realize the universal renown that she had always envisioned for him. Renan who wrote bitter words of grief that, in his self-absorption in his work, he had not given full expression to his grateful love for his devoted sister, found the days of the worldwide fame of his *Life of Jesus* less disturbed by the sharp attacks of the dogmatists than saddened by the absence from his side of the one person who would have cherished most his achievement and disdained his opponents.

The *Life of Jesus* was Renan's most popular masterpiece—the adjective should not be overlooked. It sold over sixty thousand copies within five months and was directly translated into half the languages of Europe. Its leading spirit and motivation should be recognized, for they are most significant autobiographically. In his interpretation of Jesus, who was his supreme ideal and perfect master, Renan was expressing his view of the moral and spiritual perfection to which he aspired. More than once he proceeded from a declaration of some firm moral conviction to a glance of soaring recognition of it in his chosen master. Alongside or despite the aristocratic vein in his temperament, Renan was also moved by strong concern for the common people, the needy multitude. The gospel to "the weary and the heavy-laden" gripped his heart, and he declared: "I am the only man of my time who has understood the character of Jesus and of Francis of Assisi."[49] This sort of interpretation, of which other instances might be given, would scarcely justify the ironical comment that Renan extolled Jesus for coming up to his, Renan's, standard. The truer judgment is rather the reverse: Jesus was the only one Renan would follow as a disciple. Did he not write some fifteen years earlier: "Oh Jesus, Thou surpassest them all, and I shall demonstrate it, *je le montrerai.*"[50] There is a promise of insight in this view of Renan's interpretation of Jesus, but only provided it is kept within limits. On the one hand, as it has been remarked by a perceptive critic, "all biographers are liable to draw their heroes after their own likeness"; on the other hand, "every attempt to *Renanize* Jesus seems a sacrilege to the believer, an impossibility to the historian, and an error of taste to the artist."[51]

The leading spirit and motivation of Renan's work was a profound and intense devotion to the gospel *of* Jesus, to the perfection of the personality and the spiritual ideals of his chosen Master. But in his portrayal he was directed, or may we say controlled, by his conscience as a sound historian. He was severely critical of the traditional dogmatism in the interpretation of the gospels *about* Jesus. As he stated it himself, his method was moderate: he sought the reasonable course between two unwarranted dogmatisms: the orthodox adherence to a theological formulation which taxed rational belief and was unsupported or in many ways contradicted by the Gospel texts themselves, and the outright skeptical dismissal of the supreme spiritual event in history.

In dealing with a theme of such epochal importance as the origin of Christianity, the true historian must not depart from the ascertained facts, which are very few in the case before us; but he must also recognize and express the broader and deeper significance of the evidence before him, even when it is partial. A true history is a statement of factual data, envisioned and portrayed with reliable imagination. In Renan's judgment, a few lines would suffice to state what we know for certain in the biography of Jesus; and he recited the meager evidence. Jesus "existed. He was from Nazareth in Galilee. He preached with charm and left in the memory of his disciples aphorisms of profound impression. His two principal disciples were Cephas and John the son of Zebedee. He roused the hatred of the orthodox Jews, who contrived his condemnation to death by Pontius Pilate, then procurator of Judea. He was crucified outside of the city gates. It was believed afterwards that he had been resuscitated. That is all we know with certitude. Beyond that, doubt is permitted." Renan arrays half a page of questions to which, in his judgment, no reliable answers are available.[52] But while these specific inquiries about the career of Jesus may tax the historian's assured record, the spirit and character of his supreme personality stands revealed before us and should guide our reverent interpretation.

Renan noted and was wary of trusting accounts in which the evangelists disagreed. Even in their unanimous narrative of alleged events, he was unconvinced by whatever ran counter to reasonable belief and seemed to reflect the popular bias for the miraculous and the supernatural. But the Gospel accounts did reveal to him moral and religious ideals of the highest excellence which could not be denied; as a historian of culture he knew nothing that surpassed them. As a historian and as himself a seeker after perfection he felt bound to recognize and to extol these superlative values.

What impressed Renan most was the living immediacy of Jesus's experience of God. Jesus was not a systematic theologian; he did not advance proofs of God; he felt God in himself and himself in God. This loving conviction he urged on his disciples: to be his disciple did not require acceptance of any creed or doctrine, but only loving communion with him. In the early stages of his career Jesus seemed to have been attracted for a while by John the Baptist, with much of whose pleading he sympathized. Like John the Baptist, he opposed the ceremonial emphasis in the orthodox Judaism. He and his few followers had been baptized by John; but that sort of ritual also lost its claim to his conviction. His gospel was to be one of the most thorough spirituality. The Kingdom of God which he proclaimed was not one to be attained by political revolt, in the manner of insurgent zealots; nor was it to be a restoration of Jewish orthodox dominion of a Pharisaic pattern. It was and it could be only in the inner life of each godly soul. "The Kingdom of God is within you."[53] Jesus preached "a religion free of all external forms," a theology which consisted in one's direct conviction of God as loving Father.[54] This direct communion in love set the tone and direction of his moral teaching, of loving fellowship of all men, Jew or Gentile. When Jesus declared to the Samaritan woman that God is Spirit, to be worshipped in spirit and in truth, in Jerusalem or Samaria or anywhere, he, according to Renan, "pronounced for the first time the word upon which the edifice of the eternal religion would rest."[55]

In this interpretation of the religion of Jesus, Renan was also expressing his conviction of the essence of true Christian discipleship. The genuine Christians are not the systematic orthodox theologians, firmly adhering to their dogmas, but those whose spirit has been penetrated by the sublime truths of the Sermon on the

Mount. The dogmatist and the ecclesiastic ritualist are like Martha, "anxious and troubled about many things"; but the true Christian must be like Mary, choosing "the good part, the one thing needful."[56] Renan felt, or rather hoped, that in rejecting the unsound orthodoxy and walking out of the gates of St. Sulpice he had started on his true Christian course as a disciple of Jesus, who also broke with the Pharisees and spoke forth the truth of his communion with God.

It should be noted that in a real sense Renan never broke altogether with the Church. Even when the Roman hierarchy denounced his work, he did not reply with counter-vilification. He revered the virtues of his priestly teachers even after he had disproved and rejected many of their beliefs and doctrines. He recognized in the Church supreme spiritual values; but the spirit of Jesus was a spirit of ever-living and growing power, not one of static conformity. So towards the close of his life he wrote to a Sulpician: "Two things are certain: Catholicism cannot perish; Catholicism cannot remain such as it is."[57] This religious conviction expressed also Renan's basic philosophy of life: "The goal of humanity is not repose; it is intellectual and moral perfection"[58]—an eternally progressive ideal. "The cult of Jesus will ever rejuvenate itself," but the best of men will never rise higher than in the spirit of loving devotion to him, as his disciples, looking up to him as their Master. "Jesus will never be surpassed."[59]

CHAPTER VIII

COUNT LEO TOLSTOY

The conventional, the ordinary, produces slight impression on us, nor do we feel drawn towards the entirely respectable; but the unusual personality is likely to engage our attention, especially if it is in some ways negative. Men have repeatedly been stirred by those who have defied "the establishment." The sophisticated days of Athenian culture and Corinthian luxury were just right for Diogenes of Sinope. He spat at the Hellenic amenities as artificial barriers to unbound self-expression. Spurning all social honor and conformity as empty, he found his satisfaction in suiting his own passing mood, fareing on garlic and lodging in his proverbial tub. Yet he commanded the respect of those whose proprieties he scorned. Even so the rich sensuous Florentines of the Renaissance were gripped by the scathing sermons of Savonarola. The formal conventional eighteenth century was similarly shocked and engrossed by Rousseau's romantic plea for a return to primitive nature. Coming closer home, we may note the spreading renown of Thoreau, who shrugged off New England respectabilities, to worship the Goddess of Sincerity and live his own simple life of daily self-penetration. In all these cases the daring challenge of the simple or austere or nonconformist prophet has had engrossing influence.

This reflection may help us to understand why the strong impression of Tolstoy's religious and social criticisms of our traditional culture exceeded even the worldwide fame of his literary

201

mastery. We may understand, but still we are puzzled. How was it possible for him to command such attention, and sympathy too, when he repudiated the basic principles of our modern life? In an age of most intense struggle for self-advancement and conquest, Tolstoy preached nonresistance. In an age whose proudest boast is that of its technical mastery, he scorned material dominance. In an age of the division of labor, he considered no man moral unless he produced for himself the necessities of life. Yet in spite of all this dissidence, millions have been drawn to him.

So extreme have his denials of the orthodox and the respectable seemed to some of his critics that they have even doubted the sincerity of this Russian nobleman who put on the peasant's blouse and went to the fields to plow side by side with his former serfs, and more than that, tried to learn from their dull minds moral wisdom and Christian piety. But Romain Rolland, in his response to Tolstoy's work, has spoken for great multitudes: "Ours it was by its ardent love of life, by its quality of youth; ours by its irony, by its disillusion, its pitiless discernment, and its haunting sense of mortality. Ours by its dreams of brotherly love, of peace among men; ours by its terrible accusation of the lies of civilization, ours by its realism; by its mysticism ours; by its savour of nature, its sense of invisible forces, its vertigo in face of the infinite."[1] Few readers of Tolstoy would subscribe to every clause of Rolland's panegyric; the various selections that are likely to be made would indicate the unlikelihood of any adequate formula to describe Tolstoy's outlook on life: criticism of Russian orthodoxy, or populism, or pacifism, or Christian anarchism, or whatever. Distrusting labels and prejudgment, we should pursue in his works his own struggle with the problems of life. If his solution of those problems should strike us as too bold, we would find the actual decisions which he made in his own life much bolder; and if they puzzle us, who shall say that Tolstoy is entirely to blame? "When a book and a head strike against each other, and a dull sound ensues, is the trouble always with the book?"

Before tracing the journeys and the arrivals of the great Russian pilgrim, we may consider his starting points: his ancestral background; what he finally refused to live up to; or rather, as he would have said, what he resolved to live down. Leo Nikolayevitch Tolstoy came from the topmost cream of Russian society. If one is to trust the traditional Book of Nobility (1686), the first recorded founder of the family was a certain Indris who came to Russia during the fourteenth century, perhaps from Germany but more likely from Lithuania. By the time of Peter the Great, the Tolstoys rose high in the Tsarist regime, but their fortunes swayed with the dynastic repercussions in Petersburg, politically and economically. Our Tolstoy's grandfather, generous to others and most aristocratically extravagant in self-indulgence, consumed his own fortune as well as that of his rich wife, Princess Gorchakov. His very handsome son Nikolai entered the army, fought in the Napoleonic wars, and at the death of his father found the Tolstoy estate so debt-ridden that he refused his inheritance. There was only one way ahead for him if he was to save the requirements of nobility; he found it in marrying the rich heiress Princess Marya Volkonsky, moved to the Volkonsky manor house at Yasnaya Polyana, in the Tula district, and espoused her estate of eight hundred serfs. Tolstoy's mother had ancestry as ancient as any in Russia, bar none; it reached clear back to Rurik and by marriages through the centuries was allied with every renowned name in Russia.

This was the ancestral setting and standing in which Lyof (Leo) Tolstoy was born, in 1828. As he grew up, he would be told the names of his forebears, paternal and maternal, whose portraits hung on the walls around him; some of them stiff

Tsarist conservatives, others venturing liberals, but all of them distinguished aristocrats and good orthodox churchmen. One portrait was missing, that of his mother, who died when little "Lyovotchka" was two years old, His father's death followed seven years later. The boy and his three brothers and one sister were to be brought up by various aunts as the family moved to Moscow, to Kazan, and back to Yasnaya Polyana. Leo cherished the memories and the eulogies of his parents and of the Tolstoy family tradition: if he could only come up to it, himself!

Tolstoy was deeply impressed by those before him and around him. Searching students have traced in his novels and stories the portraits for which his imagination drew upon his family environment; most notably those of his parents, whom he had in mind in telling the romance of Nikolai Rostov and Princess Maria Bolkonsky in *War and Peace*. But stronger than biographic strains in his novels were the autobiographic. It was evident in his first sketches, *Childhood, Boyhood,* and *Youth;* in *The Cossacks,* as well as in some of his later works; and especially in *Anna Karenina*.

Keen mentally but not diligent and not at all outstanding in performance, suspicious and generous in turn; reserved yet athirst for loving attention; morbid, with a certain deep melancholy, and nonetheless a reckless and quite mischievous abandon—he was a boy of a thousand questions, the despair of his tutors but also the darling of his aunts. Among his games with his three brothers, one in particular remained a cherished memory throughout life. It was directed by his eldest brother Nikolai, whom he greatly admired. Nikolai disclosed to them that there was a great secret, "how to banish all unhappiness from life, all dispute and anger, and to make people happy forever. This secret, as he told us, he had written on a green stick, and the green stick was buried near the road along the hollow by the old wood." But the first condition to be fulfilled in order to find this green stick was "to stand in a corner and not think of a white bear." All his life Tolstoy sought that green stick of blessedness. He sought it in the transports of passion, in the thrill of the gambling table, in the calm vastness and grandeur of untamed nature, in the daredevil intoxication of ever-present death and in the hardening of the soul by war; in the serene joys of a happy family life, in the glowing sense of widespread fame, social prestige, power of wealth. And then, when he had scaled the heights of human ambition, as he recoiled from it all, on the brink of an abyss, he was still in quest of that occult talisman. "As I believed then in the existence of a green stick on which was written the secret which would do away with all evil in humanity and give great happiness, so I believe now that there exists such a truth; this will be divulged to mankind and all promises will be fulfilled."[2] At the age of eighty he dictated to his secretary his request that at his death his body was to be buried near where that green stick was hidden, along the hollow by the old wood.

The problem of life and death and the meaning of it all troubled his unquiet spirit from early years. The orthodox conformity and assurance in which he had been brought up were disturbed when he was only ten years old, by the announcement made by a grammar school pupil of a latest discovery— "that there is no God, and that all we are taught about Him is a mere invention." This announcement and later ones like it, and also reading Voltaire when he was very young, did not alter Tolstoy's church conformity, but they affected his spirit in the conforming. He still said his prayers and observed the orthodox practices, but his real faith was being gradually dissipated. "A man very often lives on, imagining that he still holds intact the religious doctrine imparted to him in childhood, whereas not a trace of it remains."[3]

After the death of his father the family had moved to Kazan, where his aunt and appointed guardian lived. He followed his brothers to the University of Kazan, starting in the Department of Oriental Languages, changing to that of Law the second year; but disappointed in both educational ventures he left the university without his diploma. Unsteady in his purposes and decisions, shifting from lofty sentiments to low hankerings, scarcely twenty years old, he started to write down in his *Dnevniki (Diaries)* a list of elaborately classified rules for the manifold direction of his mind and character and development of will and emotions and daily conduct. There were over forty of them. And yet he wrote that same spring, "I do not accomplish what I resolve to do; what I do accomplish is not done well."[4] He read the entire shelf of Rousseau's writings, was swept away by Rousseau's romantic ideals, wore around his neck a medallion with Rousseau's portrait, and planned to live a simple life close to nature. But in his conduct, on returning to Yasnaya Polyana, he imitated the vagabond practices related in Rousseau's *Confessions.* Gypsy dancers and revelers, gamblers and roisterers became his daily and nightly company. Months passed in riotous living, which later necessitated the sale and removal of the house in which he had been born, to pay his gambling debts. But with the objectivity with which he described his moral degradation he also recorded the deeper yearnings after ideal purposes which stirred in his soul, unrealized. Resolving one day to turn a really new leaf, he went south with his brother Nikolai, to the Caucasus, to find worthy satisfaction in primitive unspoiled nature. His story, *The Cossacks,* was the literary fruit of his venture in the simple life like Rousseau.

The hero in *The Cossacks,* Olyenin, (a transparent self-portrait) is a Moscow society young man who has squandered half his patrimony, and has not entered any career or carried out any resolution firmly; who feels in himself energies but does not decide in what channel to direct them: a character without spiritual orientation. In the midst of wild nature he is ever in his own way, unable to become one with his environment, unable to bridge the gap between himself and others or to find happiness in generous fellowship with them. Tolstoy was writing this in his story, and in his *Diaries* and letters he was expressing similar feeling and problems in his own person. "The man who strives only for his own happiness is bad; he who aims for the good opinion of others is weak; he who seeks the happiness of others is virtuous; he whose aim is God is great."[5]

His life—thought and feeling and action—was embroiled by conflicting motives. He was in the Caucasian wilds seeking meaningful existence in primitive simplicity, but he was still the proud young aristocrat with his high demands and standards. This contention of motives showed itself unawares in minor ways. Despite his love for his brother he disapproved of Nikolai's untidiness; Nikolai in his turn laughed at Lyof's changing his linen twelve times a day. So on an earlier occasion, in Kazan, the two had argued about Leo's expressed scorn for an apparent gentleman who was out walking in the street without gloves. This same aristocrat in later life would be putting on a peasant's smock and would advocate keeping on one's soiled shirt, or washing it oneself, so as to lessen one's demands on the service of others.[6]

At deeper levels this inner conflict may be noted in his disdainful self-analysis, over against the loftiest religious and moral aspirations. He had entered military service in the Crimean War, which was to take him from the Balkans to Sevastopol. At the outset of it he probed himself ruefully, as in this extract: "I am ugly, awkward, uncleanly, and lack society education. I am irritable, a bore to others, not modest, intolerant, and as shame-faced as a child. I am almost an ignoramus. What I do know, I have learned anyhow, by myself, in snatches, without sequence, with-

out a plan, and it amounts to very little. I am incontinent, undecided, inconstant, and stupidly vain and vehement, like all
characterless people. I am not brave. I am not methodical in life,
and am so lazy that idleness has become an almost unconquer-
able habit of mine.'" And much more to the same dismal tune.
As Maude observed, this sort of self-opprobrium by a young man
in his twenties who already had mastery or good knowledge of
half-a-dozen languages, whose first stories were welcomed by the
editor of Russia's leading magazine, and it may be added, whose
early fame, together with his reported bravery on the battle-
front, had led the Tsar to send orders for special care of his personal safety in Sevastopol—all this should show the real meaning
of Tolstoy's self-reproach, in his discontent with his failure to
come up to his own high aspirations.

A page from his diaries of that period expresses the lofty
religious ideals to which later in his life he was to become utterly
consecrated:

> A discussion on God and Faith brought me to a great,
> a stupendous idea, to the realization of which I feel able
> to devote my life. The idea is to create a new religion
> corresponding to the development of mankind, a religion
> of Christ purified from dogma and mysticism, a practical
> religion, not promising bliss in future, but giving happi-
> ness on earth. I understand that this idea can be realized
> only by generations consciously working for that pur-
> pose. One generation will bequeath this idea to the next,
> and some day by fanaticism or by reason it will be
> realised. To work consciously for the union of mankind
> by religion—that is the foundation of the idea which I
> hope will inspire me.[8]

After the Crimean War Tolstoy went to St. Petersburg, where
he was received with virtual ovation in the literary circles. The
fame he had gained by his early stories was sealed by his Sevastopol war sketches. Even in their censored form they reported

the soldier's life on the battlefield in a way which gripped the reader. The poet-editor Nekrasov wrote him: "Truth—in such a form as you have introduced it in our literature—is something completely new among us." But the life of the literary elite of the capital began to weary him. Literature ought to be a guide of the people to a higher life, and here were its leaders in Russia, "who did not care who was right and who was wrong, . . . for the most part men of bad, worthless character, . . . but they were self-confident and self-satisfied as only those can be who are quite holy or who do not know what holiness is. These people revolted me, I became revolting to myself, and I realized that that faith was a fraud."[9]

Tolstoy took his only trips to Western Europe, three of them, to study social and agricultural conditions, and in 1861 returned to Yasnaya Polyana. He anticipated Tsar Alexander II's emancipation of the serfs by freeing his own peasants and devoted his time to their education and their general betterment. During a siege of illness the doctors ordered him to go to his estate in Samara to recover his health on a diet of sour milk. On his way he stopped overnight in Moscow and backslid into a gambling party. The man to whom he lost, Katkov, was the editor of *Russky Vyestnik,* who accepted as payment of Tolstoy's gambling debt the manuscript of *The Cossacks.* The spiritual pilgrimage had, and was still to have, its deviations.

In the summer of 1862 Tolstoy was in Moscow, wooing Sophia Behrs and experiencing the anguish to which the memory of his past debauches drove him when he thought of offering his life to a pure young woman. But at least he would be honest, and just before his wedding he unburdened his dismal conscience to his betrothed.

If family happiness could ever satisfy a normal person's full expectations of life, it should have satisfied Tolstoy. Sophia Behrs—or Sonya, as he called her—was a most helpful and utterly devoted wife. Her direction of the daily round of duties and the care of her large family at Yasnaya Polyana was smooth perfection. And she was more than a good mother and competent housekeeper; she was Tolstoy's literary assistant. And what a man she had to assist! He was probably the most inveterate reviser and proof corrector among all authors of masterpieces. He would insert not only words but whole sentences between the lines or even across them until the pages would be scarcely legible, and had to be copied clean, so that he could resume his further revisions and corrections. The Countess undertook this task, again and yet again. Seven times over she transcribed in longhand the whole manuscript of *War and Peace.*

The sixties and the seventies, 1863-1878, were Tolstoy's most productive years as a creative artist. To those years we owe *War and Peace* and *Anna Karenina.* Reflecting on those fifteen years, he wrote: "The new conditions of a happy family life completely diverted me from all search for the general meaning of life. My whole life was centered at that time in my family, wife and children, and therefore in care to increase our means of livelihood. My striving after self-perfection, for which I had already substituted a striving for perfection in general, *i.e.,* progress, was now again replaced by the effort simply to secure the best possible conditions for myself and my family."[10] Diverted he was from his basic aim, as he wrote, but not completely. The concern for the general welfare and the quest for the ultimate meaning of life, which had engrossed his deepest reflection, were not dismissed altogether. This must be clear to any thoughtful reader of his two greatest novels.

It is a mistaken notion that at the age of fifty, after having written *Anna Karenina,* Tolstoy suddenly turned right about face and changed his entire course of life. The true account is different. Tolstoy's conversion was dramatic, decisive; it did change radically his course and career during the remaining thirty years of his life. But it was not sudden and abrupt. In the later Tolstoy we can note the fuller and more resolute recognition of a truth which was lurking in his spirit during his entire life, despite divergences and deviations and backslidings and seeming oblivion—until finally his pitiless sincerity brought him squarely before the inevitable issue, and he confronted it and grappled with it as a man and a devotee.[11]

The moral and religious crisis in the late seventies, which led to Tolstoy's writing his *Confession* and indicated clearly the new paths he had resolved to follow, was anticipated almost twenty years earlier, when the death of his brother Nikolai confronted him sharply with the problem of the finalities of value and meaning in human existence. His intense creative activity which produced his two masterpieces postponed the great reversal in his own life quite as much as the spreading happiness of his married life. But already in *War and Peace* he was grappling imaginatively with the problem of the lasting significance of human life and the moral issues of love and marriage. These two problems Tolstoy took up imperatively in his next novel.

Anna Karenina has impressed most readers and critics by its masterly portrayal of the adulterous love of Anna and Alexey Vronsky: its ominous invasion of an honest soul, its feverish intensity and abandon, its dissolution of the emotional and moral personality, and its disastrous final ruin. But *Anna Karenina* does not stop with the exposure of pestilential illicit passion. Tolstoy's probing of the problem of love and marriage reached a deeper issue. The seeker after the decisive meaning of life asked whether human existence can be justified and blessed by love alone, be it even as stainless as his own, Tolstoy's love for Sonya. This is the autobiographical significance of the story of the love and married life of Konstantin Levin and Kitty Shtcherbatsky, which forms the counterpart in the novel to the adulterous passion of Anna and Alexey Vronsky.

Tolstoy's portrait of Levin is autobiographic. Levin is a wealthy landowner of an intensely serious and self-critical turn of mind. He is not a saint; the book of his life has filthy pages of debauch; but the miserable memory of them is countered by an eroding thought of the futility of his outwardly blameless mature life. Gloomy he is not because he is still hankering after vice but because he cannot see clearly what gives a virtuous life enduring worth. He had realized his dream of marrying Kitty, and his new life satisfied him for some time; but before very long the old doubts and discontent returned. The death of his brother and the birth of his own child—two events described unforgettably in the novel—bring Levin face-to-face with ultimate problems. He takes good care of his peasants; he is honest in his dealings; he is true and loving to his wife: but what is it all about? " 'Without knowing what I am, and why I am here, it is impossible to live. Yet I cannot know that, and therefore I can't live,' he said to himself. 'In an infinity of time, matter, and space, a bubble organism separates itself, maintains itself awhile, and then bursts, and that bubble is—I!' . . . And though he was a happy and healthy family man, Levin was several times so near to suicide that he hid a cord he had lest he should hang himself, and he feared to carry a gun lest he should shoot himself."[12]

It is quite clear that in *Anna Karenina* we have not only a portrayal of a man in spiritual struggle and anguish, but the portrayal of him by an author who was himself struggling and anguished spiritually. We know what the people who read the novel when it was first published did not understand: the struggle of life and death that was going on in Tolstoy's soul—the struggle of a man whose genius the world admired and approved, but who was not sure that God approved it, or approved him, or was in any way concerned with him; worse, was not certain whether there was any God to approve or be concerned, and was utterly dismayed by the uncertainty. The novelist of *Anna*

Karenina would soon be engrossed in the writing of his *Confession*.
The more he saw of life and the more he thought about it, the less satisfied he became. What was the meaning of it all? He had some fifteen thousand acres of land in the Samara province and three hundred horses. He was a nobleman of most distinguished parentage, with an enviable military record, a devoted wife, a happy family: but what did it all matter in the end? He was a world-famous writer, but suppose that he were to become "more famous than Gogol or Pushkin or Shakespeare or Molière, or than all the writers in the world—and what of it?" Was there any meaning in his life that would not be gone the moment he died? "I felt that what I had been standing on had collapsed, and that I had nothing left under my feet." While the public marveled at the genius revealed in Tolstoy's portrayal of Levin's spiritual anguish, in *Anna Karenina,* that genius himself battled with Levin's problems and, despairing in his failure to master them, contemplated hanging himself from the crossbeam of his study and "ceased to go out shooting with a gun, lest I should be tempted by so easy a way of ending my life."[13]

He remembered an Oriental fable about a traveler running away from a wild beast. The traveler seeks refuge inside a dry well, but sees at its bottom a dragon with gaping jaws. He seizes and clings to a twig growing in a crack of the wall and barely holds on; in dismay he sees two mice, a black one and a white one, gnawing at his branch. Thus menaced any moment to lose his last grip on life, the poor traveler licks some drops of honey which drip from the leaves of his already bending branch. "And this is not a fable, but the real unanswerable truth intelligible to all. . . . The two drops of honey, . . . my love of my family, and of writing—art as I called it—were no longer sweet to me."[14]

Like his Levin, Tolstoy reflected: "In infinite space, in infinite time, infinitely small particles change their forms in infinite complexity, and when you have understood the laws of those mutations of form, you will understand why you live on the earth."[15] You will understand why you live, and why you die, too; but not what is the meaning and the worth of it all. Neither science nor philosophy could give Tolstoy an answer to that last vital question. Yet despite this fatal quandary men all about him still somehow kept on living: Was there some understanding of life of which he was ignorant? The various answers of the people of his own class—he listed them in turn—were of no avail; but what about any possible wisdom of the ignorant peasants, who lacked the pleasures and comforts of their masters yet lived on contentedly to a ripe old age? Perhaps they, the benighted ones by the standards of society, perhaps they had this true wisdom. He had to understand why those millions of humble folk should endure their poverty while he found his opulent life unendurable. Was it due to their plain dullness; or did those peasants, after all, possess some saving insight?

And so, as Tolstoy wrote, "I began to draw near to the believers among the poor, simple unlettered folk: pilgrims, monks, sectarians, and peasants. . . . I began to look well into the life and faith of these people, and the more I considered it the more I became convinced that they have a real faith, which is a necessity to them and alone gives their life a meaning and makes it possible for them to live."[16] When he asked them they told him that they tried to follow the law of God; but what could be the meaning of that law? For their simple minds that law included all manner of beliefs and practices and rituals which to his intelligence were rank superstition. But might not there be, along with this dull credulity, "the one thing needful" of which he read in the Gospel? This possible basic truth in religion, and first of all in the Christian religion of his peasants, he must discover and grasp. It was for him personally a matter of life or death.

Tolstoy, resolved to hold fast that which is good and true, would "prove all things." He would not prejudge the dogmatic theology or the ceremonials of the Orthodox Church. He joined the peasants in attending the church services, liturgy and genuflexion and holy water sprinkling and the Eucharist and all. At home he stacked his library with religious books and Bibles and Gospels in many languages. And before long, in his forthright study of Scriptures and orthodox treatises, he began separating the wheat from the chaff, the kernel from the shell. As he grasped and cherished the teachings of Jesus in the Four Gospels, he reached the conclusion that dogmatic orthodox theology had distorted their straightforward meaning and misplaced the center of true religious devotion. His study of other religions showed him similar obscuring of their glad tidings, in fogs of ritualism and abstruse theology. But despite dogmatism and superstition, the true message of all great religions was unmistakable. There is a divine reality; it is present in every one of us, and in our way of life we can increase or repress it. The godlike life is expressed in the Golden Rule; it is the heart of Christ's religion. Jesus aimed to point out to you and to me the way to God. What he taught was not a system of doctrines but a divine ideal of life. We are all children of the same Father, but most of us are prodigal sons; we have forgotten our divine origin and destiny; we have forsaken the home of our Father and are wasting our substance in riotous living. Jesus would rouse us to come to ourselves, to return home, to seek and to find the meaning of life, to learn how we can live for God and for our fellowmen. And Tolstoy set himself most earnestly to learn in detail what Jesus taught about this godlike life.

This earnest inquiry, study and exposition of the Gospels, absorbed Tolstoy's energies. Neither his wife nor his friends could understand his new direction. Countess Tolstoy could not fathom her husband's upset, as she called it. "We all love one another. He is loved and respected by us all. All submit to him and live happily with such a wise and loving guide. He is occupied with the literary work which he loves; it brings him the people's affection, and fame, and money. What more is he looking for?"[17] Devoted as she had always been to all his work, she wrote to her sister: "He reads and thinks till his head aches, and all to show how incompatible the Church is with the teaching of the Gospel. Hardly ten people in Russia will be interested in it; but there is nothing to be done. I only wish he would get it done quicker, and that it would pass like an illness."[18] Countess Sonya's entries in her *Diaries* record in far more poignant words the tragedy in her family life: her inability to share what she regarded as her husband's religious obsession and her sore irritation by his altered way of life; his inability to realize that to her nothing finally mattered except her absolute need of his love. "He cried out aloud today that his most passionate desire was to get away from his family. To my last breath shall I remember this candid exclamation, which seemed to tear out my heart. . . . I am begging God to let me die, for I cannot live without his love. . . . He is full of Christianity and the idea of self-perfection. I am jealous."[19]

His friends and former admirers complained that he had turned his back on life; but Tolstoy replied that it was because they, not he, had mistaken the true meaning of life. He did not write another *War and Peace,* but, doubtless feeling his wife's anxiety about him, he tried to reassure her: "Now it is clearing up. . . . Ah, God willing, what I am going to write will be very important." He was not like his good friend, the poet Fet who, as Tolstoy put it, "at sixteen wrote: 'The spring bubbles, the moon shines, and she loves me,' and who went on writing and writing, and at sixty wrote: 'She loves me, and the spring bubbles, and the moon shines.' "[20] He, Tolstoy, was learning new and better tunes. His chief aim as an artist now was not merely to describe life as it was but also to draw life as it should be, to understand and to proclaim the moral and religious ideals of Jesus.

The fallacy of men's lives is this, that the average person devotes his endeavors to devising means of self-gratification and self-aggrandisement. Man seeks his own interest, his own pleasure and profit and power; he thinks he can never be so happy as when he can enforce his will on the will of others. This egoism, this lust for self-assertion and self-indulgence—sexual, economic, political, intellectual—this is responsible for the evils in life. Egoism poisons the home; it twists the social fabric of our civilization; it leads thinking to cynicism instead of yielding spiritual peace. The Gospel of Jesus, Tolstoy declared, consisted precisely in pointing out and rejecting this evil, this fallacy of life. "Man gives himself to the illusion of egoism, lives for himself—and he suffers. It suffices that he begin to live for others, and the suffering becomes lighter, and there is obtained the highest good in the world: love of people."[21] By denying the low aims in life we can turn towards higher spiritual realization: "Whosoever would save his life shall lose it: and whosoever shall lose his life for my sake shall find it. For what shall a man be profited, if he shall gain the whole world, and forfeit his life?"[22]

To match the Decalogue of Mount Sinai, Tolstoy pointed out five commandments in the Sermon on the Mount which Jesus stated with unquestionable clearness and simplicity and which should be recognized as the foundation of the genuine Christian religion.[23]

"Ye have heard that it was said to them of old times, Thou shalt not kill; and whosoever shall kill shall be in danger of the judgment: but I say unto you, that every one who is angry with his brother shall be in danger of the judgment."[24] This first commandment is hard—so hard indeed that some old readers or copyists must have sought to soften it by adding after the clause "everyone who is angry with his brother" the words "without a cause," thus nullifying the force and indeed the real sense of the commandment. (As we know today, the modern revisions of the Gospel have recognized and excluded this interpolation.) According to Tolstoy, Jesus stated plainly and simply: Anger in the heart is murder; be not angry. And when Jesus added the admonition against calling one's brother "Raca" or "thou fool," he emphasized the moral claim which each man has upon us. We are not to excuse our anger or the evil we do to some man by scorning him as foolish and worthless, a nobody, of no account.

Tolstoy obeyed this commandment by allaying animosity in his own personal relations. Had he not quarreled with Ivan Turgenev, challenged him to a duel, and despite some formal pacifications remained estranged from him? In April, 1878 he wrote Turgenev that he was overjoyed to find in his soul no longer any hate but only hope for their renewed mutual friendship. Would his old friend forgive him for all his blame and be assured of all the comradeship of which he is capable? It was reported that Turgenev wept when he read that letter. For his part he not only responded readily to the friendly appeal but later when almost from his deathbed, wrote to Tolstoy a letter in the noblest spirit. He, Turgenev, could not share Tolstoy's religious devotion, and he urged his friend, "great writer of our Russian land," to return to his former creative activity; but he sent him his warmest friendly farewell.[25]

The second commandment of Jesus stresses the spiritual principle in a most intimate personal relation. Here Jesus is likewise perfectly clear: "Ye have heard that it was said, Thou shalt not commit adultery; but I say unto you, that every one that looketh on a woman to lust after her hath committed adultery with her already in his heart. . . . It was said also, Whosoever shall put away his wife, let him give her a writing of divorcement: but I say unto you, that every one that putteth away his wife, saving for the cause of fornication, maketh her an adulteress; and whosoever shall marry her when she is put away committeth adultery."[26] By very persistent examination of the Greek text and various translations, Tolstoy supported his interpretation of this commandment by correcting the clause "saving for the cause of fornication" (as if it referred to the wife) to read "besides the sin of dissoluteness," as referring to the husband who divorces his wife so that he can marry another.[27] In this second commandment, Tolstoy insisted, Jesus condemned sensuality, lust. Whether a union of passion is sanctified by the Church or is in secret or overt defiance of social and religious conventions: it is all the same debased so long as it is not transfigured by a motive nobler than the urge for self-gratification. If the incentive to marriage is merely sexual pleasure, that marriage is adultery in God's eyes; it is surely damned. The family relation includes sex, but it can yield a moral homelife only as it is transfigured by higher purposes and more integral personal communion. Tolstoy's moral reason sought to grasp this interpretation of Jesus's second commandment, and his creative imagination also gave it living portrayal, as in his works, *The Kreutzer Sonata* and *Resurrection*.

The third commandment in the Sermon on the Mount affects the political sphere and official relations. "Again ye have heard that it was said to them in old time, Thou shalt not forswear thyself, but shall perform unto the Lord thine oaths: but I say unto you, Swear not at all, . . . but let your speech be Yea, yea; Nay, nay: and whatsoever is more than that is of the evil one."[28] To Tolstoy this commandment did not mean a condemnation of profanity and cursing, taking the name of God in vain. It was interpreted by Tolstoy to signify the attitude of Jesus towards government and official oaths of obligation. Jesus charged us to keep—respect and preserve—our spiritual freedom. Do not pledge yourself absolutely to duties and alliances of which your better conscience may disapprove tomorrow. Do not surrender to another man nor to an institution or system your moral right and duty to act at any future time in accordance with your own best light. How can you, taking an oath, lay your hand on a cross or on the Gospels, when the crucified Lord declared strictly in the Gospels, *Swear not at all?* Your oaths in any assumed official position, military or civil or whatever, subject your will to the order of someone else; but the responsibility for your actions is and must remain yours alone.

Related to the third commandment, which concerns a person's relation to the official social system, Jesus taught in another commandment the right principle in our attitude towards aliens, and more broadly in the whole problem of international relations. "Ye have heard that it was said, Thou shalt love thy neighbor and hate thine enemy; but I say unto you, Love your enemies, and pray for them that persecute you. . . . For if ye love them that love you, . . . what do ye more than others? Do not the Gentiles do the same?"[29] The reference to "the Gentiles" elucidates the expanded meaning of Jesus's basic teaching of love as the guiding motive of life. The term "neighbor," in the Jewish usage, signified a Jew, as may be seen clearly in the Parable of the Good Samaritan; it meant "a fellow-countryman, a man of one's own people." The term "enemy" signified the alien, the Gentiles, the national foes. Against this narrow nationalistic outlook Jesus declared: "Know that all men are brothers, sons of one God; and do not infringe peace with any one for the sake of national aims."[30] You have been taught patriotism, the exclusive love for your own people; but I tell you, love all nations, love all men. Jesus would replace narrowly patriotic devotion by all-human fellowship. In this spirit Tolstoy wrote emphatically: "I now know that my unity with others cannot be destroyed by a frontier line, or by a governmental decree that I am to belong to this or that nation. I now know that all men, everywhere, are equals and brothers. . . . I now understand that welfare is only possible to me on condition of my acknowledging my oneness with all people in the world without exception."[31]

The commandment which Tolstoy regarded as the most fundamental of all and as the keystone of the truly Christian moral edifice and the heart of the religion of Jesus has been called the law of nonresistance. "Ye have heard that it was said, An eye for an eye, and a tooth for a tooth: but I say unto you, Resist not him that is evil: but whosoever smiteth thee on thy right cheek, turn to him the other also. And if any man would go to law with thee, and take away thy coat, let him have thy cloak also. And whosoever shall compel thee to go one mile, go with him two. Give to him that asketh thee, from him that would borrow of thee turn not thou away."[32] Theological commentators through the centuries have qualified this teaching so as to adapt it to our own worldly practices. Of course, they have said, Jesus condemned relentless vindictive retaliation; but he surely did not mean to prohibit the restraint or punishment of the wrong-doer so as to safeguard public and private security. Both orthodox dogmatists and freethinking liberals come to his commandment with the unquestioned assumption that the preservation of our social order is the sacrosanct first principle. But, according to Tolstoy, that is precisely what Jesus questioned when he declared his universal law of love under all conditions. By returning evil for evil you can make the wrongdoer no longer dangerous, but not better. Now, you may say, when I have once rendered him harmless, then I can with safety try to convert him to a good life. This is moral confusion. By force you may cow the evildoer into submission, but you can get him to follow God freely only by love. Do not resort to violence in any circumstances, private or public. Love is the law of the Christian life, and only love can arouse love.

This commandment may be criticized as impracticable and

inexpedient. That in fact is the most common and persistent criticism of it. So we read in Tolstoy's *Diaries* of his discussion with the Countess and with the poet Fet: "The Christian teaching is unworkable."—"So it is folly?"—"No, but impracticable."—"Have you tried to practise it?"—"No, but it is impracticable."[33] Now it is precisely against our worldly pursuit of the practicable and the expedient that Jesus protests. Whether we follow him or not, we should at least not be confused or evasive about his crystal-clear teaching. In his Gospel Jesus upset the worship of expediency and put in its place the worship of God, who is not the ideal of practicality and expediency, but of holiness, who does not as a reasonable shepherd remain prudently with his ninety-nine sheep that are safe in the fold, but like a loving shepherd goes out in search of the one lost sheep.

The average man is much more conformist in his beliefs than he is in his daily conduct. Most men seem quite ready to include in their doctrine any creed which is solemnly pronounced to them and to which they nod assent and which is to take them to heaven, if only it is reasonable in its practical applications and does not interfere unduly with their worldly affairs. And that is the usual way in which people judge each other, as Tolstoy observed in his own case. But then his earnest study of the Gospels revealed to him the supreme truths of the good and godlike life. He adopted the explicit teachings of Jesus, which required a radical reformation of a person's life and of the established social system. As he pointed out in his *Critique of Dogmatic Theology* and other writings, his conversion to the spiritual ideals of the Gospels was also a radical departure from the system of beliefs and practices and ritual of traditional Christianity. He repeated his conviction that the religion of Jesus was not a theological system but a Gospel of the blessed life. He endeavored to follow it by striving to rid his soul of anger, of lust and violence and all selfishness and to cherish the spirit of love and universal fellowship.

The Holy Synod of the Russian Orthodox Church, which was closely allied with the autocratic regime of the Tsar, was more and more alarmed by the spreading popular influence of Tolstoy in "Holy Russia" and finally resolved to excommunicate him officially. In February, 1901, the Holy Synod issued its anathema of "the new false teacher—Count Leo Tolstoy. . . . In his works and letters, distributed in great numbers by him and his followers throughout the whole world, and particularly within the borders of our dear land, he preaches with zealous fanaticism the overthrow of all the dogmas of the Orthodox Church and the very essence of the Christian faith. . . ." Contrary to the full confidence of the Church hierarchy in its sovereign authority over the people, its edict evoked universal protest which spread throughout the world and found expression in countrywide demonstrations of admiration for Tolstoy. Countess Sonya, declaring her own unalterable orthodoxy, wrote in indignation to the Holy Synod for their excommunication of her earnestly religious husband who, like many others outside the Church, led a more truly Christian life than certain high ecclesiastics "wearing diamonded miters and stars." Tolstoy himself answered the Holy Synod in a spirit of Christian charity but firm rededication to his Gospel convictions, and continued devoutly in his search and practice of the teachings of Jesus.[34] But in a certain sense the Holy Synod was right, for Tolstoy's teachings did aim at the repudiation of the institutional system of orthodox beliefs and practices. In his *Diaries* he wrote explicitly that the chief service to mankind in our time would be the destruction of the distorted Christianity and the establishment of the true Christian religion.[35]

Tolstoy's beliefs were not beliefs about things but beliefs in principles, commitments, and loyalties. Thus believing in the

Gospel of Jesus, he was resolved to follow it in directing every part of human life. It became for him the program of all reform—political, social, economic, artistic, intellectual—and not only as a general principle, but as applied to himself, to Leo Tolstoy.

He considered the teachings of Jesus as they should apply to his career as a literary artist, and more generally as a member of the intelligentsia. People speak loftily of the "division of labor"—but what is right division of labor? Do the scientist, the novelist or dramatist, the poet, the musician, the artist serve directly the spiritual needs of the workers who by their labor satisfy directly his physical needs? When a scientist compiles a catalogue of a million beetles, when an artist paints opulence, when a poet indulges in sophisticated fancies, and all help themselves to the products of the peasant's toil, is there any fair division or exchange of labor?

Tolstoy pursued this problem in his essay entitled *What is Art?* Great art is to be judged by its capacity to communicate itself to universal humanity: not only to some aesthetic coterie but to all men and women however simple and humble. A work of art which fails or refuses to perform this chief function for a part, and that by far the greater part of humanity, is bad art, no matter how highly it might be praised by those who, in lauding it, aristocratically isolate themselves from the common people. "The destiny of art in our time is to transmit from the realm of reason to the realm of feeling the truth that well-being for men consists in being united together, and to set up, in place of the existing reign of force, that Kingdom of God, *i.e.*, of love, which we all recognize as the highest aim of human life."[36] "Art is only one and consists in this: to increase the sinless general joys accessible to all—the good of man."[37] Tolstoy applied this principle in a radical and negative rejudgment of traditionally proclaimed literary and artistic masterpieces, and of his own works also; discarding *War and Peace* and *Anna Karenina* and saving only stories like "The Prisoner of Caucasus" as an example of universal art communicating the very slightest feelings common to all men, and "God Sees the Truth" ("The Long Exile") as belonging to religious art, transmitting feelings of love of God and our fellowmen.

Tolstoy applied his understanding of the Gospel of Jesus in dealing with the problems of social-economic reform. He offered his services as a worker to the Russian census bureau, choosing for his district the slums of Moscow, to see directly the homes and lives of the submerged masses. There he learned that those people cannot be saved from squalor and degradation merely by almsgiving. Organized charity cannot cure the ills of poverty, for the idle and wasteful affluence of the upper classes not only impoverishes the multitudes but also corrupts them by rousing in their souls greed and envy and distorted ideas of happiness through mere possession.

The pursuit of pleasure and sensual enjoyment and idle luxury is not repellent to us aristocrats only because we are all morally dull and do not realize the daily enormity of our lives. Consider, my titled friends, Tolstoy exclaimed, bethink yourselves: what are you about? Here are a hundred women at a festive ball. "Each woman at this ball whose dress costs a hundred and fifty rubles was not born at the ball, but she has lived also in the country, has seen peasants, knows her own nurse and maid, whose fathers and brothers are poor, for whom earning one hundred and fifty rubles to build a cottage with is the end and aim of a long, laborious life; she knows this; how can she, then, enjoy herself, knowing that on her half-naked body she is wearing the cottage which is the dream of her housemaid's brother?"[38]

But what is to be done? For this is the title of the book from which we are quoting—*What Is to be Done?* Stop thinking all the time of yourselves, of your desires and pleasures and so-called cultural demands, and think a while of your fellowmen. But you may insist: what difference would it make in the end? My philanthropic drop in the ocean would make no real change; things will go on as they are just the same. "If I came among savages," Tolstoy replied, "who gave me chops which I thought delicious, but the next day I learned (perhaps saw myself) that these delicious chops were made of a human prisoner who had been slain in order to make them; and if I think it bad to eat men, however delicious the cutlets may be, and however general the custom to eat men among the persons with whom I live, and however small the utility to the prisoners who have been prepared for food my refusal to eat them may be, I shall not and will not eat them."[39]

An Oriental proverb has the truth in a nutshell: If there is one man idle there is another dying of hunger. This problem is quite simple; it needs only willingness and resolution to solve it. "If a horseman sees that his horse is tired out, he must not remain on its back and hold up its head, but first of all get off." Feed the horse, Tolstoy said, but first of all get off the horse's back! Make sure, first of all, that by your own personal way of life you are not enslaving the lives of others. The more you spend on yourself, the more you oblige others to labor for you; the less you spend and consume, the more you yourself work, the better member of society you are. Give to the poor, yes, but first, stop the spread of poverty by your own excessive drain of the social resources. The realization of this truth was compared by Tolstoy to the experience of a man who, having started on a certain errand, finds out that it is futile and wrong, and turns back home. What had been on his right hand would now be on his left, and what had been to the left would be to the right. This is the meaning of our conversion to the social gospel of Jesus in brief: a gospel to the weary and heavy-laden, but also to a certain rich man.

This teaching could not remain mere preachment; it was initially and finally a self-probing and self-judgment. Tolstoy asked himself: How can I, Lyof Tolstoy, how can I stop exploiting others and using them as my servitors? Well, I can take care of my own room; I can clean my own boots; indeed I can make my own boots; I can go out in the fields and by my own work produce the equivalent of the food which I consume. And only after I have done this, only then shall I have a right to offer my help to my fellowmen without feeling like a robber who returns part of the booty. Nor am I, in so doing, rejecting the true dignity of mental work. The maximum time that I can spend in really productive mental activity is five hours a day. I sleep eight hours. What do I do with the remaining eleven hours? Let me, during this time, relieve the peasant of some manual labor; let me allow him some little rest, a chance to have a cup of tea and think may be for half an hour.

Still, what was Tolstoy to do with his large property, with his thousands of acres of land, with the copyrights of his writings? The rich young man of the Gospel, whom Jesus asked to give his wealth to the poor, was presumably a bachelor; Tolstoy's case was quite different. Would he be justified in giving away all his estate to the poor, to the peasants? That would have compelled his wife and his five sons and three daughters to give up their rich life and follow him, maybe contrary to their personal convictions—and compulsion is wrong, according to the Gospel. Besides, Countess Sonya had helped to increase his wealth: he could not give away her and her children's shares. On the other hand, he could no longer keep it up and remain honest in his convictions. Tolstoy's solution was to renounce all rights to his estate; he turned it over to the Countess to manage as she saw fit. In his own house he remained as a guest.

Each day he spent several hours in manual labor, earning his own bread directly. He wrote steadily but declared all his work, from then on, free of copyright, free for anyone to publish and circulate. Only when the Dukhobors faced punishment for their refusal to serve in the army, Tolstoy copyrighted his novel *Resurrection* to raise funds for their planned emigration to Canada where freedom and respect for their religious convictions were promised them. In his stories and essays he advocated the gospel teaching of universal love and fellowship, in opposition to all violence and selfishness.

But still he felt that he was not able to live as unselfishly as he ought, even though only a guest at Yasnaya Polyana. In the year 1897, he wrote the following letter to his wife and put it among his papers, asking that it be delivered to her after his death—only the beginning of it is cited here:

"My dear Sonya:

"Already for a long time I have been tortured by the contradiction existing between my life and my religious convictions. I could not oblige you to change your life—the habits to which I myself accustomed you . . . but I cannot continue living as I have lived here sixteen years; . . . and now I have decided to carry out that which for a long time I have wished to do—to go away. . . ." More than thirteen years elapsed before Tolstoy carried out this decision, and on November 10, 1910, fled from his house at Yasnaya Polyana to seek his peace in seclusion with God. He was eighty-two years old and, as it turned out, very seriously ill. He was unable to continue on his road in the cold weather and had to stop over at the railway station of Astapovo, where his condition worsened; inflammation of the lungs set in, and his life slowly ebbed away. His last words as he was losing consciousness were: "All is well, . . . all is simple and well . . . well . . . yes, yes."[40]

Who is to judge Tolstoy's faith and his life? His own parable of "The Two Old Men" is addressed as much to himself as to the rest of us. Two peasants, Yefim and Yelisei, set out on a pilgrimage to Jerusalem. But Yelisei is delayed on his journey by the call of mercy and, having spent on a poor family most of the money which he had saved up for his pilgrimage, he is obliged to return to his village. Yefim proceeds on his way alone, wary of strangers and prudently calculating from beginning to end. But when he finally reaches his goal, arriving just in time to elbow his way inside the Church of the Holy Sepulchre, behold! he catches sight of Yelisei, there ahead of him, clear up towards the altar. It is only Yefim's vision, of course, and it is Tolstoy's parable; but its message is unmistakable.

CHAPTER IX

ALBERT SCHWEITZER

Long shelves of autobiographies and journals include the lives of no persons more versatile than Albert Schweitzer. Only two come readily to mind: Leonardo da Vinci and Goethe, and no contemporary has approached him. His four doctorates—in theology, philosophy, medicine, and music—indicate the broad range of his mind's domains. During his first thirty years he pursued with seemingly equal interest philosophical studies, New Testament criticism, preaching and teaching, and organ-playing and construction, devoted mainly to the art of Johann Sebastian Bach, on which he became an outstanding authority. Then he decided to carry out a vow which he had made in a spirit of putting the Gospel of Jesus in daily practice, to consecrate his main energies to medical service to the primitive multitudes of central Africa. He went through the hard discipline of a German medical school and then proceeded to the Congo region where he built a hospital for the black natives, to which he was committed for more than half a century. In his healing ministration to human ills he was guided by a farther reaching spiritual principle: reverence for all life wherever found.

Dr. Schweitzer has been called a modern saint, and he was doubtless one of the greatest men of our age. The self-recorded accounts of his life and his writings on many important subjects express the highest aspirations and are bound to impress his readers with mingled admiration and humility. Where else in our world could we find a better example of living Christianity in practice than in his jungle hospital at Lambaréné, on the bank of the equatorial African river Ogowe?

Schweitzer's books, *Memoirs of Childhood and Youth* and *Out of My Life and Thought,* chronicle the very early manifestations of the dominant ideas and interests of his versatile spirit. He was born in 1875, the second child of a German Lutheran pastor in upper Alsace, when that province was under German rule, following the Franco-Prussian War of 1870-1871. His forebears had been ministers, schoolmasters, organists: these three—religious service, education, music—marked the Schweitzer family tradition. Young Albert continued the tradition along all three lines, by training himself for the careers of a university professor, a Lutheran pastor, and an organ concert artist. When he was only six months old his family moved to Grünzbach, in the Münster valley; but he remembered that his birthplace was Kaysersberg, the early home of Geiler von Kaysersberg, the contemporary of Savonarola, whose preaching at the Strassburg cathedral had enduring renown. Did Schweitzer, in his critical review of scores of modern alternative interpretations of the character and career of Jesus, mention the comment attributed to his fifteenth-century predecessor: "The Holy Scripture is like a wax nose, every one twists it to serve his notion"?[1]

Schweitzer's memoirs of his childhood, as we might surmise, include both anticipation of his later convictions and radical shifts in his attitudes. His strong distaste for writing his thankyou Christmas letters was partly due to his difficulty in composition and also to his having to do his writing in his father's study which smelled so disagreeably of the old leather-bound books. He vowed that he would never bury himself in such an illsmelling den: not he—the future lifelong reader and writer by midnight oil! The spirit of compassion which was to mark his career as a medical missionary found early expression in his aversion to killing or mistreatment of any living thing. He recalled his remorse when he had switched his dog that barked at the postman, although he knew that patting it would have served his purpose; or when he whipped his overtired horse to keep it trotting. Once or twice he went hunting and fishing with boys who urged him to come along, but had to give it up. The commandment "Thou shalt not kill" sounded in his ears. After saying his prayers at night he would add one of his own: "O, heavenly Father, protect and bless all things that have breath; guard them from all evil and let them sleep in peace." It was a lad's reach towards his ultimate principle of Reverence for All Life.[2]

In his schooling he had his ups and downs, or better, his downs and ups. His first school terms were very disappointing; he was given to daydreaming and desultory reading rather than to steady attention to his studies, and his grades were so low that questions were raised regarding his withdrawal. Happily for him, a new teacher gripped his attention from the outset, showed him what carefully prepared mastery meant and what real zeal could accomplish. Young Albert's performance rose up the scale and erelong he was moving towards the top. Without evasion and without boasting he recounted his lapses as well as his accomplishments, in his poor attempt at drawing and verse-making but also in his extraordinary advance in music. His father started giving him piano lessons when he was only five. Two years later he surprised his schoolmistress by improvising on the harmonium. Organ-playing was in the family tradition, and he felt at home as soon as he touched the keyboard. After only a year's practice the nine-year-old boy was able to take the place of the church organist when the latter had to be absent one Sunday. Of course he needed instruction in technique and interpretation. Fortunately he could go to a fine organist, Eugène Münch, who taught him more than finger exercises. He showed him the difference between correct playing and genuine musical interpretation, and, very important, he introduced him to the great organ music of Johann Sebastian Bach.[3]

Young Schweitzer's compassionate sensitiveness was not limited to his treatment of dogs and birds and fishes. The humanitarianism that was to mark his later career in the African jungles expressed itself in his boyhood in his eagerness to feel and to be felt as a real comrade by the poorer boys in school. Being the pastor's son he was regarded by them as a sprig of the gentry, and he could never be really one of them so long as the external marks of exclusiveness set him apart. They would twit him with being well fed, with his evening meal of hot meat broth. So he resolved to be as much like them as possible. He insisted on wearing wooden clogs to school, for no village lad wore leather shoes on weekdays. In winter, like them, he would put on only fingerless gloves and the plainest brown cap. He had been given an overcoat made out of one of his father's; but the tailor's praise—"By Jove, Albert, now you're a regular gentleman!"— was enough to make him refuse to appear on the street in it. No amount of parental urging or even punishment for his strange obstinacy could alter his decision: he simply would not seem to be acting in any superior way but be only like the village boys.[4]

At his monthly missionary services his father read to his congregation one season the memoirs of a missionary to the Basuto tribesmen in South Africa. Those accounts of lowly primitive lives made a deep impression on the pastor's boy. This compassion for suffering humanity in the Dark Continent was stirred further by his seeing in Colmar the monument to Admiral Bruat, at the base of which was the stone figure of a Negro, the carved sadness of whose face young Schweitzer could not get out of his memory. In later years, on his periodic trips from Lambaréné to Europe, he made it a point to revisit Colmar and see that statue.[5]

We are not to expect thorough consistency in the youth's

convictions. For all his self-leveling, he could not deny himself an exception. He did see his first bicycle and how the rider could wheel along like the wind into the beautiful countryside. He had earned some money tutoring pupils in mathematics and invested it in a secondhand bicycle on which he was soon riding out into the woods which he loved. But pastor's sons were not expected to ride bicycles in Grünzbach; well, he would avoid exclusiveness in externals, but in some important matters he did not propose to conform to popular ideas; and that did not apply only to bicycles. Even as a lad he was bent on raising questions and doing his own thinking. His career in Biblical criticism started very early. "When I was eight my father, at my own request, gave me a New Testament, which I read eagerly. Among the stories which interested me most was that of the Three Wise Men from the East. What did the parents of Jesus do, I asked myself, with the gold and other valuables which they got from these men? How could they have been poor after that? And that the Wise Men should never have troubled again about the Child Jesus was to me incomprehensible. The absence, too, of any record of the shepherds of Bethlehem becoming disciples, gave me a severe shock."[6]

Later, when he was being prepared for confirmation, though he felt deeply the religious striving in his heart, he also had questions which, as he was aware, he was not supposed to ask, and, as he wrote, "I kept myself closely shut up." The old Lutheran pastor to whom he had been sent could not fathom the seeming indifference of the youth. On one point, as Schweitzer felt though he did not speak out, they differed radically. The pastor instructed the confirmation class that "in submission to faith all reasoning must be silenced." But Schweitzer held: "I was convinced—and I am so still—that the fundamental principles of Christ have to be proved true by reasoning, and by no other method."[7]

In a section with a Latin title Schweitzer described some hard times at home during his last years at school. His father's meager income was overtaxed by the needs of his family of five children. Albert had outgrown his winter clothes and had to face the cold in his thin summer suit, unlike the other pupils; this was exclusiveness in the reverse. He knew his mother's daily worry to economize in every way possible and did his best to make no demands. But when the day of the final examinations approached, the problem of the required formal attire confronted him. The family did have a black frockcoat which fit him, and his uncle lent him his black trousers for the occasion. But they were far too short for him; when he put them on he had to lengthen his suspenders, which left a yawning gap below the waistcoat. Willy-nilly he had to appear in that attire, only to arouse a roar of laughter when he entered the examination room. Embarrassment was hard enough, but it all might have turned out badly for him, for the visiting examiner thought that the young fellow was trying to play the buffoon and took him through the paces with a drilling examination. Fortunately he turned to history, his own and also Albert's special interest, and the test ended happily, with a special praise for the youth in the graduation certificate. Conditions at home also improved materially before long. A better manse was provided for the pastor's family, and the inheritance of a small fortune from a relative of his mother's eased the home budget all around.[8]

At the age of eighteen, with greater assurance for his future, young Schweitzer was looking forward to his studies at the University of Strassburg. But he also wished to make further progress in his music. His mother's brother who was a businessman in Paris, invited him to spend his summer vacation in the capital, and he was accepted as a pupil by the famous organist Charles Widor. Widor was attracted to the Alsatian youth; the two became close friends and later collaborated in advancing the appreciation of the music of Bach.

At the University of Strassburg Schweitzer took up chiefly theology and philosophy. Before long he became absorbed in Biblical research; for good scholarly work he required not only Latin and Greek, which he already had from his gymnasium years, but also Hebrew, of which he had acquired only an elementary knowledge at school and the further more solid study of which cost him much persistent work. He passed his preliminary examination in it at the end of the first semester. Within weeks he had to begin his year of military service, but fortunately did not have to leave Strassburg and by the kindness of his captain was allowed to attend some university lectures.

When his term of summer manoeuvers in the uplands began, he put in his haversack his Greek Testament and his Professor Holtzmann's commentary. Thus began Schweitzer's searching critical inquiries into the early records of the Christian teachings. Several generations of New Testament scholars, mainly Germans, had traced the likely order in the composition of the Four Gospels: the later date of the profound theology of the Fourth Gospel following the three so-called Synoptic Gospels, of which that of Mark was the earliest, with Matthew and Luke using partly Marcan materials and partly another source no longer available to us in its entirety, the *Logia,* or reported Sayings and Acts of Jesus. This in broad terms was the view of his Professor Holtzmann; Schweitzer kept it in mind, but he chiefly studied the Gospel accounts themselves. We should remember him, at the age of eight, raising questions about the Three Wise Men and the shepherds at the manger of Bethlehem. Here at the army summer camp the university student-soldier was being confronted with passages in the Gospels which perplexed him in his interpretation of the historical character and teaching of Jesus. How did Jesus regard himself and his mission? Two chapters in the Gospel of Matthew, the tenth and the eleventh, engrossed him and left him "sorely puzzled." Jesus is reported as sending his disciples to spread his gospel, warning them of persecutions which they would suffer, but assuring them: "Ye shall not have gone through the cities of Israel, till the Son of Man be come."[9] Other passages in the Gospels also indicated that Jesus believed in this speedily forthcoming fulfillment. But the actual course of events, as related by the evangelists, did not realize these expectations. How are we, then, to understand and to interpret this view of the character and outlook of the historical Jesus, in relation to the other view also found in the Gospels, where Jesus is reported as giving a wholly spiritual interpretation of the Kingdom of God, as not a localized state or event, "lo here or there," but as a spiritual presence in us: "The Kingdom of God is within you"? And one other question: Why was Jesus seemingly evasive in his reply to John the Baptist's inquiry, whether he, Jesus, is the one who is to come, "he that cometh"?[10]

The systematic development and exposition of Schweitzer's interpretation dealing with these and other problems found expression in solid treatises to which he devoted many years of research, some of them in the primeval African forest. His most concise statement of his view may be cited from his autobiography, *Out of My Life and Thought:* "Of this I was certain: that Jesus had announced no kingdom that was to be founded and realised in the natural world, by Himself and the believers, but one that was to be expected as coming with the almost immediate dawn of a supernatural age."[11] His first systematic statement of this view was given in his work *The Secret of Jesus's Messiahship and Passion,* translated in English under the title, *The Mystery of the Kingdom of God.* This was followed by his extensive and thorough examination of the works of some threescore of his predecessors in New Testament Criticism, *From Reimarus to Wrede,* translated in English as *The Quest of the Historical Jesus.*

He proceeded next to a most searching study of Pauline theology, in two treatises, *Paul and his Interpreters* and *The Mysticism of Paul the Apostle*.

Schweitzer was, as he stated, "dealing with the most vital thing in the world's history." The vision of the coming of the Kingdom of God through the Gospel of Jesus was bound to be affected by the actual historical course of events. "We must always make a fresh effort to realize to ourselves that Jesus and His immediate followers were, at that time, in an enthusiastic state of intense eschatological expectation. We must picture them among the people, who were filled with penitence for their sins and with faith in the Kingdom, and the revelation of Jesus as the Son of Man, seeing in the eager multitude itself a sign that their reckoning of the time was correct. . . ."[12] But this expectation was not fulfilled, and in the ongoing course of history Christian eschatology underwent revisions. "What did the disciples do between Easter and Pentecost? The answer is that day by day they waited with the other believers. . . ."[13] The immediate rebound may be noted in the Epistles of St. Paul. "The apostle Paul had to wrestle with the problem, but it did not seriously affect him, because he took the view that the coming of the Kingdom was only postponed for a short time."[14] His eschatological vigilance and eagerness are expressed throughout his Epistles in a series of passages which Schweitzer quoted in detail. Yet though Paul expected that many of the converts to whom he wrote and whom he exhorted to watch and pray would themselves live to see the great consummation, he and all of them lived and died, and Christ the Lord did not return in his glory. Writing at the age of seventy-five, Schweitzer comments on the readjustment of ideas in Christian eschatology: The early Church as a whole held "that the death and resurrection of Jesus simply made it possible for the Kingdom to come some time, and that they must be content to wait for it. From the second generation onwards the arrival of the Kingdom becomes 'one far-off divine event,' and in later days it is infinitely far away. This change of necessity affects the nature of the expectation. Originally it had a dominant position at the very centre of the faith; now it falls into the background."[15]

We may return to the early stage of Schweitzer's studies in New Testament criticism, at the University of Strassburg. His conclusions were in sharp variance not only with traditional doctrines of orthodoxy but also with many modern liberal interpretations. Did he wonder how he would fare with his theological professors when he came up for his final examinations which were to include historical and textual and dogmatic studies? Fortunately for him he was entirely successful and received his degree. Despite disagreements in scholarly conclusions, his consecration to the Christian Gospel was as genuine and convincing as his intellectual integrity in Gospel research. Religion, he held, has "no reason for trying to avoid coming to terms with historical truth." But he was disturbed by "the painful consciousness that this new knowledge in the realm of history would mean unrest and difficulty for Christian piety." It was bound to be a shock to many to learn that the historical Jesus was capable of error, "because the supernatural Kingdom of God, the manifestation of which he announced as imminent, did not appear." But, Schweitzer pled, "what can we do in the face of what stands clearly recorded in the Gospels?" He cited St. Paul's words to the Corinthian church: "We can do nothing against the truth, but for the truth." His own conclusion was a confession but also a resolution: "I find it no light task to follow my vocation, to put pressure on the Christian Faith to reconcile itself in all sincerity with historical truth. But I have devoted myself to it with joy, because I am certain that truthfulness in all things belongs to the spirit of Jesus."[16] His words echo a magisterial declaration by St. Augustine.

The interests and activities of his versatile spirit were developing along several lines. The licentiate in theology was hard at work on his studies for the doctorate in the department of philosophy. For his doctoral dissertation he chose the subject of the religious philosophy of Kant. Meanwhile it was not to be understood that philosophy and theology were to rule out organ-playing. Schweitzer returned to Paris, planning to continue his training in organ-mastery under Widor while also working on his doctor's thesis. He made little use of commentaries and devoted all his study to Kant's own works. This combination of musical training and philosophical research involved a schedule of severe overwork that would have ruined a person of less sturdy constitution. He wrote that many times he would work all night at his philosophy and then go to Charles Widor for his organ lessons, without having had a wink of sleep. As if all that were not enough, he was also taking piano lessons, under two distinguished teachers! As it was, he did survive and was able to return to Germany with his completed thesis, and, after a summer at the University of Berlin, took his examination for the doctorate in philosophy at Strassburg. He was encouraged to qualify as a *Privatdozent* in philosophy, but, so it was hinted to him, he would have had to give up preaching, and that he regarded as a necessity of his being. So he preferred to remain a theologian with philosophical interests and competence. He did receive appointment in the Faculty of Theology, and at the age of twenty-seven gave his inaugural lecture on "The Logos Doctrine in the Fourth Gospel."

His bent for critical exposition, already productive in historical, theological, and philosophical research, manifested itself also in music. Widor who regarded him no longer as a pupil but as a young colleague, had been urging him to write a volume in French on the musical art of Bach. With his characteristic zeal and energy Schweitzer devoted himself to this work, and his published volume was received with wide acclaim. A growing demand for a German edition led him not to translate but to rewrite and expand his work from 455 to 844 pages. In contrast to the interpretations of Bach's art as pure music, Schweitzer regarded him as "poet and painter in sound. . . . His music is poetic and pictorial because its themes are born of poetic and pictorial ideas. Out of these themes the composition unfolds itself, a finished piece of architecture in lines of sound. . . . A soul which out of this world's unrest longs for peace and has already tasted peace, allows in this music others to share its own experience."[17]

From Bach's organ music and organ-playing Schweitzer proceeded to studies in the right and wrong way of organ construction. This led him to much toilsome but also instructive and very productive work in the rebuilding of old church organs, for which before long he was receiving tributes of praise from fellow musicians but also much resistance from managers of organ factories who disputed his exposure of their mechanical instruments. So here was another line of activity in his incredibly versatile career which was engrossing his seemingly inexhaustible energies. Yet another chapter of his life story was in prospect, and that the most inspiring.

Thus Schweitzer recorded the fertile years of his young life in its third decade. He was Principal of the Theological College of St. Thomas, with very pleasant living quarters; he was professor at the University of Strassburg, engaged in teaching and research in his favorite subjects; he was a devoted preacher; he was gaining wide recognition for his historical and critical scholarship; in his music he was an acknowledged authority on Bach, a concert organist, a respected specialist in the design and construction of organs throughout Europe. In all this various success in so many fields of what we call the higher life, what more could he desire or hope for himself? Yet he was oppressed by a sense of spiritual unfulfillment. Despite his exposure of the perplexities of orthodox Christian theology to which his New Testament studies had led him, he never wavered in his conviction that the Gospels contain the heart and soul of God's message to men. Jesus was and always remained for Schweitzer the supreme teacher who pointed the one true way to the blessed life. To grasp firmly the teaching—not so much the traditional doctrine about Jesus, but the living Gospel of Jesus, his great word to us—that was the deepest yearning and the highest aim of Albert Schweitzer: What is God's message to you and to me which Jesus brought and ever brings to us?

What does believing in Jesus mean, what must it mean in his, Schweitzer's, life? In all his achievements and satisfactions in his cultured world, he had around him on all sides the dismal evidence of the crying need and destitution of numberless human failures. What had he done, what was he doing to relieve all that distress? The concern for the woeful lot of the weary and the heavy-laden, which he had recognized as central in the teachings of Jesus—was this to remain simply a part of his religious study and learning, or did it not need also to be translated into his own daily life? "While at the university and enjoying the happiness of being able to study and even to produce some results in science and art, I could not help thinking continually of others who were denied that happiness by their material conditions or their health. . . . Many a time already had I tried to settle what meaning lay hidden for me in the saying of Jesus: 'Whosoever would save his life shall lose it, and whosoever shall lose his life for My sake and the Gospels shall save it.' "[18]

This whole problem had disturbed him since his early years; it had become more insistent just because of his own personal well-being. "It became steadily clearer to me that I had not the inward right to take as a matter of course my happy youth, my good health, and my power to work. Out of the depths of my feeling of happiness there grew up gradually within me an under-standing of the saying of Jesus that we must not treat our lives as being for ourselves alone. Whoever is spared personal pain must feel himself called to help in diminishing the pain of others. We must all carry our share of the misery which lies upon the world."[19] He reached his decision for himself when he was twenty-one. Until he reached his thirtieth year he would devote his life to his cultured pursuits; but after that he would undertake to help his fellowmen directly. For some years he considered various ways in which he must serve to alleviate distress, until as it happened, circumstances pointed out clearly his road to equatorial Africa.

His thirtieth birthday was approaching when he read an appeal by the Paris Missionary Society of their dire need of a physician for their mission field in the Gabon, the northern province of the French Congo colony in Africa. "Men and women who can reply simply to the Master's call, 'Lord, I am coming,' those are the people whom the Church needs." Then and there Schweitzer reached his decision. He wrote to his parents and friends that he had resolved to take a course in the medical school as a preparation for his chosen career as a medical missionary in wild Africa. He described their reactions to his declara-tion, most of them negative, discouraging, quite uncomprehend-ing. Charles Widor compared him to a general who would leave his directing headquarters to plunge into the thick of the battle. Others tried to fathom his real motive that might have led to his outlandish decision: discontent in his professional career or his popular fame as an artist, or maybe some sore disappointment in love? He preferred as a real kindness the "persons who made no attempt to dig their fists into my heart, but regarded me as a precocious young man, not quite right in his head, and treated me condescendingly with affectionate mockery."[20]

On the top of all, he had his doubts whether the Paris Mis-sionary Society, which had leaders of very dogmatic Protestant convictions, would accept such a known advocate of unorthodox ideas as himself. Just the same he was unwavering in his choice and settled down to the severe discipline of the medical school. Once again, as formerly in Paris, it was only his vigorous constitution which saw him through the tangled trail of mastering the entirely new field of scientific study and practice. At last he became a diplomaed doctor of medicine. The preparation for his new career was over; and the day for his active starting in it was at hand.

He had no illusions regarding the arduous character of the course which he was undertaking. There were problems of equipment and supplies, of reliable support, and first of all, of policies. The mission station of the Paris Society was at Lambaréné, on the Ogowe River in the general region of the Congo. The work had been started by American Protestant missionaries, but they had found complications in their operation in a French colony. The French government had no official Catholic objection to their Protestant affiliation, but it did insist that all instruction of and conference with the natives was to be carried on in the French language. The continued efforts of the Americans became too difficult on those terms, and so their work was taken over by the Paris Missionary Society. The leaders of the Society were quite glad to receive support from anyone or any group irrespective of their religious views, but they did insist on strict orthodoxy in selecting the missionaries whom they sent out.

Schweitzer foresaw trouble if he consented to a regular examination by the Society's committee; so he preferred to meet individually with a number of their leaders, explaining to them that his projected work in Africa was to be simply that of Christian medical ministration to the black natives. He planned to be merely a doctor who surely shared with the Society in true Christian love for the needy, who may not share all their beliefs but had no intention of preaching or teaching any doctrines. If they would only accept him and help him to start his hospital work, he would tend exclusively to his medical and surgical practice and would be "as mute as a fish" on any matters of Biblical doctrine. On this clear understanding, that he would not say or do anything that might give offense to the missionaries already at Lambaréné, he was accepted by the Society, but not without opposition. One of the more unyielding members of the committee sent in his resignation. He would not have an unorthodox Schweitzer curing black natives in Africa!

An interesting light on the wide range of Schweitzer's mind and character is thrown by his accounts of some details in his preparation for putting the Gospel into daily practice along the Equator. He would be going into the primeval forest, away from libraries or other materials for intellectual work. Despite the hard toil of his medical studies he took time to complete some of his theological writings. And was he going to say farewell for aye to his music? No more concerts, yes; but his Paris friends did provide him with a piano that had pedal attachments to simulate organ playing. He wrote an amusing account of the adventure which that heavy musical instrument had in being transported from the river steamer on an oversize dugout boat, then hoisted and tugged and almost sunk in the slimy bank and finally pulled up safely to dry ground.

We are moving ahead of our story. Before there could be any dry roof over that piano, there had to be a roof, and a cabin under that roof, and a clearing in the primeval forest; and earlier than that, the collection of funds to buy building materials, to say nothing of medicines and hospital supplies. The Missionary Society offered him some ground for his hospital and some initial help; but he soon understood that he would have to find himself the main support for his extensive undertaking. This he was to some degree successful in doing. Again and again through the years he would have to return to Europe where he used his fame as a concert artist to raise money for his hospital and staff, native or brought from Europe. There had to be a beginning, however modest. With a fair supply of the most immediately needed materials he at last sailed for his faraway African destination, on Good Friday, 1913. He was not alone on his voyage, for here we learn of his bride, Helene Bresslau, daughter of a Strassburg university professor. She shared his devotion to the relieving of human distress. With her at his side he was to begin the second and longer part of his life, in Christian service which was to tax all his powers and to sanctify his career.

Up and down the Ogowe River and its tributary streams Dr. Schweitzer's future patients were going to arrive in their canoes. He had read books on the tropical diseases that afflicted the African natives; he was not long in dealing with them at firsthand. The principal ones included malaria, leprosy, sleeping sickness, dysentery, but also surprisingly, pneumonia and heart disease; happily, no cancer or appendicitis. Surgery would be needed for cases of hernia, especially in painful, emergency cases of neglected and strangulated hernia, and for elephantiasis tumors.[21] All this was bound to be an immediate and staggering challenge to a beginning doctor who was just starting to unpack his medicines and supplies, and whose future hospital and patient wards were to be established in some run-down shacks on a strip of land that had been allotted to him out of the mission grounds.

The new doctor was helped from the outset, in his dealing with the natives, by their grateful memory of the good work done by an earlier doctor. They submitted to his treatment without the native, superstitious fears about which he had worried in advance. More immediately he had the devoted and competent help of his wife who had been trained as a nurse and proved of invaluable help to him in his surgery. All the same it had to be a rough primitive undertaking. Before they could move into the hut where they were to live they had a battle royal with the spiders and the cockroaches which had taken full possession of the place.

He had to begin with the very limited materials and building provisions which were on hand or were likely to be made available to him. We should also be warned that all the way through, his was to be a hospital in the jungle. The criticisms which have been made from time to time of Dr. Schweitzer's primitive hospital installation and conditions have been quite undeserved. He would have been glad and grateful if some of his critics had offered him sufficient funds to establish a truly modern hospital. The miracle is what he did achieve with his very limited resources in his wild tropical jungle. He wrote with grim humor that when he arrived at Lambaréné the only large structure allotted to him was a henhouse which he had to clean out and whitewash; after repairing the roof he "decided to promote it to the rank of hospital."[22] A little later, happily, he moved into a large corrugated-iron building. He had no finished lumber for his medicine cabinet shelves and had to use the boards of the packing cases in which the supplies had been shipped. He roofed his buildings with thatch of palm leaves; thus protected from the burning sun as well as from the tropical rains he could proceed with his medical treatments and surgery. In the course of time European medical associates joined him, but he had to start on his own. His first surgical assistant and interpreter was a former cook, whose French was definitely slanted towards the kitchen vocabulary. After hearing the report of a native suffering from hernia, he would inform the doctor that the man's right leg of mutton hurt him badly; or else that a woman had a pain in her upper left cutlet and in her loin. As the hospital work expanded and he needed larger quarters, Schweitzer had to construct new buildings, first clearing the thick jungle, cutting down the trees and using the heavy trunks for his beams and uprights—all this with such native labor as he could find or induce to do the work. To his many arts and professions was added that of a jungle architect. Many Negroes who had had schooling regarded themselves as above manual labor. When he asked a man in a white suit who had come to visit a patient to lend him a hand with the construction, the gentleman declined, as that sort of work was unbefitting an intellectual. "You're lucky," Schweitzer told the Negro, "I too wanted to become an intellectual, but I didn't succeed."[23]

The Schweitzers had barely unpacked their cases and supplies when long rows of native patients thronged the grounds from early morning. They waited their turn in the shade outside the henhouse hospital. Every day one of the assistants read out the Doctor's Standing Orders, which described the primitive people and conditions that somehow had to be kept in order. Schweitzer's problems and difficulties were not merely those of inadequate equipment and the natives' almost unmanageable lack of sanitation, which complicated medical and surgical treatment. He had to contend also with the mentality of superstitious patients. They compared him to their own medicine men who explained the deaths of those who had not been cured as having been due to some witch poisoning. Poisons, some of them claimed in exculpation, were quite outside their practice; though the natives did suspect that they could be bribed to poison someone's enemy. The white doctor, they felt sure, was a good man who never poisoned, and yet he did kill the sick men before he cut them up. In this way they explained to themselves his use of anesthetics; only he could somehow cure those whom he first killed and then marvelously brought back to life. That was the miracle of the strange European-Christian medicine.

Native superstition was not the only problem for doctors and missionaries. The African had primitive disregard for truth-telling and was an inveterate thief. Schweitzer had to keep everything every hour under lock and key. He could not trust even his assistant Joseph who was relatively enlightened. Not only medicines and instruments but axes, saws, machete knives, and also kitchen utensils and supplies had to be under constant supervision. All this was on the wrong side of the ledger. But he also recorded his surprise, as he came to know his natives better, to find that they had real concern for what they considered to be right and wrong. Their moral laws differed from his, but such as they were, they mattered to them strictly in their daily conduct. What they mostly sought to understand in their dealings with the white men was their different ways and laws, their Christian rights and wrongs, many of which seemed to them quite strange.

Schweitzer remarked the strong impression which the sermons of the missionaries to the natives made upon him, quite different from those which he heard at the meetings of the missionaries themselves which he attended. In the latter, and in their discussions with him, he felt clearly their distrust of his own departure from their theological orthodoxy, notwithstanding their high regard for his medical service. To the blacks, as they explained, another approach was needed. The mind of the native could not grasp theological doctrines; he must just be led to accept the plain teachings of Jesus about the right way of life. Now as they felt assured that their doctor was in main agreement with them in *that* view of the Christian Gospel, before long they said to him that they would not object to his speaking to the natives about moral and religious matters as well as about medicines and daily health and sanitation. Thus they themselves released him from his promise to keep strictly to his medicine and surgery and not to preach.

In the tropical jungle Schweitzer found the truth of the Gospel verse in full evidence: "Not he that saith unto me, Lord, Lord, shall enter into the Kingdom of heaven, but he that doeth the will of my Father who is in heaven."[24] And as he was meeting with the natives, patients and their families alike, in circumstances of grave emergency, he had the greatest opportunity to bring to them the Gospel of Jesus, a gospel to the weary and the heavy-laden. There is an unforgettable page in which he described one of his surgical operations for strangulated hernia:

> . . . In the hardly-lighted dormitory I watch for the sick man's awakening. Scarcely has he recovered consciousness when he stares about him and ejaculates again and again: "I've no more pain! I've no more pain!" His hand feels for mine and will not let it go. Then I begin to tell him and others who are in the room that it is the Lord Jesus who has told the doctor and his wife to come to the Ogowe, and that white people in Europe give them the money to live here and cure the sick negroes. The African sun is shining through the coffee bushes into the dark shed, but we, black and white, sit side by side and feel that we know by experience the meaning of the words: "And all ye are brethren."[25]

He had not been long in Africa before he learned that the natives's ideas of the white men's religion were greatly perplexed by the course of world events. The year after he landed in Africa the First World War broke out in Europe, and before long its repercussions reached the African jungles. Dr. Schweitzer's and his wife's medical service was sorely needed and was gladly acceptable at the French missionary station of Lambaréné; but when France was attacked by Germany the French colonial officials informed the two Alsatians that, as German citizens, they should consider themselves prisoners of war. Hospital activities were ruled out, and they were placed on a sort of house arrest. This gave Schweitzer unwelcome leisure; in his characteristic way he used it to advance work on his books. At first he thought of proceeding further with his theological treatise on St. Paul, but he soon turned to a larger subject, the Philosophy of Civilization. This problem was plainly imposed on his mind by his confrontation with the natives in wartime. The African black man could not understand how the white Christians, who had taught him the gospel of neighborly love, how they could fight and kill each other. What was their real directive belief after all? Schweitzer himself was probing the basic problem of the true principles of civilization: "What is the nature and the attitude towards life in which the will to general progress and to ethical progress are alike founded and in which they are bound together?"[26]

The problem with which he was grappling had religious as well as moral significance. His New Testament critical studies had led him to conclusions of radical disagreement with traditional orthodoxy, and in a different way at variance with many modern interpretations; but they had also confirmed him in his conviction of the basic and saving truths of Jesus's Gospel of the blessed life. Jesus declared that the Kingdom of God is within us. We are living in a world of mechanism and conflicting forces, but in this world we can and we ought to live in fellowship, as we are all children of God. There is a divine spiritual strain in the physical world. Schweitzer compared it to the warm current of the Gulf Stream coursing through the cold ocean. "There is the God of love within the God of the forces of the universe— one with Him and yet so totally different. We let ourselves be seized and carried away by that vital stream."[27] This is our true spiritual career. As a doctor and a scientist he recognized that he is rooted in the physical world and is subject to its laws; but his deepest insight revealed him to himself as a personality acknowledging and pursuing the realization of spiritual values and contemplating their perfection as divine. The Kingdom of God is within us, within him, Schweitzer, and in morals and religion alike the Christian gospel was to be expressed in the resolution to realize the Kingdom of God in our daily life. Did this ideal appear to be lofty sentimentality to the cold secular mind? So was the Gospel of Jesus to the judgment of the pagan intelligentsia: foolishness. "We are fools for Christ's sake," St. Paul wrote.[28] So

Schweitzer exclaimed one day, when his patience had been worn threadbare by his trials with the natives: "What a blockhead I was to come out here to doctor savages like these!" Whereupon his black assistant Joseph remarked quietly: "Yes, Doctor, here on earth you are a great blockhead, but not in heaven."[29]

Schweitzer had this basic conviction, religious and moral, of the supreme and imperative ideal of brotherly love, but how was he to grasp and express its fundamental principles? He was writing a philosophy of civilization. The best statement of the basic idea which he had found in the theories that he studied was the principle of thoroughgoing philanthropy, respect and reverence for the dignity of human personality. Philosophy and poetry as well as religion have given it powerful expression. It is the heart of Kant's social ethics: "So act as to treat humanity, whether in thine own person or in that of any other, in every case as an end withal, never as a means only."[30] And Robert Burns expressed it in seven short words: "A man's a man for a' that." This truth in its various expressions had not only been recognized by Schweitzer; he had been practicing it in his services to the African natives. But he felt that the fundamental principle was not limited, could not be limited to men's relations with each other. Its roots reach deeper into the nature of reality, even as our human nature is rooted in the rest of nature and is integral with it. In the African jungle, he was in daily intimate contact with the teeming tropical life; in the spirit of the Gospel he was ministering to the ailing blacks, his brothers. But they and he must also feel their common kinship and fellowship and communion with all life whatever. Soon after his arrival in the tropics, while he was on a long trip up the Ogowe River, he recorded the day when the universal principle of *Reverence for All Life* dawned upon him as supreme and imperative.

Schweitzer explained and developed this principle without evasion but also without the rigidity which would have involved confusion and unreasonableness. How are we to understand this principle of Reverence for Life, for All Life? Even as a child he had felt it wrong to kill or mistreat any living thing. But still he had had his usual diet at his mother's table. And here in Africa he noted that the natives would plainly and simply starve if it were not for their successful hunting and fishing. Besides, in his professional service medicine and surgery would be impossible without the disinfectants which killed microbes to save human lives. In dramatic ways he saw that throughout nature life fed on life. He had to wage daily war with the termites that would have gnawed away his wooden buildings, or with the invasions of ants that would attack his poultry and clean up every chicken to the bones. The jungle around him was alive with monkeys which the natives killed for food. He cited a white settler's remark that he was oddly squeamish about cooking a little monkey that looked so much like a black baby: "Doctor, eating monkeys is the first step in cannibalism."[31]

Suppose that he tried to avoid all these perplexities in his principle of Reverence for Life, at least as far as his diet was concerned, by adopting strict vegetarianism: still, even before he could plant a garden or preserve it he had to spray or otherwise destroy the swarms of tropical bugs and pests of all sorts. Besides, as a vegetarian he would be feeding on plant life: should he not respect it also, desist from all destruction? But then he could not survive. Schweitzer would not brush aside all these objections as pointless; they had to be met by the right restatement of his principle. The right attitude was important here. He declared: In my diet, in my daily program generally, I should avoid all *needless* destruction of any life whatever. So fishing and hunting for food would be allowable, but not for pure sport, for getting trophies. What matters here is the motive, the guiding purpose. I disinfect the patient's wound, I kill the germs—in order to preserve human life; I sweep out the ants from my chicken coop, to save the chickens, to save them for the food which all of us in the hospital need if we are to do our work of healing native ills. But I must always be on the alert to avoid needless and thoughtless destruction of life, of any living thing. Am I digging the postholes for my next building? Let me carefully rake away the toads and other beasties to safety. Do I notice an insect struggling in the water where it has fallen by chance? Surely I can stretch a branch to it so it can crawl out of danger. Of course I must mow the meadows for the hay which our cattle need for the winter; but on my way home I surely need not and should not thoughtlessly flick off with my cane the flowers or tall grasses that grow and flourish along my path.

But I may be told, surely this is all so petty; what does it really matter? It does matter greatly in my own spirit, which it expresses and which it nourishes towards further fruition. This sort of natural piety is of utmost importance—this my living communion with all life, which uplifts and spiritualizes our every action. Like God, in a godly way, we mark the sparrow's fall and consider the lilies of the field. "A man is ethical only when life, as such, is sacred to him, that of plants and animals as that of his fellow man, and when he devotes himself helpfully to all life that is in need of help. . . .The ethic of Reverence for Life, therefore, comprehends within itself everything that can be described as love, devotion, and sympathy whether in suffering, joy, or effort."[32] Moral tests and standards rest upon this universal foundation: "The essence of Goodness is: Preserve life, promote life, help life to achieve its highest destiny. The essence of Evil is: Destroy life, harm life, hamper the development of life."[33]

Schweitzer knew full well that his basic idea was not congenial to our common ways of thinking, especially in the West, that it was likely to invite ridicule as maudlin sentimentality.

It is the fate of every truth to be the object of ridicule when it is first acclaimed. It was once considered foolish to suppose that colored men were really human beings and ought to be treated as such. What was once foolishness has now become a recognised truth. Today it is considered an exaggeration to proclaim constant respect for every form of life as being the serious demand of a rational ethic. But the time is coming when people will be amazed that the human race was so long before it recognised that thoughtless injury to life is incompatible with real ethics. Ethics is in its unqualified form extended responsibility with regard to everything that has life.[34]

Throughout his later life and since his death in 1965 Albert Schweitzer has seemed to millions of men and women to be the exemplar not only of the living Gospel of Jesus but also of a sort of secular saintliness: an exemplar of the perception and expression of the higher and upbuilding spirit in our civilization. True civilization and essential Christianity, in his view, are grounded in the same ultimate principle. "Civilization I define in general terms as spiritual and material progress in all spheres of activity, accompanied by an ethical development of individuals and of mankind."[35] And likewise the kernel of our religion: "The essential element in Christianity as it was preached by Jesus and as it is comprehended by thought is this, that it is only through love that we can attain to communion with God. All living knowledge of God rests upon this foundation: that we experience Him in our lives as Will-to-love."[36]

CHAPTER X

POPE JOHN XXIII

Pope John entitled his autobiography *Il Giornale dell' Anima, Journal of a Soul*. It is a wholly exceptional book. Unlike most autobiographies, written late in life and therefore consisting largely of recorded memories, Pope John's *Journal* is a diary which he started as a seminary pupil at the age of fifteen and continued for sixty-six years. Almost one fifth of it was written before his eighteenth year. In his *Confessions* St. Augustine during his forties recalls his early sins: the orchard raids of his childhood, the profligacies of his youth. But in the first part of Pope John's *Journal* we read a youth's recorded hopes, anxieties, compunctions. We can follow his intimate career as it actually develops: the experiences, ideas, and feelings of an intensely devout religious person in his lifelong endeavor to pursue an ideal of Christian perfection which he never felt sure of attaining. The *Journal* recounts the spiritual pilgrimage of a priestly soul.

What makes this book doubly striking, in our day, is its revelation of an utterly consecrated Catholic spirit unfolding itself, not in a medieval setting, but directly in our midst, in the worldly currents and tensions of our contemporary scene. Imagine a St. Augustine or a St. Teresa living in our day, to whom we ourselves could have mailed a letter of inquiry. The Vatican Council which Pope John convened was in session almost yesterday. He died on June 3, 1963.

Our diarist was the son of Giovanni Battista Roncalli and his wife Marianna, of the small town of Sotto il Monte, in the district of Bergamo in Lombardy. Baptized in the evening of his birth, on November 25, 1881, he was given the name Angelo Giuseppe. He called himself Angelo and, as we shall note, honored St. Joseph above all other saints. The Roncalli family were simple devout people of plain but respectable, if not distinguished, ancestral tradition reaching back to the fifteenth century. While there was no destitution in their homelife, their daily state was that of frank poverty. Recalling his years of childhood, Pope John remarked: "We were poor, but content with our condition and full of confidence in the Lord's help. There never was bread on our table, only *polenta;* no wine for the children or young people, and seldom meat; only at Christmas and Easter did we have a slice of home-made cake. Clothes and shoes for going to church had to last for years. . . . And yet when a beggar appeared at the door of our kitchen, where the children—twenty of them—were impatiently waiting for their bowl of *minestra,* there was always room for him, and my mother would hasten to seat the unknown person beside us."[1] As to his material condition, he preferred to end as he had begun. This he wrote in his "Spiritual Testament": "Born poor, but of humble and respectable folk, I am particularly happy to die poor, having distributed, according to the various needs and circumstances of my simple and modest life in the service of the poor and of the holy Church which has nurtured me, whatever came into my hands—and it was very little— during the years of my priesthood and episcopate."[2]

Pope John's literary executor, Don Loris Capovilla, writes that one day the Holy Father handed over to him a handful of notebooks, the *Journal.* When asked if they might be published, together with his other writings, the Pope replied: "You may do so. At first I felt some reluctance about publishing and letting others republish my private papers. . . . I am well aware that people want to know everything about a Pope, and everything may be useful to historians. But they are a more intimate part of me than anything else I have written; my soul is in these pages." He was moved to recall his earliest years, and his mild face suffused with tears:

> I was a good boy, innocent, somewhat timid. I wanted to love God at all costs and my one idea was to become a priest, in the service of simple souls who needed patient and attentive care. Meanwhile I had to fight an enemy within me, self-love, and in the end I was able to get the better of it. But I was mortified to feel it constantly returning. I was troubled about my distractions during prayer and I imposed severe sacrifices on myself to get rid of them. I took everything very seriously and my examinations of conscience were detailed and severe. . . . Now at a distance of more than sixty years, I can look upon these first spiritual writings of mine as if they had been written by someone else, and I bless the Lord for them.[3]

His beginning years in school were not marked by any unusual success, but he showed great capacity for growth, so that he rose eventually towards the top of his class. This promising advance, together with his very convincing desire to prepare for a priestly calling, led to his being chosen, when only fourteen years of age, to assume the clerical habit at the Seminary of Bergamo where he had been a pupil for three years. There as a young seminarist he began the writing of his *Journal of a Soul,* as he inscribed his diary on its first page, a continual spiritual confession in writing "to the honor and glory of God." The first year of this boy's autobiography yielded little self-expression. He began by copying down for himself the so-called "Little Rules" prepared by his spiritual director for the guidance of boys and young men who had committed themselves to the Lord's service.

The second year he translated and adapted these rules in more personal terms as his own spiritual exercises of Christian resolution. Many of them concerned details of his daily ritual of worship, but some already indicated his keen sense of special spiritual needs, the dangers and pitfalls that beset him, which he ever strove to overcome with divine Grace, especially pride, vanity, self-love: "Above all, I will watch myself carefully, lest the tree of pride should grow in me; I will beware of this, keeping myself humble-minded and the lowliest of all, both in pious practices and in study. . . . I will make a special effort to mortify myself, above all and at all times chastising my self-love, my besetting sin, avoiding all occasions which might foster it. Therefore I will not try to display my learning in conversation, . . . I will not use phrases or words which give me an air of superiority. . . ."⁴ This and more of the sort he wrote at the age of fifteen.

In his resolution to avoid all worldly interests or inclinations or thoughts or actions, this Italian boy urged himself to remember that he is never alone but always a seminarist in the sight of God and the Madonna. He should ever watch his eyes and hands and mind, both in public and in private, ever on his guard against the temptations of the devil who was always lurking to seduce him. Even seemingly innocent attractions, when they diverted him from his concentration on his pious devotion, were evils to be avoided. We recall that St. Augustine remarked how at church services he would be moved by the beauty of the choir's music, and how he felt that he had sinned, for a musical appeal had prevailed over his feelings of pure piety. So our young seminarist warned himself to beware of being lured by mere beauty, not only in the world outside but even in church. "I will set a special guard on my eyes, which St. Ambrose called 'deceitful snares,' and St. Anthony of Padua 'thieves of the soul.' . . . Even in the churches, besides behaving with edifying decorum during the sacred functions, I will never gaze at beautiful things of any sort, such as pictures, carvings, statues or other objects of art which, however slightly, offend against propriety. . . ."[5] Despite his Italian blood he was able to withstand the urges of sensuality. Late in his life, at the age of seventy, in a solemn written confession to God, while reviewing his sins of youth and adult years, he thanks the Lord that he had never departed from the strictest chastity: "In relations with others, 'through the eyes, or through touch, in the time of puberty, or youth, or maturity, or old age, or in the reading of books or newspapers or in looking at statues and pictures, God's grace, God's grace I say, never once permitted temptation or failure, never, never.' "[6]

Contritely the septuagenerian confessed his inability to make a similar disavowal about other offenses. The transgressions which he had striven to overcome in early youth continued to embroil him through the years. The rueful rehearsal of them recurs on his pages. The vices which he found hardest to master were egotism and vaingloriousness, pride in speech and manner; as he put it, "wanting to be a Solomon," ready to stand in judgment of others and to parade his own wisdom. The repeated use of this and similar expressions indicates his unending struggle to control his self-love.[7] "Vanity squirts out of every word; . . . I am only a little Lucifer in my pride, and worse." He must stamp "I" and "me" like "venomous snakes."[8] He prayed the Lord for grace to cultivate self-abasement; on page after page we read the same self-exhortation, written at the age of seventeen, and twenty-three, and forty-three: he needs humiliation, to realize what a good-for-nothing he is in the sight of God, he that cannot overcome even drowsiness, and at holy communion! "Humility, humility, still more humility. . . . I want to love humiliations. . . . To humble myself constantly I will tell myself that I am a lazy fellow, a beast of burden that . . . deserves to be beaten."[9] These remorseful reflections are the more remarkable when we consider the universal impression which as Bishop and Cardinal and Pope he made, of his transparent humble submission to God.

Despite his reported continual backsliding, he carried his ascetic self-control and even self-mortification to some extremes. What were his petty sufferings, compared with those of the Lord Jesus? Had he spent a miserable night with a violent toothache? Bless the pains, for they could bring his thoughts to the agonies of the Cross. Yet he confessed that he did like his comforts; so far was he from utter self-devotion to God. Like a medieval saint, he would bless pain for most swiftly bearing his mind to God. But not only pains and hardships would he bear in pious silence: he should put silence on his program in his daily career; in class, in council, he should listen more and talk less, less. Especially, in his youth he urged himself not to waste time in idle talk; he should stop "gossiping away, promising the earth"; "be careful with certain people not to touch on certain subjects which irritate them." When somebody humiliated him, he should bear it in silence, in Christ-like patience. Instead of "longing to cut a fine figure," he should aspire to make himself holy.[10]

In his waking hours he struggled with his failings, but at night the devil assailed him with hellish dreams. If he could only, only once for all, get over his vain illusions which trip him into sins and follies! "In everything I do I must behave like a boy, the boy I really am, and not try to pass myself as a serious philosopher and a man of importance. . . . All my vanities, all my distractions during my devotion, examinations of conscience, . . . all the words, the witticisms prompted only by a secret desire directly or indirectly to show off how much I have studied, . . . all these will be judged. My God, what terror I feel! What a mounting heap of sins! How shameful for me, sensitive as I am about my good name and my pride!"[11]

Not only ostentatious loquacity was he struggling to avoid, but mere merry prattle. One autumn in the seminary he rued that he had been "rather too merry," and so his mind had "fluttered about like a butterfly, neglecting the most important things." Didn't St. Bernard say that priestly joking is blasphemous? Smiling abnegation was seemly, but not jolly levity.[12] Beware of excessive mirth; of course, do not go to the opposite extreme of sour gloominess. Cultivate genial goodwill, but never transgress modest and decent sobriety. Aim at the saintly monastic cheerfulness, happiness in the Lord, not in worldly revels.

He sought the true joy, in the Lord, but that joy always had a grave aspect here on earth, this side of the grave. He had received reports of his little brother's very serious illness; he prayed: "O Mary, make my little Giovanni better." But he also reflected on his own possible even though unexpected death. How would it be with him, if he were to stand in judgment right then, at that very moment? "Every time I think of purgatory I tremble."[13] His thoughts about himself and his daily trials and problems led him to reflect on the truly Christian, Christ-like life. What does it mean to live like the Savior? Again his chief problem confronted him, his need of humility. The Son of God humbled himself. "He lived in seclusion. No one knew anything about him. To all appearances he was just the son of Mary, the carpenter's son. No sign yet of his future greatness, his divine origin. What a fine lesson of reserve for me, always so full of myself, my pride ever driving me to display my few natural gifts, which are accompanied by so many failings. I too must live in seclusion so that, far from the turmoil of the world, I may hear the voice of Jesus speaking to my heart." If Jesus was so patient with him, how could he lose his temper with anyone? "Tranquillity, calm, cheerfulness, good manners, never a cross word with anyone, no excited speech, but simplicity, cordiality, sincerity, without cowardice—no flabbiness." In his struggle to master his sins of public display, pride and self-love he even cherished holy self-abasement. "I intend that the promise which I make shall be a declaration before the whole Church that it is my will to be crushed, despised, neglected for the love of Jesus and for the good of souls, and to live always in poverty and detachment from all the interests and riches of this world."[14]

He longed to draw closer to Jesus, and he had his moments of intimate mystical devotion: "Jesus, I am here waiting for your coming. . . . Delay no longer, come, be my guest. Alas! it is already late, I am overcome with sleep and my pen slips from my fingers. Let me sleep a little, O Jesus, while you and your Mother and St. Joseph are preparing the room. . . . As soon as you come the splendour of your light will dazzle my eyes, . . . I will worship you and show you all my love. . . . Come, I am longing for you."[15] We seem to be reading a page by St. Teresa.

The mention of Mary and St. Joseph was not accidental. If we may express it without misleading implications, Angelo Roncalli, both in his youth and his maturity and when in his old age he became Pope, seems to have had, alongside of his adoration of the Holy Trinity, a direct and prayerful devotion to the triad of Jesus, Mary, and Joseph. These three were repeatedly inscribed on his pages in pious reverence. *Jesus, Mary, Joseph.* While in the seminary in Rome he wrote on the back of an image of the Madonna a vow of dedication: "On 2 June, 1903, I, Angelo Roncalli, offered my heart to the Immaculate Virgin."[16] When he was only seventeen, he wrote: "The most direct way to Jesus is through Mary. In a word, I will be all for Mary so as to be all for Jesus."[17] His daily prayers in which Jesus and Mary subtly interpenetrate his adoration also recall to our minds his repeated accounts of his pilgrimages to the many shrines of the Madonna.

The priestly soul which was revealed in all this self-searching and contrition and reaffirmed hope and holy endeavor was the soul of a youth and a man who was bound to respond actively to the problems and the struggles in which the Church itself was embroiled in the complexities of modern life and thought. Angelo Roncalli's career traversed many periods before his final elevation to the seat of Peter. He was a student at a seminary and a consecrated priest: then in turn secretary to a bishop; spiritual director and professor at the Seminary of Bergamo in his native province; President of the Central Council for Italy of the Pontifical Missionary Works; consecrated Bishop; visitor and Apostolic Delegate and later Missionary Archbishop in Bulgaria, Turkey, and Greece; Papal Nuncio in France; Cardinal Patriarch of Venice; and finally Pope. The mere recital of this outward biography indicates his active contact with the many fields of Roman Catholic activity.

There was nothing isolated or provincial in his church offices. He celebrated masses throughout the Continent, in the Middle East, and across the Atlantic. His missionary work in the Balkans brought him in intimate contact with both the lower clergy and the higher ecclesiastics of the Eastern Orthodox Churches, Bulgarian and Greek. In those Christian countries he was supervising Christian missions, Roman Catholic, emphasizing his keen sense of a divided Christendom, a cleavage which he regarded as a major spiritual tragedy in the Western world, itself disrupted and chaotic and needing woefully the undivided guidance of the Church Universal. While still a student at the seminary, before he had come in direct touch with Eastern Orthodoxy, young Angelo had recorded his resolution to pray "for the conversion of sinners and the return of the dissident churches."[18] This was the formal reaction of a Roman Catholic: Rome was and is the home of the Church of Christ, from which other churches have strayed and to which they should one day return, like prodigal sons.

His set resolution in dealing with Eastern Orthodox Churches was "to leave an impression of dignity and loving kindness, a radiant kindness and a pleasing dignity." He must avoid any superior detachment; serving in Bulgaria he must reach the people directly and learn the Bulgarian language. The day after he began his residence in Sofia he paid a courtesy visit to the Bulgarian Holy Synod and then and also later had conferences with the Metropolitan. Similar was his approach to the other Eastern Churches. He had a meeting with the Armenian Archbishop of Nicomedia. As Papal Representative in Turkey and Greece he conferred with the Greek Patriarch Benjamin and later with the Archbishop of Athens. His various appointments in the Balkans lasted more than fifteen years; they gave him the most thorough and intimate preparation for the ecumenical work to which he dedicated himself later, as Pope: one of the major purposes in the convening of the Vatican Council. Beyond his concern for the winning of the Eastern Orthodox Churches, he was not forgetting the Mohammedans: "I want to study Turkish with more care and perseverance. I am fond of the Turks, to whom the Lord has sent me; it is my duty to do what I can for them. . . . Jesus, Holy Church, the souls in my care, and the souls of these Turks, too, no less than those of our unfortunate brethren, the Orthodox."[19]

This grievous sense of the cleavage in Christendom, which his missionary relations with Eastern Orthodoxy in the Balkans had emphasized, was doubly keen when it concerned the various Protestant sectarians. For these were modern straying dissidents, not ancient Christian bodies, some of which were as old as Rome. He had had occasion in his youth to note the tenacious Protestant heresies. In his twenty-third year, when he was ordained priest, he was asked to serve as a guide to a young Protestant who was being prepared for his conversion to Rome. He found him a difficult pupil: "He has been thoroughly imbued with the instruction which the Protestants are so expert in giving. There is not a single prejudice against the Catholic Church that he does not know, not one article of heretical teaching that he has not learnt. . . . Meanwhile this has convinced me of my tremendous obligation to thank God for the great gift of faith: one has only to talk to a Protestant for a few hours to understand all the importance of this. . . . As for the poor unfortunates outside the Church, we must feel sorry for them, poor children, pray hard for them, and work with all our hearts and strength for their conversion."[20]

The Protestants had power and majesty in the West, but eventually they must return to Holy Church. Thus he reflected as he wrote about the solemn audiences at the Vatican and the grand public festivities attending the visit to Rome of Edward VII, "a heretical King of Protestant England which has persecuted the Catholic Church for more than three centuries," and following him, the visit of Kaiser Wilhelm of Germany. He commented ironically on all that pomp and circumstance: "Flags, festoons, decorations in the streets, glittering uniforms, plumes, soldiers, military reviews, receptions . . . it is a bewildering succession of events, an uproar, a racket, a confusion, a frenzy."[21] The English visit, to be sure, was mainly political, but King Edward

> did one really good thing while he was in Rome: . . .
> He did not disdain, indeed he considered it an honour,
> to visit and pay homage to another man, a poor per-
> secuted old man, whom he acknowledged to be greater
> than himself: the Pope, the Vicar of Jesus Christ. . . .
> It is a sign of the times that after such a night of storm
> we see the new dawn rising from the Vatican, a slow
> but real and sincere return of the nations to the arms of
> their common Father who has long awaited them, weep-
> ing over their foolishness, and the triumph of Christ the
> King who, upraised on the Cross, once more draws all
> things to himself.[22]

These were words of a young seminary student of theology, but they expressed a deep lifelong conviction which should be kept in mind in considering the later convening of the Vatican Council. Kaiser Wilhelm's visit to Rome took place within a fortnight after that of King Edward, and Angelo Roncalli once more reflected on the empty pomp and might and grandiose vanities of this world against which the eternal authority of the Catholic Church must one day prevail. "A Protestant Emperor, after centuries of hostility, ascends the Vatican stairs with unusual, almost unique ceremony and splendour, and humbles himself before the greatness of the papal throne!"[23]

Long years of broad experience and varied contacts in his outspreading ecclesiastical career taught Angelo Roncalli the need of a more thorough mutual understanding, not only of Roman Catholics and other Christian bodies, but of all churches and the large world of modern thought, with its secular scientific outlook on the world and on modern life. What concerned him even more directly in his position of rising ecclesiastic responsibility was his recognition in the Church itself of the tensions between conservatives and liberals, which in a different form were controversial in the larger crisis of modern life. These contending issues concerned his own spiritual peace but also the disturbed unfolding of the intellectual life of the young seminarist and priest and bishop and cardinal and Pope.

During his seminary course he had shown a somewhat dual attitude towards study and learning and mastery of doctrine. He had high regard for intellectual competence, but alas, he reflected, how the pursuit of it had tempted him to vain display of it and sinful pride! He was wary of it also in a deeper sense, for is not the intellectual commitment, if it dominates the soul, itself misleading and quite the wrong emphasis for a true Christian? Did not Jesus admonish us to become as little children, devout and trusting in faith, not learned Pharisees?

A very significant passage in his *Journal,* dated during his twenty-third year, records a self-analysis of his mind:

> A careful examination of myself and the motives of my self-love has enabled me to perceive that within me, besides my imagination, always the crazy inmate of the house, are two reasoning minds, as it were, both of which do their utmost to make themselves heard. They are the reasonable reasoning mind, my own real mind, and the other reasoning mind, which is my inveterate foe. When I am meditating seriously, and considering goodness in general and in practice, this other mind always discovers a lot of ifs and buts, makes fun of my resolutions and always finds some objections or some soothing arguments in its own favour. Wonderfully aided and abetted by my imagination, it does all it can to cloud my understanding and to pour cold water over my good intentions; it gets the better of my reasonable mind and gives it no mercy, always bold and importunate, always a tyrant.[24]

Study and learning, the Roman seminarist reflected, are not to be neglected, not at all; but they do not suffice. The Christian life requires more than conclusive theological arguments and historical competent learning. It demands commitment of the devout will, to resist the lures of intellectual mastery, if it leads us astray from the love of the crucified Lord. Was young Roncalli remembering the answer which St. Bonaventura made, when asked about his studies and his library, and he simply pointed to his worktable and the sole crucifix on the wall in front of it?

> My great book, from which I must henceforth learn with greater care and love the lessons of divine wisdom, is the crucifix. I must make a habit of judging all human concerns and knowledge in the light of the principles of this great book. It is too easy for me to be deceived by empty appearances and to forget the true source of truth. When I look at the crucifix I shall feel all my dif-

> ficulties dissolve—all those modern problems, theoretical
> and practical, in the field of study. The solution of all
> difficulties is Christ. . . . One thing only I desire, to
> stay always in your holy love, one with you as you are
> one with your Father.[25]

In this spirit of devout resolution, eight months later, the
young seminarist confronted full front the problem of modern
religious criticism as it concerns the issues between reason and
faith. What was he willing to venture, and what was he resolved to
safeguard and insure? He recorded it very clearly:

> I want to guard my faith carefully, like a sacred treas-
> ure. Most of all I want to be true to that spirit of faith
> which is gradually being whittled away before the so-
> called requirements of criticism, in the atmosphere and
> light of modern times. . . . It will always be my prin-
> ciple, in all spheres of religious knowledge and in all
> theological and biblical questions, to find out first of all
> the traditional teaching of the Church, and on this basis
> to judge the findings of contemporary scholarship. I do
> not despise criticism, and I shall be most careful not to
> think ill of critics or treat them with disrespect. On the
> contrary, I love it. I shall be glad to keep up with the
> most recent findings, I shall study the new systems of
> thought and their continual evolution and their trends;
> criticism for me is light, is truth, and there is only one
> truth, which is sacred. But I shall always try to introduce
> into these discussions, in which too often ill-considered
> enthusiasms and deceitful appearances have too much
> to say, a great moderation, harmony, balance and seren-
> ity of judgment, allied to a prudent and cautious broad-
> mindedness. On very doubtful points I shall prefer to
> keep silent like one who does not know, rather than
> hazard propositions which might differ in the slightest
> degree from the right judgment of the Church.[26]

Did he not include among the matters that he may have indicated in this latter class the traditional Catholic devotion to

saints's holy relics and shrines of miraculous agencies? As Cardinal and Patriarch of Venice he preached a homily at the Portuguese Shrine of Fatima which concluded as follows: "O Our Lady of Fatima, through the virtue of your Immaculate Heart, obtain for us from blessed Jesus, the fountain of every grace, justice, charity and peace! Amen." And likewise to the Virgin of Lourdes: "Renew the miracles of a century and let new wonders follow the old. In this place add new glory to your hand and your right arm."[27] These words and many others like them should be kept in mind in our view of the Cardinal's mental and spiritual outlook. Again, as Pope, he prayed to Our Lady of Loretto for her motherly intercession to bless and crown the success of the Vatican Council.

This undeviating intellectual loyalty to the Church had also a practical expression, ecclesiastic and social. In the preparation for his consecration as Bishop he meditated persistently and wrote down eleven specific principles of personal commitment. The concluding one is very significant: "I insert in my coat of arms the words *Oboedientia et Pax* (Obedience and Peace) which Cesare Baronius used to say every day, when he kissed the Apostle's foot in St. Peter's. These words are in a way my own history and my life. O may they be the glorification of my humble name through the centuries!"[28]

His resolution was devout, but it was not unwavering, for as he read the works of the modernists he felt the instability of much traditional assurance. His intellectual demand for real evidence, genuine proof and conviction, contended with his pious insistence on utter commitment of his will. A real struggle was going on in his soul, and he would not dissemble or ignore it; but he was determined that whatever might befall, it should not end in the collapse of his faith.

> My studies! What a great many preconceived ideas I
> have about these! I have ended by judging them as the

world does. I have let my head be turned by modern ideas. Learning is always a fine thing, a secondary ingredient of a useful priestly life, and also a secondary means of saving souls in these modern times. God preserve me from underestimating study, but I must also beware of attaching to it an exaggerated and absolute value. Study is one eye, the left eye; if the right eye is missing, what is the use of a single eye, of study by itself? . . . Of course I shall always go on studying, I shall never give it up, but "all according to order and measure; we must seek knowledge soberly."[29]

The passage which we have quoted was written in 1904. Eighteen years later, in his tribute to the former spiritual director of the Roman seminary, he reaffirmed his refusal to let any modern critical research set him adrift in his faith. He was not at all insensible of the strong impact of the spirit of liberalism; he recognized its strength not only in the world but in himself, but more decisive than his recognition of it was his firm resolution not to yield or surrender to it. He recalled the strong lure of modernism among the seminarists from which their director safeguarded them:

The wind of modernity, sometimes impetuous and other times gentle and caressing, which was afterwards to degenerate in part into so-called Modernism, was blowing almost everywhere, and was to poison the heart and soul of many. . . . The spirit of modernity, liberty and criticism is like good wine, bad for weak heads. . . . All we who were students in that school of strict orthodoxy and the true Roman spirit, combined with lively and enlightened asceticism, may now congratulate ourselves on the fact that not one of us has faltered or strayed from the straight path of being "of one mind with the Church" in all things.[30]

A careful search of the *Journal* has not disclosed any significant counter-passages that would indicate a basic change in Pope

John's attitude towards the tension between conservatives and liberals in the Catholic Church. The period before and after the middle of our century has been marked by two movements which have represented two alternative reactions to the medieval Scholastic tradition. On the one hand we should note the work of a number of very thorough and also very critical scholars who were continuing within the Roman Catholic fold the literary-historical or so-called "higher" criticism of the Bible pursued by their predecessors of Protestant or nondenominational adherence. Over against this movement of thought, which involved much radical negation of traditional orthodoxy, the Neo-Scholastic movement has represented a positive and constructive demand for a modern restatement of the medieval, chiefly Thomist doctrines that would deepen the appeal of the Catholic Church to contemporary minds and make it more convincing, without surrender of its traditional and authoritative values. The present theological leadership in the Roman Catholic hierarchy is marked by a liberal current of widespread covering both of the aforementioned alternatives, some of them of a definitely radical turn, some tending towards an acceptably moderate position, but most of them opposed to, as they are opposed by, the rigid intransigent conservatives in the Roman Curia and their adherents.

While the *Journal* does not record any fundamental change in Roncalli's attitude towards modernism, it does show, both in his expressed thought and in his chosen policy as rising prelate and as Pope, a growing and then a decided readiness for a straightforward and, as he hoped, a fruitful dialogue by Christian minds of different outlooks, both those within the Catholic Church and the dissident outsiders. As has been noted already, his readiness to proceed to conference rather than to solemn isolation was manifested in his initial approach to the ecclesiastics of the Eastern Churches among whom he was working as Apostolic Delegate in directing missionary activities, in Bulgaria, Turkey,

Greece. He recorded his difficulties in dealing with the august Greek prelates, but his firm policy was one of unmistakable Christian goodwill. Later as Papal Nuncio in France, he related with deep sorrow the spread of negative secularism in that land which had been a citadel of Catholic Christian devotion during the Middle Ages. But what mainly concerned him was to understand the tensions in contemporary life which find expression in modern secularism, and to consider the right ways in which the Church could deal with them.

In this spirit of positive construction through frank conference, when he became Pope, he chose his course of policy which led to the convening of the Second Vatican Council. This chosen policy expressed also his personal view of the holy office to which he had been elected. God's elevation of him, lowly and unworthy as he regarded himself, signified to him a needed clear view of his entire remaining span of life, as devoted wholly to God and to mankind: no longer merely himself or provincial in any way, no longer just Angelo Roncalli with his title, but God's alone and hence universal in outlook and devotion, Catholic in the ancient sense of ecumenical in his hopes and practices. Not without significance was the choice of his title as Pope, John XXIII, thus dismissing to oblivion the *anti*-pope John XXIII of Avignon.

He did not consider his election to the papacy as his own ecclesiastic promotion, lifting him to the summit in his priestly career. Early in his life he had written down his decision not to be over-impressed by churchly dignities nor to make the pursuit of them a purpose in his life. "Poor or rich, honoured or despised, poor priest in a mountain parish or Bishop of a vast diocese, it must be all the same to me, as long as in this way I do the will of my Master, fulfill my duty as a faithful servant and save my soul."[31] His robes of office were not to be vestments of pomp and proud display: in whatever station, he was always to be a bare contrite soul alone with God. Thus he settled it for his career, a seminary student in Rome: "Even if I were to be Pope, even if my name were to be invoked and revered by all and inscribed on marble monuments, I should still have to stand before the divine judge, and what should I be worth then?"[32] While serving as Apostolic Delegate in Turkey and Greece, he heard murmurs that "greater things are in store," rumors of a coming advancement in his career, but he checked any natural stir of proud ambition as ungodly: "For the little, or nothing, that I am worth to Holy Church, I have already my purple mantle, my blushes of shame in finding myself in this position of honour and responsibility when I know that I am worth so little."[33] In the same spirit, after his elevation to the Papacy, he declared solemnly that he had done nothing to promote his election: "Absolutely nothing; indeed I was most careful and conscientious to avoid anything that might direct attention to myself. As the voting in the Conclave wavered to and fro, I rejoiced when I saw the chances of my being elected diminishing, and the likelihood of others, in my opinion truly most worthy and venerable persons, being chosen."[34] When the reader of the *Journal* recalls Angelo Roncalli's continual confession of his major sins of pride and self-will and his contrite prayers to overcome them, the above three cited passages, at three stages of his career, reveal his lifelong resolution and his humble recognition of the divine Grace that had sustained him throughout.

Once established in the Vatican, he regarded his exalted position as a demand of new duties and as requiring a reconsideration of himself. Most immediately it affected a revision of his relation to his family. He had always felt a close attachment to his family, to his mother, "for whom, after God, Mary, and the saints, I bear the greatest love of which my heart is capable."[35] There is a page of poignant emotion in which he wrote of his grief that, in remaining loyal to his churchly status, he had offended his mother by rebuking her curiosity in asking him a question about a certain matter which he could not discuss with her. This problem of his personal intimate relations with his parents, simple folk who could not understand the restrictions which their son's offices in the Church placed on him, must have taxed his tact. When he reached the summit of his rise in the hierarchy, it was not papal pride and dignity but rather a deep sense of his duties which led him to write down that thenceforward his family was to be the entire world. He was Pope, Papa, Father of the Church Universal, and this supreme commitment must surmount his other attachments to family or class or country. "Since the Lord chose me, unworthy as I am, for this great service, I feel I have no longer any special ties in this life, no family, no earthly country or nation. . . . This sense of belonging to everyone must give character and vigour to my mind, my heart and my actions."[36] He did not neglect the Roncalli clan, not at all; but he wrote to them as the shepherd of the flock. This attitude is reflected in the wording and provisions of his will and last testament. The reader is reminded of the words of Jesus in the Gospel: "He who loves father and mother more than me is not worthy of me."[37] But he regretted deeply their inability to understand the true motivation of his chosen way of dealing with them. More than thirty years before entering the Vatican, he had felt an unavoid-able tension between his family attachment and his episcopal duties and loyalties. "The law of the apostolate and the priest-hood is above the law of flesh and blood. . . . My closest rela-tions, brothers, sisters, nephews and nieces, with very few excep-tions, are exemplary Christians and give me great joy. But it would never do for me to get mixed up in their affairs and con-cerns, so as to be diverted from my duties as a servant of the Holy See, and a Bishop!"[38]

This adopted principle—the primacy of his pastoral duties, above other personal attachments no matter how dear and inti-mate—applied also to his public secular loyalties. Even before his elevation to the Papacy, he charged himself to remember that in his ordination to his priestly office he was no longer Angelo Roncalli of Sotto il Monte, even though he did spend many of his vacations in his native town. He was Bishop of his See, yes, but consecrated to minister to all souls regardless of locality or land. He not only celebrated mass throughout the world; everywhere he was at the Lord's feet. In moving to the Vatican the former Cardinal Patriarch of Venice did not forget the poor multitudes of his former diocese, but he felt bound now to develop a broader sense and range of his ministration. During the Second World War this primarily episcopal view of himself in his office determined his attitude towards all political and social partisanship: "Patriotism, which is right and may be holy, but may also degenerate into nationalism, which in my case would be most detrimental to the dignity of my episcopal ministry, must be kept above all nationalistic disputes. The world is poisoned with morbid nationalism, built up on the basis of race and blood, in contradiction to the Gospel."[39]

It is in this spirit, as presiding over the Church Universal, that Pope John XXIII conceived his project for the Second Vatican Council. First of all, he was convinced of the need to prepare his own, the Pope's, soul for that holy undertaking. He set aside a week to concentrate each day in turn on his own spiritual need: "I have resolved to fix my mind on the three theological virtues: faith, hope and charity, and the four cardinal virtues: prudence, justice, fortitude and temperance; precisely seven points, altogether worthy of concentrated meditation, not only on the part of every good servant of the Lord but above all for the perfection of the holy and sanctifying virtue of a Bishop, and especially of the Bishop of Bishops, whose virtue must stand like the chief point of splendour in the glory of a Council."[40]

The opening pleas of his prayer expressed the intensity of his devout commitment:

O Divine Spirit, sent by the Father in the name of Jesus, give your aid and infallible guidance to your Church and pour out on the Ecumenical Council the fullness of your gifts. O gentle Teacher and Consoler, enlighten the hearts of our prelates who, eagerly responding to the call of the Supreme Roman Pontiff, will gather here in solemn conclave. May the Council produce abundant fruits: may the light and power of the Gospel be more widely diffused in human society; may new vigour be imparted to the Catholic religion in its missionary function; may we all acquire a more profound knowledge of the Church's doctrine and a wholesome increase of Christian morality. . . ."[41]

Especially deep were his desires as former Apostolic Delegate to Bulgaria, Turkey, and Greece for a true Catholic rapprochement with the Eastern Orthodox Churches: "Oh Mary, why should not your Eastern children be reunited with us, in the house of our common Father who awaits them? . . ."[42] His high hopes for the Vatican Council were expressed in his Apostolic Exhortation: "We may already say that we all feel we are within sight of a new era, founded on our fidelity to our ancient treasury of faith, and opening on to the wonders of real spiritual progress: a progress which from Christ alone, the glorious and immortal King of all ages and peoples, can draw dignity, prosperity and blessing."[43]

The above passages breathe the spirit of genuine universal goodwill, but they are not utterances of a modernist mind. The position of Pope John was that of an unmistakable conservative, but of a conservative profoundly convinced of the imperative need of mutual understanding by persons, churches, and organizations of different outlooks, and of the zeal for the cultivation in them all of an ecumenical perspective. Alongside of the conservatism or liberalism of one's own ideas, it is important to distinguish one's conservative rigidity, or one's liberal tolerance, *about* one's ideas and convictions. In this latter sense of the terms Pope John's convening of the Vatican Council expressed a genuinely liberal ecumenical spirit, of utmost importance and hopeful promise for the future. Where so much is granted much more is to be expected.

The worldwide outlook which found expression in the Vatican Council was not limited to problems of theological doctrine or ecclesiastical order. Its broad purpose may be noted also in Pope John's appeals for world peace and the establishment of a world system of effective law, to replace flagrant and destructive violence. In this devotion to the cause of universal justice and peace Pope John's leadership has been followed by that of his successor, Pope Paul VI. Reasonable spirits of whatever variety of intellectual adherence are bound to salute the sustained advocacy of worldwide conciliation which issues today from the Vatican.

NOTES

CHAPTER I.

ST. AUGUSTINE

[1]A. Harnack, *Monasticism . . . and the Confessions of St. Augustine* (Engl. transl. by E. E. Kellett and F. H. Marseille), London, Williams & Norgate, 1913, p. 123.

[2]From *The Confessions of St. Augustine* translated by John K. Ryan. Copyright © 1960 by Doubleday & Company, Inc. Reprinted by permission of the publisher. I:i:1.

[3]*Confessions*, III:i:1.

[4]*Confessions*, II:i:3.

[5]Quoted by R. L. Ottley, *Studies in the Confessions of St. Augustine*, London, Robert Scott, 1919, p. 12.

[6]*Confessions*, III:iv:8.

[7]*Confessions*, III:v:9.

[8]*Confessions*, V:x:18.

[9]*Confessions*, IV:vii:12.

[10]*Confessions*, V:xiv:24.

[11]II Corinthians 3:6; cf. *Confessions*, VI:iv:6.

[12]*Confessions*, V:xiv:24.

[13]*Confessions*, V:xiv:25.

[14]*Confessions*, VI:i:1.

[15]*Confessions*, VI:ii:2.

[16]*Confessions*, VI:iii:3.

[17]Cf. *Confessions*, VI:xii:22.

[18]*Confessions*, VI:xiii:23.

[19]*Confessions*, VII:i:1.

[20]*Confessions*, VII:xx:26.

[21]*Confessions*, VII:xxi:27.

[22]*Confessions*, XVII:xvii:23.

[23]*Confessions*, VII:iii:7.

[24]*Confessions,* VIII:xi:27.
[25]*Confessions,* VIII:vii:18.
[26]*Confessions,* VIII:v:12.
[27]*Confessions,* VIII:xii:28.
[28]*Confessions,* VIII:xii:28-29.
[29]*Confessions,* IX:i:1.
[30]St. Augustine, *The City of God,* XII:6 (transl. by Marcus Dods), Edinburgh, Clark, 1872, revised.
[31]*Confessions,* VII:xvi:22.
[32]Genesis 1:31.
[33]I Corinthians 15:41.
[34]Luke 15.
[35]*Enneads,* III:ii:17 (transl. by Stephen Mackenna), New York, Pantheon, 3rd ed., n.d.
[36]Cf. Harnack, *History of Dogma* (transl. by James Millar), London, Williams & Norgate, 1898, Vol. V, pp. 79 f.
[37]*The City of God,* XIV:28.
[38]*Confessions,* XIII:ix:10.
[39]This and the following passages are cited from the English translation by William H. Draper, reprinted in part in H. H. Blanchard's *Prose and Poetry of the Continental Renaissance in Translation,* New York, David McKay, 2nd ed., 1955, pp. 31-57.

CHAPTER II.

ST. TERESA OF ÁVILA

[1]From *The Complete Works of St. Teresa,* translated and edited by E. Allison Peers from the critical edition of P. Silverio de Santa Teresa, C.D., Published in Three Volumes by Sheed & Ward Inc., New York. Volume III, p. 74. Cited hereafter as *Works.*
[2]Cited in *Saint Teresa of Jesus,* by E. Allison Peers, London, Faber and Faber, 1953, p. 22.
[3]*Book of the Foundations, Works,* Vol. III, p. 105.
[4]*Ibid.,* p. 194.
[5]*Constitutions, Works,* Vol. III, p. 222.
[6]Cf. V. Sackville-West, *The Eagle and the Dove,* London, Michael Joseph, 3rd impression, 1944, p. 77.
[7]Cf. E. Allison Peers, *Saint Teresa of Jesus,* p. 75.
[8]*Constitutions, Works,* Vol. III, p. 222.
[9]*Ibid.,* p. 227.
[10]*Ibid.,* p. 237.
[11]*Life, Works,* Vol. I, p. 56.
[12]*Ibid.*

[13]*Ibid.*, p. 10.
[14]*Ibid.*, p. 11.
[15]*Ibid.*, p. 32.
[16]*Ibid.*, p. 40.
[17]R. A. Tsanoff, *Religious Crossroads*, New York, Dutton, 1942, p. 231.
[18]*Bhagavadgita*, VI, in *Sacred Books of the East* (transl. by K. T. Telang), Oxford, Clarendon Press, 1882, p. 71.
[19]Translation by Edward Fitzgerald, quoted here from Sir Frederick Pollock's *Spinoza*, p. 317.
[20]II Corinthians 12:12 ff.
[21]*Itinerary of the Mind to God*, last chapter; cited here from H. O. Taylor, *The Medieval Mind*, 3rd ed., Vol. II, pp. 448 f.
[22]Quoted by E. Allison Peers, *Saint Teresa of Jesus*, p. 81.
[23]*Life, Works*, Vol. I, p. 64.
[24]John 9:25.
[25]Luke 10:38 ff.
[26]*Way of Perfection, Works*, Vol. II, p. 71.
[27]*The Letters of St. Teresa* (transl. by John Dalton), London, Thomas Baker, 1902, p. 60.
[28]*Life, Works*, Vol. I, p. 65.
[29]St. Augustine, *Soliloquies*, I:7, in W. J. Oates (ed.), *The Basic Writings of St. Augustine*, New York, Random House, 1948, p. 262.
[30]*Interior Castle, Works*, Vol. II, p. 203.
[31]*Life, Works*, Vol. I, p. 92.
[32]*Way of Perfection, Works*, Vol. II, p. 127.
[33]*Ibid.*, p. 129.
[34]*Life, Works*, Vol. I, p. 88.
[35]*Ibid.*, p. 95.
[36]*Ibid.*, p. 96.
[37]*Ibid.*, p. 97.
[38]*Ibid.*, pp. 97-98.
[39]*Ibid.*, p. 102; cf. *Interior Castle, Works*, Vol. II, p. 253.
[40]*Spiritual Relations, Works*, Vol. I, p. 329.
[41]*Ibid.*, p. 340 f.
[42]*Life, Works*, Vol. I, p. 275.
[43]*Ibid.*, p. 122, note.
[44]*Ibid.*, p. 180.
[45]*Ibid.*, pp. 189 f.
[46]*Ibid.*, p. 231.
[47]*Ibid.*, p. 271.
[48]*Ibid.*, p. 267.
[49]Cf. *ibid.*, p. 289.
[50]*Ibid.*, p. 292.

[51]Wordsworth, *The Prelude*, 1850, XII, 272 f.

[52]William James, *The Varieties of Religious Experience*, London, Longmans, Green, 30th impression, 1919, p. 387.

[53]Plato, *Phaedo*, 69, in *Plato's Dialogues* (transl. by Benjamin Jowett), Oxford, Clarendon Press, 3rd ed., 1892.

[54]Matthew 7:16.

[55]Shakespeare, *Midsummer Night's Dream*, V:i.

CHAPTER III.

GEORGE FOX

[1]Cf. Rufus M. Jones, in his Introduction to *The Journal of George Fox*, paperback edition by Capricorn Books, New York, 1963, pp. 22 ff. This edition will be cited below as *Journal*. It is in modern English. Fox's own written or dictated manuscript version, with its peculiar spelling, is hard to read. In our study, however, we have consulted throughout the extensively annotated edition of Fox's own text, edited in two volumes by Norman Penney and published in two volumes by the Cambridge University Press in England and by the John C. Winston Co. in Philadelphia, 1911.

[2]Cf. Vernon Noble, *The Man in Leather Breeches; The Life and Times of George Fox*, New York, Philosophical Library, 1953, pp. 13, 29.

[3]Cf. Rufus M. Jones, in *Journal*, pp. 28 f., note.

[4]*Journal*, pp. 92, 97, 99.

[5]*Ibid.*, pp. 65 f.

[6]*Ibid.*, pp. 66, 67.

[7]*Ibid.*, pp. 79, 82.

[8]*Ibid.*, p. 83.

[9]Luke 17:21.

[10]*Journal*, p. 101.

[11]Cf. Vernon Noble, *op. cit.*, p. 50.

[12]*Journal*, pp. 66, 67.

[13]Matthew, 5:34, 37.

[14]*Journal*, p. 414.

[15]*Ibid.*, p. 427.

[16]*Ibid.*, p. 256.

[17]Quoted by Rufus M. Jones, *The Story of George Fox*, New York, Macmillan, 1919, p. 81.

[18]*Journal*, pp. 214 f.

[19]*Ibid.*, p. 355; cf. pp. 389 ff.

[20]Quoted by Samuel M. Janney, *The Life of George Fox*, Philadelphia, Lippincott, Granbo & Co., 1853, p. 189.

[21]*Journal*, p. 75.

[22]Cf. Vernon Noble, *op. cit.*, pp. 115, 122.

[23]*Ibid.*, chaps. viii-x.

[24]Josiah Royce, "George Fox as a Mystic," in *Harvard Theological Review*, Vol. VI, 1913, p. 31.

[25]*Journal*, pp. 132 f.

[26]*Ibid.*, p. 187.

[27]*The Journal of George Fox*, edited from the MSS. by Norman Penney, Vol. I, p. 348.

[28]*Journal*, p. 457.

[29]*Ibid.*, p. 97.

[30]*Ibid.*, p. 578.

[31]Rufus M. Jones, *The Story of George Fox*, pp. 168 f.

CHAPTER IV.

JOHN BUNYAN

[1]Cf. G. B. Harrison, *John Bunyan, a Study in Personality*, Garden City, New York, Doubleday, Doran, 1928, p. 217.

[2]John Bunyan, *Grace Abounding to the Chief of Sinners* (ed. by Roger Sharrock), Oxford, Clarendon Press, 1962, p. xii. In quoting from this and the other works of Bunyan, we shall follow his peculiarities in spelling and in the use of capitals and italics.

[3]*Ibid.*, p. 5.

[4]*Ibid.*, p. 8.

[5]*The Bedside Bunyan* (ed. by Arthur Stanley), London, Eyre and Spottiswoode, 1947, pp. 172, 150.

[6]*Grace Abounding*, p. 6.

[7]*Ibid.*, p. 94.

[8]*Ibid.*, p. 7.

[9]*Ibid.*, p. 94.

[10]*Ibid.*, pp. 11 f.

[11]*Ibid.*, pp. 20, 28, 31.

[12]*Ibid.*, p. 42.

[13]*Ibid.*, p. 58.

[14]*Ibid.*, p. 14.

[15]*Ibid.*, pp. 81 f.

[16]*Ibid.*, p. 85.

[17]Harrison, *op. cit.*, p. 133.

[18]*Grace Abounding*, pp. 109 f.

[19]*Ibid.*, pp. 117 f.

[20]*Ibid.*, p. 128.

[21]John Bunyan, *The Pilgrim's Progress* (ed. by James Blanton Wharey; second edition, rev. by Roger Sharrock), Oxford, Clarendon Press, 1960, pp. 8, 9.

[22]*Ibid.,* p. 8.

[23]Cf. R. Sharrock, *John Bunyan,* London, Hutchinson's University Library, 1954, p. 78.

[24]*The Pilgrim's Progress,* pp. 14, 15.

[25]*Ibid.,* p. 97.

[26]*Grace Abounding,* p. 76; cf. pp. 47, 48, 50.

[27]*The Pilgrim's Progress,* p. 162.

[28] Sharrock, *John Bunyan,* p. 144.

[29]John Bunyan, *The Life and Death of Mr. Badman* and *The Holy War* (ed. by John Brown), Cambridge University Press, 1905, pp. 21, 24, 28, 31.

[30]*The Life and Death of Mr. Badman,* p. 167.

[31]*The Holy War,* p. 184.

[32]*Ibid.,* p. 207.

[33]*Ibid.,* p. 313.

[34]*Ibid.,* p. 325.

[35]*First Esdras,* iv:41.

[36]*The Holy War,* p. 431.

[37]J. A. Froude, *Bunyan,* London, Macmillan, 1908 ed., p. 175.

[38]Sharrock, *John Bunyan,* p. 9.

[39]*The Bedside Bunyan,* p. 18.

[40]*Ibid.,* p. 19.

[41]Froude, *op. cit.,* p. 93.

CHAPTER V.

JOHN WESLEY

[1]John Wesley, *The Journal of John Wesley* (abridged by Nehemiah Curnock, with an introduction by Bishop Gerald Kennedy), New York, Capricorn Books, 1963, p. xiii.

[2]Julia Wedgwood, *John Wesley and the Evangelical Reaction of the Eighteenth Century,* quoted by S. Parkes Cadman, *The Three Religious Leaders of Oxford: John Wycliffe, John Wesley, John Henry Newman,* New York, Macmillan, 1916, p. 243.

[3]Cf. *Journal,* p. xii.

[4]Cf. F. J. McConnell, *John Wesley,* New York and Nashville, Abingdon Press, 1939, pp. 11 f.

[5]John Wesley, *The Journal of the Rev. John Wesley, A.M.* (ed. by Nehemiah Curnock), Standard Edition, Bicentenary Issue, London, The Epworth Press, 1938, Vol. I, p. 465. This edition is hereafter cited as *Journal.*

[6]Cf. *Journal,* Vol. I, p. 466.

[7]Edward Gibbon, *The Autobiography of Edward Gibbon* (ed. by Dero A. Saunders), New York, Meridian Books, 1961, p. 72.

[8]Cf. Cadman, *op. cit.,* p. 196.

[9]Cf. *Journal*, Vol. I, pp. 96 f.

[10]Cf. Cadman, *op. cit.*, p. 185.

[11]Cf. Albert M. Lyles, *Methodism Mocked*, London, The Epworth Press, 1960, pp. 21 ff.

[12]Cf. Umphrey Lee, *The Lord's Horseman: John Wesley the Man*, New York and Nashville, Abingdon Press, 1954 ed., p. 38.

[13]*Journal*, Vol. I, pp. 112 f.

[14]*Ibid.*, p. 407.

[15]Cf. *ibid.*, p. 31.

[16]*Ibid.*, pp. 290 ff., 317 ff., 329, 337, 376 f.

[17]*Ibid.*, p. 418.

[18]*Ibid.*, p. 424.

[19]*Ibid.*, p. 442.

[20]*Ibid.*, pp. 464, 472.

[21]*Ibid.*, pp. 472, 481.

[22]*Ibid.*, Vol. II, p. 310.

[23]*Ibid.*, pp. 328 ff., 320.

[24]*Ibid.*, p. 494.

[25]*Ibid.*, p. 321.

[26]*Ibid.*, p. 167.

[27]*Ibid.*, p. 172.

[28]*Ibid.*, Vol. III, p. 83.

[29]*Ibid.*, pp. 94, 171.

[30]*Ibid.*, pp. 84, 236.

[31]*Ibid.*, Vol. V, pp. 266-274.

[32]*Ibid.*, p. 265; cf. *ibid.*, Vol. VI, p. 109.

[33]Cf. *Ibid.*, Vol. III, pp. 18, 17.

[34]*Ibid.*, Vol. V, p. 354.

[35]Umphrey Lee, *op. cit.*, p. 153.

[36]John Wesley, *Works*, London, Wesleyan-Methodist Book-Room, n.d., Vol. VII, p. 383.

[37]*Ibid.*, Vol. X, p. 413.

[38]Some of the hostility assumed the form of satire. A selection of it has been compiled by Lyles, *op. cit.*

[39]*Journal*, Vol. II, pp. 256 f.

[40]Cited by Albert C. Outler, in *John Wesley*, New York, Oxford University Press, 1964, p. 72.

[41]*Journal*, Vol. III, pp. 99 f.; Vol. IV, p. 21.

[42]*Ibid.*, Vol. IV, p. 90.

[43]*Ibid.*, Vol. VII, p. 59.

[44]*Ibid.*, p. 389; cf. *John Wesley*, ed. by A. C. Outler, p. 99.

[45]*Journal*, Vol. VII, pp. 408 f.

[46]*Ibid.*, Vol. VIII, pp. 35, 127, 128.

[47]*Ibid.,* Vol. VI, p. 507.

[48]Cf. *Ibid.,* Vol. VII, p. 182.

[49]Cf. McConnell, *op. cit.,* pp. 118, 120.

[50]*Journal,* Vol. VII, p. 377.

[51]*Ibid.,* Vol. V, p. 55.

CHAPTER VI.

JOHN HENRY CARDINAL NEWMAN

[1]John Henry Cardinal Newman, *Apologia pro Vita Sua* (with an introduction by Philip Hughes), Garden City, New York, Image Books, Doubleday, 1956, p. 110. This edition will be cited hereafter as *Apologia.*

[2]*Ibid.,* p. 124.

[3]Cf. Wilfrid Ward, *The Life of John Henry Cardinal Newman,* London, Longmans, Green, 1927 ed., Vol. I, p. 27, note 2.

[4]*Apologia,* pp. 125 ff.

[5]*Ibid.,* pp. 127 ff.; cf. Henri Bremond, *The Mystery of Newman* (transl. by H. C. Corrance), London, Williams & Norgate, 1907, pp. 183 ff.

[6]St. Augustine, *Soliloquies,* I:7, in W. J. Oates (ed.), *The Basic Writings of St. Augustine,* New York, Random House, 1948, p. 262.

[7]Cf. William Barry, *Newman,* London, Hodder and Stoughton, 1904, p. 20.

[8]Cf. Henry Tristram, in *A Tribute to Newman,* Dublin, Browne and Nolan, 1945, p. 259.

[9]Cf. *Apologia,* p. 15.

[10]*Ibid.,* p. 163.

[11]Cf. *A Newman Synthesis* (arranged by Erich Przywara), London, Sheed and Ward, 1930, p. 143.

[12]*Apologia,* p. 166.

[13]*Letters and Correspondence of John Henry Newman during his Life in the English Church* (ed. by Anne Mozley), London, Longmans, Green, 1891, Vol. I, pp. 358, 378; cf. Ward, *op. cit.,* pp. 53 f.

[14]S. Parkes Cadman, *The Three Religious Leaders of Oxford and their Movements,* New York, Macmillan, 1916, p. 455.

[15]*Apologia,* pp. 177 f.

[16]*Ibid.,* p. 179.

[17]*Ibid.,* pp. 180 f.

[18]*Ibid.,* p. 188.

[19]*Ibid.,* p. 210.

[20]*Ibid.,* p. 219.

[21]Cf. Eugene R. Fairbrother, *The Oxford Movement,* New York, Oxford University Press, 1964, pp. 151, 154 ff.

[22]*Apologia,* pp. 247 f.

[23]*Ibid.*, p. 288.

[24]*Ibid.*, p. 315.

[25]John Henry Cardinal Newman, *Loss and Gain: The Story of a Convert,* London, Burns Oates & Washbourne, n.d., p. 289.

[26]A. W. Hutton, in article on Cardinal Newman, *The Encyclopedia Britannica,* 11th ed.

[27]*Apologia,* p. 317.

[28]Ward, *op. cit.,* Vol. I, p. 395.

[29]*Discourses on the Scope and Nature of University Education,* in *Newman, Prose and Poetry* (sel. by Geoffrey Tillotson), Cambridge, Harvard University Press, 1957, p. 385.

[30]*Ibid.*, pp. 486, 505, 522.

[31]Charles Sarolea, *Cardinal Newman,* Edinburgh, T. & T. Clark, 1908, p. 53; cf. chap. v.

[32]*Apologia,* p. 317.

[33]*Ibid.*, p. 318.

[34]*Ibid.*, p. 327; cf. pp. 318, 330.

[35]*Ibid.*, p. 332.

[36]Ward, *op. cit.,* Vol. I, p. 158.

[37]*Apologia,* pp. 391, 382.

[38]Ward, *op. cit.,* Vol. II, p. 234.

CHAPTER VII.

ERNEST RENAN

[1]*Recollections of My Youth* (transl. of Ernest Renan's *Souvenirs d'enfance et de jeunesse* by C. B. Pitman), London, George Routledge & Sons, 1929, p. xxxv. This work will be quoted hereafter as *Recollections.*

[2]G. C. Coulter, in his Introduction to the *Recollections,* p. xxiii.

[3]*Recollections,* p. xxxi.

[4]*Ibid.*, p. xxxii.

[5]*Ibid.*, p. 82.

[6]Cf. the discussion of the Breton-Celtic strains in culture in Pierre Lasserre's *La jeunesse d'Ernest Renan,* Paris, Garnier, Vol. I, Chap. i: "Renan Breton." Cf. also the more extensive study by René Galand, *L'Ame celtique de Renan,* New Haven, Yale University Press, and Paris, Presses universitaires de France, 1959.

[7]Cf. Raymond Poincaré, *Ernest Renan,* Paris, Champion, 1923, p. 3.

[8]Renan, *Essais de morale et de critique,* Paris, Calmann-Lévy, n.d., p. 147.

[9]*Ibid.*, p. xix.

[10]Cf. Galand, *op. cit.,* p. 175.

[11]Jacques Boulenger, *Renan et ses critiques*, Paris, Editions du siècle, 1925, chap. ix.

[12]*Recollections*, p. 67.

[13]*Ibid.*, p. 9.

[14]*Ibid.*

[15]*Ibid.*, p. 163.

[16]*Ibid.*, pp. 196, 192 f.

[17]Acts 8:30.

[18]Renan, *Cahiers de jeunesse, 1845-1846*, Paris, Calmann-Lévy, n.d.

[19]*Recollections*, pp. 262, 263.

[20]Renan, "Ma soeur Henriette," in *Lettres intimes, 1842-1845*, Paris, Calmann-Lévy, 5th ed., 1896, p. 23.

[21]Cf. *ibid.*, pp. 96, 97, 100, 186; cf. *Souvenirs d'enfance et de jeunesse*, Paris, Lévy, 5th ed., 1883, p. 405.

[22]Renan, *Lettres intimes, 1842-1845*, pp. 197, 239.

[23]Renan, *Lettres du séminaire, 1838-1846*, Paris, Calmann-Lévy, n.d., pp. 111 f., 185 f.

[24]*Ibid.*, p. 250.

[25]Renan, *Cahiers de jeunesse, 1845-1846*, p. 240.

[26]Renan, *Souvenirs d'enfance et de jeunesse*, Appendice, pp. 382, 383.

[27]*Recollections*, p. 255.

[28]*Ibid.*, p. 173.

[29]Renan, *Souvenirs d'enfance et de jeunesse*, p. 389.

[30]Cf. Jean Pommier, *Renan*, Paris, Perrin, 1923, p. 45.

[31]*Recollections*, p. 273.

[32]Cf. *ibid.*, pp. 285, 289.

[33]*Ibid.*, p. 359.

[34]Renan, *Lettres intimes, 1842-1845*, p. 313.

[35]Renan, *Lettres du séminaire, 1838-1846*, pp. 262, 281, 306.

[36]*Ibid.*, pp. 319 ff.

[37]Cf. Renan, *Nouvelles lettres intimes, 1846-1850*, Paris, Calmann-Lévy, 1923, pp. 5 f., 56, 50 f., 69.

[38]Renan, "Ma soeur Henriette," in *Lettres intimes, 1842-1845*, pp. 43 f.

[39]*Recollections*, pp. 306 f.

[40]*Ibid.*, p. 281.

[41]*Ibid.*, pp. 280, 274.

[42]Renan, *Cahiers de jeunesse, 1845-1846*, pp. 304, 351, 353 f.

[43]Renan, *Nouveaux cahiers de jeunesse, 1846*, Paris, Calmann-Lévy, 1907, p. 232.

[44]*Recollections*, p. 327.

[45]Renan, *L'Avenir de la science*, Paris, Calmann-Lévy, 8th ed., 1894, pp. i, 364 ff.

[46]*Ibid.*, pp. viii f., 5.

[47]Job 13:7; Spinoza, *Ethics,* iv, preface; *Spinoza's Short Treatise on God, Man, and His Well-Being* (transl. by A. Wolf), London, Black, 1910, pp. 78, 103; St. Augustine, Epistle 166, cited in A. E. Burn's article, "Creeds," *Encyclopedia Britannica,* 11th ed.

[48]Cf. Sir M. E. Grant Duff, *Ernest Renan: In Memoriam,* London, Macmillan, 1893, p. 79.

[49]*Recollections,* p. 136.

[50]Renan, *Cahiers de jeunesse, 1845-1846,* p. 304.

[51]Albert L. Guérard, *French Prophets of Yesterday,* London, T. Fisher Unwin, 1913, p. 240.

[52]Renan, *Vie de Jésus,* Paris, Calmann-Lévy, 13th ed., n.d., pp. xvi f.

[53]Luke 17:21.

[54]Renan, *Vie de Jésus,* pp. 48, 119, 79.

[55]*Ibid.,* p. 244.

[56]Luke 10:41 f.

[57]Renan, *Correspondance, 1872-1892,* Paris, Calmann-Lévy, 1928, Vol. II, p. 272.

[58]Cf. *Pages choisies des grans écrivains: Ernest Renan,* Paris, Armand Colin, Calmann-Lévy, n.d., p. 54.

[59]Renan, *Vie de Jésus,* p. 475.

CHAPTER VIII.

COUNT LEO TOLSTOY

[1]Romain Rolland, *Tolstoy* (transl. by Bernard Miall), New York, Dutton, 1911, p. 5.

[2]*The Life of Tolstoy* by Tolstoy's very close friend and biographer, Paul Birukoff (Engl. transl.), London, Cassell, 1911, pp. 15 f.

[3]Tolstoy, *A Confession* (transl. by Aylmer Maude), Oxford University Press ed. of 1945, pp. 3, 5. This work is cited hereafter as *Confession.*

[4]Lev Tolstoy, *Sobraniye sotchinenii* (Collected Works), Moscow, Khud Literatura, 1965, Vol. XIX, pp. 33, 41-46. Cited below as *Sobraniye sotchinenii.*

[5]*Sobraniye sotchinenii,* Vol. XIX, p. 95; transl. in Paul Birukoff, *The Life of Tolstoy,* p. 35.

[6]Cf. Aylmer Maude, *The Life of Tolstoy: First Fifty Years,* London, Cassell, 1911, p. 60.

[7]*Ibid.,* pp. 128 f.

[8]*Sobraniye sotchinenii,* Vol. XIX, p. 150; transl. in Paul Birukoff, *The Life of Tolstoy,* pp. 37 f.

[9]Cf. Maude, *The Life of Tolstoy: First Fifty Years,* p. 132; *Confession,* p. 11.

[10]*Confession,* p. 17.

[11]Cf. Countess Tatiana Tolstoy's essay in *Family Views of Tolstoy* (transl. by Louise and Aylmer Maude), Boston, Houghton Mifflin, 1926, p. 87, note.

[12]Tolstoy, *Anna Karenina* (transl. by Louise and Aylmer Maude), Oxford University Press, Vol. II, 1944 ed., p. 405.

[13]*Confession*, pp. 19 ff., 28.

[14]*Ibid.*, pp. 23 f.

[15]*Ibid.*, p. 31.

[16]*Ibid.*, p. 66.

[17]Tatiana Tolstoy's essay in *Family Views of Tolstoy*, p. 89.

[18]Aylmer Maude, *The Life of Tolstoy: Later Years*, London, Constable, 1911, p. 13.

[19]*The Diary of Tolstoy's Wife, 1860-1891* (transl. by Alexander Werth), London, Gollancz, 1928, p. 200.

[20]Maude, *The Life of Tolstoy: Later Years*, pp. 13, 7, 372.

[21]*Sobraniye sotchinenii*, Vol. XX, p. 105; transl. by Rose Strunsky, *The Journal of Leo Tolstoy, 1895-1899*, New York, Knopf, 1917, p. 255.

[22]Matthew 16:25 f.

[23]Cf. Tolstoy, *What I Believe* (transl. by Aylmer Maude), Oxford University Press, 1945 ed., chap. vi.

[24]Matthew 5:21 f.

[25]*Sobraniye sotchinenii*, Vol. XVII, pp. 237, 488 f.; Sergei Tolstoy, *Tolstoy Remembered by His Son* (transl. by Moura Budberg), New York, Atheneum, 1962, pp. 162 f.

[26]Matthew 5:27 f., 32 f.

[27]Tolstoy, *What I Believe* (with *A Confession*) (transl. by Aylmer Maude), Oxford University Press, 1945 ed., pp. 194 ff.

[28]Matthew 5:33 f., 37.

[29]Matthew 5:43 f., 46 f.

[30]Tolstoy, *What I Believe*, p. 224.

[31]Quoted by Aylmer Maude, *The Life of Tolstoy: Later Years*, p. 57.

[32]Matthew 5:38-42.

[33]*Sobraniye sotchinenii*, Vol. XIX, pp. 285 f.

[34]Cf. Ernest J. Simmons, *Leo Tolstoy*, Boston, Little Brown, 1946, chap. xxxiv, especially pp. 594 ff.

[35]Cf. *Sobraniye sotchinenii*, Vol. XX, p. 165.

[36]Tolstoy, *What Is Art?* (transl. by Aylmer Maude), New York, Crowell, 1899, p. 184.

[37]*Journal of Leo Tolstoy, 1895-1899*, p. 26.

[38]Tolstoy, *What Is to be Done?* (transl., ed. by Isabel F. Hapgood), New York, Crowell, 1890, p. 153.

[39]*Ibid.*, p. 156.

[40]Birukoff, *op. cit.*, pp. 148, 154.

CHAPTER IX.

ALBERT SCHWEITZER

[1]Cf. Petavell-Olliff, *Le problème de l'immortalité*, Vol. I, p. 95.

[2]Schweitzer, *Memoirs of Childhood and Youth* (transl. by C. T. Campion), New York, Copyright 1929, 1957 by Macmillan, pp. 18 ff., 28 ff. This work will be cited hereafter as *Childhood and Youth*.

[3]*Ibid.*, pp. 38 f., 40 ff.; Schweitzer, *Out of My Life and Thought: An Autobiography* (transl. by C. T. Campion), Copyright 1933, 1949, (c) 1961 by Holt, Rinehart and Winston, Inc., cited hereafter as *My Life and Thought*. (Page references are to the paperback edition by New American Library, New York, 1963.)

[4]*Childhood and Youth*, pp. 9 ff.

[5]*Ibid.*, pp. 45 f.

[6]*Ibid.*, p. 14.

[7]*Ibid.*, p. 43.

[8]*Ibid.*, pp. 58 ff.; cf. pp. 62 ff.

[9]Matthew 10:23.

[10]Matthew 11:2 ff.

[11]*My Life and Thought*, p. 13.

[12]Schweitzer, *The Quest of the Historical Jesus* (transl. by W. Montgomery), New York, Macmillan, 1959, p. 386.

[13]Cf. E. N. Mozley, *The Theology of Albert Schweitzer, for Christian Inquirers*, New York, Macmillan, 1951, p. 59.

[14]Schweitzer, Epilogue to Mozley, *The Theology of Albert Schweitzer*, p. 88.

[15]*Ibid.*, p. 89.

[16]*My Life and Thought*, pp. 45, 49, 51.

[17]*Ibid.*, pp. 55 f.

[18]*Ibid.*, p. 70.

[19]*Childhood and Youth*, p. 61.

[20]*My Life and Thought*, pp. 72 f., 74.

[21]Cf. *Ibid.*, p. 111.

[22]Schweitzer, *On the Edge of the Primeval Forest* (transl. by C. T. Campion), New York, Pyramid Books, 1963 ed., p. 32, cited hereafter as *The Primeval Forest; My Life and Thought*, p. 110.

[23]Schweitzer, *The Forest Hospital at Lambaréné* (transl. by C. T. Campion), New York, Henry Holt, 1931, p. 119; *My Life and Thought*, pp. 110 ff.; *The Primeval Forest*, p. 31 f.

[24]Matthew 7:21.

[25]*The Primeval Forest*, p. 74.

[26]*My Life and Thought*, p. 119.

[27]*Albert Schweitzer: An Anthology* (ed. by Charles R. Joy), Boston, Beacon, 1962 ed., p. 109.

[28]I Corinthians 4:10.

[29]Schweitzer, *The Forest Hospital at Lambaréné*, p. 118.

[30]Kant, *The Fundamental Principles of the Metaphysics of Morals*, in T. K. Abbott's translation, *Kant's Critique of Practical Reason and Other Works in the Theory of Ethics*, London, Longmans, Green, 6th ed., 1909, p. 47.

[31]*The Primeval Forest*, p. 114.

[32]*My Life and Thought*, p. 126.

[33]Schweitzer, *The Teaching of Reverence for Life* (transl. by Richard and Clara Winston), New York, Holt, Rinehart, and Winston, 1965, p. 26.

[34]*Albert Schweitzer: An Anthology*, pp. 273 f.

[35]*My Life and Thought*, p. 155.

[36]*A Treasury of Albert Schweitzer* (ed. by Thomas Kiernan), New York, Citadel and Philosophical Library, 1965, p. 123.

CHAPTER X.

POPE JOHN XXIII.

[1]Pope John XXIII, *Journal of a Soul* (transl. by Dorothy White), New York, McGraw-Hill, 1965, p. 329, note 3. This work is cited hereafter as *Journal*.

[2]*Ibid.*, p. 343.

[3]*Ibid.*, p. xvii.

[4]*Ibid.*, pp. 12, 13.

[5]*Ibid.*, p. 16.

[6]*Ibid.*, p. 304.

[7]*Ibid.*, pp. 21, 31, 55.

[8]*Ibid.*, pp. 100, 32, 102.

[9]*Ibid.*, pp. 20, 41, 143, 198.

[10]*Ibid.*, pp. 42, 41, 36, 61.

[11]*Ibid.*, pp. 45, 67.

[12]Cf. *Ibid.*, pp. 55, 58, 255.

[13]*Ibid.*, p. 46.

[14]*Ibid.*, pp. 71, 75, 179.

[15]*Ibid.*, pp. 99 f.

[16]*Ibid.*, p. 127, note 2.

[17]*Ibid.*, p. 22.

[18]*Ibid.*, p. 23.

[19]*Ibid.*, p. 228.

[20]*Ibid.*, p. 157.

[21]*Ibid.*, pp. 122, 121.

[22]*Ibid.*, p. 122.
[23]*Ibid.*, p. 124.
[24]*Ibid.*, p. 131.
[25]*Ibid.*, p. 134.
[26]*Ibid.*, p. 144.
[27]*Ibid.*, pp. 386, 388.
[28]*Ibid.*, p. 206.
[29]*Ibid.*, p. 156.
[30]*Ibid.*, pp. 435, 436.
[31]*Ibid.*, p. 85.
[32]*Ibid.*, p. 87.
[33]*Ibid.*, p. 232.
[34]*Ibid.*, p. 325.
[35]*Ibid.*, p. 78.
[36]*Ibid.*, pp. 298 f.
[37]Matthew 10:37.
[38]*Journal*, p. 251.
[39]*Ibid.*
[40]*Ibid.*, p. 325.
[41]*Ibid.*, p. 391.
[42]*Ibid.*, p. 384.
[43]*Ibid.*, p. 445.

BIBLIOGRAPHY

FOREWORD. THE STUDY OF AUTOBIOGRAPHIES

Bates, Ernest S. *Inside Out, an Introduction to Autobiography*. New York, Sheridan House, 1937.

Burr, Anna R. *The Autobiography, a Critical and Comparative Study*. Boston, Houghton Mifflin, 1909.

Misch, Georg. *A History of Autobiography in Antiquity*. Cambridge, Harvard University Press, 1951.

————. *Geschichte der Autobiographie*. 4 parts in 7 vols. Frankfurt, G. Schulte-Bulmke, 1949-67.

Padover, Saul K. *Confessions and Self-Portraits: 4600 Years of Autobiography*. New York, John Day, 1957.

Pascal, Roy. *Design and Truth in Autobiography*. Cambridge, Harvard University Press, 1960.

University Library of Autobiography. 15 vols. New York, F. Tyler Daniels Co., 1918.

CHAPTER I. ST. AUGUSTINE

St. Augustine. *The City of God*. 2 vols. Transl. by M. Dods. Edinburgh, T. and T. Clark, 1872.

————. *The Confessions*. Transl. by E. B. Pusey. New York, Dutton, 1909.

————. *The Confessions*. Transl. by John K. Ryan. Garden City, Doubleday, 1966.

Oates, Whitney J. (ed). *Basic Writings of St. Augustine.* 2 vols. New York, Random House, 1948.

Blanchard, H. H. (ed.). *Prose and Poetry of the Continental Renaissance in Translation.* 2nd ed. New York, David Mc-Kay, 1955.

Gilson, E. H. *Introduction a l'etude de Saint Augustin.* Paris, J. Vrin, 1931.

————. *The Christian Philosophy of Saint Augustine.* New York, Random House, 1960.

Guardini, Romano. *The Conversion of Saint Augustine.* Transl. by Elinor Briefs. Westminster, Newman Press, 1960.

Harnack, Adolf. *History of Dogma.* Vol. V. Transl. by James Millar. London, Williams and Norgate, 1898.

————. *Monasticism . . . and the Confessions of St. Augustine.* Transl. by E. E. Kellett and F. H. Marseille. London, Williams and Norgate, 1913.

McCabe, Joseph. *St. Augustine and His Age.* London, Duckworth, 1910.

Martin, Jules. *Saint Augustin.* Paris, F. Alcan, 1901.

Nourrisson, Jean F. *La philosophie de St. Augustin.* Paris, Didier, 1866.

Ottley, Robert L. *Studies in the Confessions of St. Augustine.* London, R. Scott, 1919.

Papini, Giovanni. *Saint Augustine.* Transl. by Mary Prichard Agnetti. London, Hodder & Stoughton, 1930.

West, Rebecca. *St. Augustine.* London, P. Davies, 1933.

CHAPTER II. ST. TERESA OF ÁVILA

The Complete Works of St. Teresa. 5th ed. Transl. by E. Allison Peers. London, Sheed & Ward, 1957.

The Letters of St. Teresa.   Transl. by John Dalton. London, Thos. Baker, 1902.

James, William. *Varieties of Religious Experience.* 30th ed. London, Longmans, Green, 1919.

Peers, E. A. *Handbook to the Life and Times of St. Teresa and St. John of the Cross.* London, Burns Oates, 1954.

——————. *Saint Teresa of Jesus, and Other Essays and Addresses.* London, Faber & Faber, 1953.

Sackville-West, V. M. *The Eagle and the Dove, A Study of Contrasts: St. Teresa de Ávila, Ste. Therese of Lisieux.* London, M. Joseph, 1944.

CHAPTER III.   GEORGE FOX

The Journal of George Fox.   2 vols. Ed. by Norman Penney. Cambridge University Press, 1911.

The Journal of George Fox.   Ed. by Rufus M. Jones, New York, Capricorn Books, 1963.

Jones, Rufus M.   *The Story of George Fox.* New York, Macmillan, 1919.

Knight, Rachel. *The Founder of Quakerism; a Psychological Study of the Mysticism of George Fox.* London, Swarthmore Press, 1922.

Noble, Wilfred V. *The Man in Leather Breeches; the Life and Times of George Fox.* New York, Philosophical Library, 1953.

CHAPTER IV.   JOHN BUNYAN

The Bedside Bunyan; an Anthology of the Writings of John Bun-

yan. Ed. by Arthur Stanley. London, Eyre and Spottiswoode, 1947.

Bunyan, John. *Grace Abounding to the Chief of Sinners.* Ed. by Roger Sharrock. Oxford, Clarendon Press, 1962.

————. *Life and Death of Mr. Badman* and *The Holy War.* Ed. by John Brown. Cambridge University Press, 1905.

————. *The Pilgrim's Progress.* Ed. by J. B. Wharey. Oxford, Clarendon Press, 1960.

Froude, J. A. *Bunyan.* London, Macmillan, 1908.

Harrison, G. B. *John Bunyan; a Study in Personality.* New York, Doubleday, Doran, 1928.

Sharrock, Roger. *John Bunyan.* London, Hutchinson Universal Library, 1954.

CHAPTER V. JOHN WESLEY

John Wesley's Journal. Abridged by Nehemiah Curnock. New York, Philosophical Library, 1951.

The Journal of the Rev. John Wesley. 8 vols. Ed. by Nehemiah Curnock. London, Epworth Press, 1938.

Wesley, John. *A Representative Collection of his Writings.* Ed. by A. C. Outler. New York, Oxford University Press, 1964.

————. *Letters.* 8 vols. Ed. by John Telford. London, Epworth Press, 1931.

Cadman, S. P. *The Three Religious Leaders of Oxford and their Movements: John Wycliffe, John Wesley, John Henry Newman.* New York, Macmillan, 1916.

Lee, Umphrey. *The Lord's Horseman: John Wesley the Man.* Nashville, Abingdon Press, 1954.

McConnell, F. J. *John Wesley.* New York, Abingdon Press, 1939.

CHAPTER VI. JOHN HENRY CARDINAL NEWMAN

Letters and Correspondence of John Henry Newman during his Life in the English Church, with a Brief Autobiography. 2 vol. Ed. by Anne Mozley. London, Longmans, Green, 1891.

Newman, John Henry. *Apologia pro Vita Sua.* Garden City, Doubleday, 1956.

————. *Apologia pro Vita Sua.* Ed. by Wilfrid Ward. London, H. Frowde, 1913.

————. *Loss and Gain: the Story of a Convert.* London, Burns Oates and Washbourne, n.d.

————. *The Idea of a University.* London, Longmans, Green, 1891.

Barry, W. F. *Newman.* London, Hodder & Stoughton, 1904.

Bremond, Henri. *The Mystery of Newman.* Transl. by H. C. Corrance. London, Williams & Norgate, 1907.

Cadman, S. P. *The Three Religious Leaders of Oxford and their Movements: John Wycliffe, John Wesley, John Henry Newman.* New York, Macmillan, 1916.

Fairbrother, Eugene R. *The Oxford Movement.* New York, Oxford University Press, 1964.

Sarolea, Charles. *Cardinal Newman and His Influence on Religious Life and Thought.* Edinburgh, T. & T. Clark, 1908.

Strachey, Lytton. *Eminent Victorians.* New York and London, Putnams, 1918.

Przywara, Erich. *A Newman Synthesis.* London, Sheed & Ward, 1930.

CHAPTER VII. ERNEST RENAN

Renan, Ernest. *Correspondance.* 2 vols. Paris, Calmann-Lévy, 1926-28.

————. *Histoire des origines du christianisme.* 7 vols. Paris, Michel Lévy frères, 1863-69.

————. *L'Avenir de la science.* 8th ed. Paris, Calmann-Lévy, 1894.

————. *Nouvelles lettres intimes, 1846-1850.* Paris, Calmann-Lévy, 1923.

————. *Recollections of My Youth.* Transl. by C. B. Pitman. London, Routledge, 1929.

————. *Souvenirs d'enfance et de jeunesse.* 2nd ed. Paris, Calmann-Lévy, 1883.

————. *The Life of Jesus.* Introd. by J. H. Holmes. New York, Modern Library, 1955.

————. Vie de Jesus. 13th ed. Paris, Calmann-Lévy, n.d.

Galand, René M. *L'Ame celtique de Renan.* New Haven, Yale University Press, 1959.

Grant Duff, Sir Mountstuart Elphinstone. *Ernest Renan.* London, Macmillan, 1893.

Poincaré, Raymond. *Ernest Renan.* Paris, Champion, 1923.

Séailles, Gabriel. *Ernest Renan, Essai de biographie psychologique.* Paris, Perrin, 1923.

CHAPTER VIII. COUNT LEO TOLSTOY

Reminiscence of Tolstoy by His Son Count Ilya Tolstoy. Transl. by George Calderon. New York, Century, 1914.

Tolstoy, Leo. *A Confession* and *What I Believe.* Transl. by Aylmer Maude. London, Oxford University Press, ed. of 1945.

—————. *Anna Karenina*. Transl. by Constance Garnett and Louise and Aylmer Maude. London, Oxford University Press, 1920.

—————. *Childhood, Boyhood, and Youth*. Transl. by C. J. Hogarth. New York, Dutton, 1917.

—————. *What is Art?* and *Essays on Art*. Transl. by Aylmer Maude. London, Oxford University Press, 1932.

—————. *Works*. Transl. by N. H. Dole, *et al.*

The Journal of Leo Tolstoy. Transl. by Rose Strunsky. New York, Knopf, 1917.

The Countess Tolstoy's Later Diary, 1891-1897. Transl. by Alexander Werth. London. V. Gollancz, 1929.

Birukoff, Paul. *The Life of Tolstoy*. London, Cassell, 1911.

Gorky, Maxim. *Reminiscences of Lev Nikolaevich Tolstoy.* Transl. by S. S. Koteliansky and Leonard Woolf. New York, Huebsch, 1920.

Lourie, Ossip. *La philosophie de Tolstoi, suivie de ses pensées.* 5th ed. Paris, F. Alcan, 1931.

Maude, Aylmer. *Leo Tolstoy*. London, Methuen, 1918.

—————. *The Life of Tolstoy: First Fifty Years.* 6th ed. London, Constable, 1911.

—————. *The Life of Tolstoy, Later Years.* 2nd ed. London, Constable, 1911.

Merezhkovsky, D. S. *Tolstoy as Man and Artist; with an Essay on Dostoyevsky.* Westminster, Constable, 1902.

Rolland, Romain. *Tolstoy*. Transl. by Bernard Miall. New York, Dutton, 1911.

Simmons, Ernest J. *Leo Tolstoy*. Boston, Little, Brown, 1946.

CHAPTER IX. ALBERT SCHWEITZER

Schweitzer, Albert. *Civilization and Ethics.* Transl. by John Naish. London, A. and C. Black, 1923.

————. *J. S. Bach.* Transl. by Ernest Newman. New York, Breitkopf & Härtel, 1911.

————. *Memoirs of Childhood and Youth.* Transl. by C. T. Campion. New York, Macmillan, 1929.

————. *On the Edge of the Primeval Forest.* Transl. by C. T. Campion. New York, Pyramid Books, ed. of 1963.

————. *Out of My Life and Thought: an Autobiography.* Transl. by C. T. Campion. New York, New American Library, ed. of 1963.

————. *The Forest Hospital at Lambaréné.* Transl. by C. T. Campion. New York, Henry Holt, 1931.

————. *The Quest of the Historical Jesus.* Transl. by W. Montgomery, New York, Macmillan, 1959.

————. *The Teaching of Reverence for Life.* Transl. by Richard and Clara Winston. New York, Holt, Rinehart, and Winston, 1965.

Joy, Charles R. and Arnold Melvin. *The Africa of Albert Schweitzer.* New York, Harper, 1948.

Mozley, E. N. *The Theology of Albert Schweitzer, for Christian Inquirers.* New York, Macmillan, 1951.

CHAPTER X. POPE JOHN XXIII

Pope John XXIII. *Journal of a Soul.* Transl. by Dorothy White. New York, McGraw-Hill, 1965.

Capovilla, Loris. *The Heart and Mind of John XXIII: His Secretary's Intimate Recollections.* Transl. by Patrick Riley. New York, Hawthorn Books, 1964.